CLASSIC

Worship

The Believer's Guide to Worship

To the Praise of His Glory

Centre for
Faith and Spirituality
Loughborough University

ISBN 0 85476 834 3

Published by
KINGSWAY PUBLICATIONS
Lottbridge Drove, Eastbourne, BN23 6NT, England.
E-mail: books@kingsway.co.uk

Designed and produced for the publishers by
Bookprint Creative Services, P.O. Box 827, BN21 3YJ, England.
Printed in Great Britain.

Reproduced from the original typesetting
of the single-volume editions.

Worship

GRAHAM KENDRICK

KINGSWAY PUBLICATIONS
EASTBOURNE

Contents

TO
the women in my life—
my wife Jill and daughters Abigail,
Amy and Tamsin

1

Celebrating the Truth about God

Who are we all hiding from?

It was the little boy's first trip to church, and his mother had hurriedly put him through the correct 'Sunday best' procedure of thorough washing, dressing in smart clothes, and the inventing of a parting in his hair—previously unknown to his startled scalp. Having been warned to 'behave', which generally meant 'shut-up and don't fidget', they proceeded to the local church under the incessant clanging of its bell.

On entering the church, the boy was instantly curious, fascinated by this strange new world. The hushed voices, the high arches, the slightly musty smell and the rows of empty wooden pews. Or were they empty? No, here and there a hat, the back of a head, a pair of hunched shoulders, would bob up or down, appear or disappear.

His mother led him in whispers to one of these dark tunnel-like rows, where she immediately knelt and bowed her head; he copied instinctively. The silence only lasted for a few more seconds, as the question that had been growing more and more urgent in his lively young mind suddenly burst out, ringing loud and clear through the ancient arches: 'Mummy, who are we all hiding from?'

11

The ensuing scene, the embarrassment and the retributions that may have befallen the boy are better left to the imagination, but it is worth pondering upon the irony of his analysis of the situation.

Who *were* they hiding from, or rather, why did their behaviour give the lad that impression? No doubt later on in the service (unless he was removed of course) the boy would have heard some singing, some readings from Scripture, a sermon, responses and so on, but I wonder if that first impression would have been totally dispelled by the end of the proceedings. What I am sure of is that he did not leave that building with a sense of wonder, excitement and awe, trembling at his first experience of being caught in the very presence of God, as the worshippers enthroned the living God in their gathering, upon wave after wave of spontaneous heartfelt praise and worship. I am sure that he did not look up at joy-filled faces or see sad ones released from their worry and fear and transformed before his eyes into expressions of happiness, peace and serenity. What I am also pretty sure of is that by the end the little boy was rather bored and wondering what he was missing on telly. In fact he was probably reduced to feeling much the same as a good many other churchgoers that morning.

I can well remember in my own childhood how going to church seemed so often to be little more than a lesson in patience and endurance. I longed for 'the service' to come to an end. I would watch the dust floating in the shafts of summer sunlight, or scratch with my 'collection penny' in the varnish of the pew in front of me. The trouble was, nothing ever *happened*; well, certain prescribed things did, but nothing unexpected or unusual—unless somebody fainted, or had a fit, or knocked over a pile of hymnbooks.

A God who never does anything?

Years and years of churchgoing taught me much about God and the Bible, and I would be wrong to underestimate the important truths and concepts that penetrated my mind. Yet, in a subtle but powerful way, I unconsciously began to believe, in total contradiction to my stated beliefs, that God is a God who never does anything. Oh, certainly he *used* to do things, and undoubtedly still did do things abroad through missionaries and in the lives of people who then wrote books about it. But to do anything tangible, real or supernatural, here and now?—that would have really scared us! Actually, I think most of us would have been delighted, having got over the initial shock.

It is interesting to note that many years later, when spiritual hunger demanded to be satisfied, my biggest barrier to entering into any experience of the Spirit of God was this pervading unbelief arising out of twenty years or so of apparent divine inactivity. I found myself trapped by a subconscious conviction that 'nothing will ever happen to me'. Of course it was in no way God's fault, and unbeknown to me at that time God was stirring his people into a dynamic awareness of his life-changing power and glory. But that is another part of the story.

A taste of heaven

Returning to our little boy for a moment, let us consider what the reality should have been. In 1 Peter 2:9 we read, 'But you are a chosen people, a royal priesthood, a holy nation, a people belonging to God, that you may declare the praises of him who called you out of darkness into his wonderful light.' The New American Standard Bible uses the phrase 'that you may proclaim the excellencies of him who has called you'. Here we see something of the marvellous plan of God for his church. He has chosen us for a reason, elevated us to a status beyond our imagination, called us together as a new eternal nation for a very definite purpose. We are to proclaim his excellencies, declare his praise.

Sometimes it seems that once we are forgiven for our sins, the 'great transaction' done and our salvation secure in terms of an entrance ticket to heaven, we slip our ticket into our back pocket and sit on it until we reach our final destination. Thus we endure our spiritual bus journey, passing the time looking out of the window and chatting to our fellow passengers.

Thankfully, this passive view of salvation is less and less in evidence today, and recent years have seen an ever-broadening understanding of God's plan to redeem our whole personalities, our relationships and finally the whole of creation. The climax of the Scriptures indeed shows us just that, and in the book of Revelation we see glimpses of a totally new order, not only 'spiritual' but physical and tangible. And worship is the dominant and all-consuming activity of the redeemed millions and countless angelic beings. Revelation 19:5–7 says:

> Then a voice came from the throne saying: 'Praise our God, all you his servants, you who fear him, both small and great!' Then I heard what sounded like a great multitude, like the roar of rushing waters and like loud peals of thunder, shouting: 'Hallelujah! For the Lord God Almighty reigns. Let us rejoice and be glad and give him glory!'

A glorious destiny

Worship is our destination, and there is no doubt that praise and worship should be the dominant feature of the journey there. Our praise and worship begins now, not then. They just get perfected somewhat when we arrive! Ephesians 1:11–12 says:

In him we were also chosen, having been predestined according to the plan of him who works out everything in conformity with the purpose of his will, in order that we, who were the first to hope in Christ, might be for the praise of his glory.

We are chosen, predestined, planned and willed by God himself to this very end!

The Westminster Shorter Catechism, in what can be seen as a kind of summing up of these and other scriptures, states, 'Man's chief end is to glorify God and enjoy him for ever.' The nature of our future heavenly worship is marvellous to ponder on, though it must be realized that we can only begin to know anything about it through the use of comparisons with things that are familiar to us. Yet we do have a foretaste, a kind of down-payment on this future glory. Ephesians 1:13–14 goes on to say:

Having believed, you were marked in him with a seal, the promised Holy Spirit, who is a deposit guaranteeing our inheritance until the redemption of those who are God's possession—to the praise of his glory.

It is the joy of many millions of Christians across the world to experience the 'streams of living water' from the Holy Spirit within, overflowing into magnificent worship to the Father, and this is just a hint of what is to come!

A friend of mine when asked why he dances in worship of God says, 'I dance because I can't fly!' If we feel down here that for safety reasons we sometimes ought to nail our boots to the floor, then what might be in store for us in the future! There may be jobs going for heavenly air traffic controllers as people like my friend finally realize their ambition! I like to think of the saints meeting their Lord at the second coming that way too, a worldwide

company of worshippers that can't be held down any
longer!

Our present concern, however, is to get ready for
heaven, and to introduce heavenly practices on earth so
that we can truly pray, 'Your kingdom come, your will be
done on earth as it is in heaven.' Our preoccupation
should not be with denominational preferences, matters
of style, tradition, personal taste or fashion, but with the
revealed will of God, 'that you may proclaim the excellencies of him who has called you out of darkness into his
marvellous light'.

Praise should match its object

So what does it mean in practice to proclaim his
excellencies or declare his praises? Is this command totally
satisfied by what normally goes on between certain set
hours every Sunday? If there is one thing that the British
are good at, despite our traditional reserve and emotional
conservation, it is pomp and ceremony. We really are
very expert at it, as evidenced by events such as the
wedding of the Prince and Princess of Wales. The greater
in standing the people involved, the more significant the
occasion, the more splendid and ornate the celebration.
The organizers demand that the event should match the
importance of the personalities featured and the majesty
they are meant to represent. On a more mundane level,
we all carry out this same principle in our family and social
lives. Heroes from the Falklands conflict were welcomed
back to their council houses or surburban streets with
banners, singing, shouting and cheering. Weddings are
celebrated as special events and the couple praised by
proud parents; new babies are doted upon and their
parents congratulated. Young people passing exams are
given presents and applauded at ceremonies for their

achievements, and at football matches even British people go wild with excitement as they praise their winning team, lifting the hero of the match on their shoulders in a victory parade, shouting or dancing themselves to exhaustion! We somehow feel that it is only right that the praise should match the importance of the person, their achievement or the occasion, even if the occasion only amounts to twenty-two men kicking a sphere of inflated leather round a muddy field!

Precisely the same principle is appropriate to our Creator God, and yet infinitely more so. Our earthly objects of praise are often unworthy of it, and frequently praised for quite the wrong reasons. God, however, is totally worthy of the praise and worship of his whole creation. He would be totally worthy of it even if he had chosen to condemn the whole human race for our sin and rebellion, without any hope of salvation, let alone his immeasurable praiseworthiness for his love in providing through his Son that marvellous hope.

The principle here is that our praise and worship should attempt to match its object. I say 'attempt' because even an eternity of praise will never do justice to the attributes and character of God, but each fresh new aeon will discover something yet more exhilarating, and another explosion of vibrant heartfelt celebration will burst across the new heaven and earth and echo to the corners of the new creation. Is there not, then, something desperately wrong if we get regularly bored in church? Do we think that the only appropriate way to worship God is to never stray from the tram-lines of liturgical rigidity (whether conformist or non-conformist!), physical rigidity, and mental rigidity, with everything predictable and undemanding? Does this match in any way our Saviour and God? What kind of a God do we think we have? Is he not endlessly creative, irrepressibly vital and alive, always doing 'new things'. Indeed God is 'the same yesterday, today and for ever', but one of his unchanging characteristics is that he is always full of surprises! If the presence of God is made known in our worship, if his Living Presence truly saturates the proceedings, then not only will there be the reverence and order that characterize the holy God of an ordered creation, but a sense of the unexpected that reflects his endless creativity as he moulds and fashions our lives together.

God in a box

People who have been to see *The Sound of Music* at the cinema umpteen times, almost religiously you might say, obviously derive some pleasure from it on each successive occasion. Quite what it is that keeps them going defies my power of understanding, but I accept that such people exist! I would imagine that even these *aficionados* will eventually (if they have not already atrophied in their seats) get tired of the same old lines, knowing exactly how the story will end. Elements of suspense and surprise, such as they are, must eventually disappear almost entirely. The same numbing effect is frequently achieved among 'worshippers', where the god who is worshipped is a god of the past, who fits neatly into the box of our predetermined patterns and, to the great relief of many, never does anything remotely unexpected, never causes his servants to move beyond the bounds of what is humanly explainable, and never does anything supernatural.

If this is the God who is being worshipped, then it is patently not the God of the Scriptures. It must be a false one, or at the very least a false image superimposed like a photo-negative upon the real God, obscuring his true dynamic nature, hiding his breathtaking and awesome power.

Telling lies about God

Hence, I would dare to say that many of our patterns and practices of worship, in a subtle but nevertheless effective manner, tell lies about God. Could it not be seen as a terribly sad but natural result of this kind of deadness in worship that some years ago it was proclaimed by Nietzsche: 'God is dead.' The irony of that gigantically presumptuous statement is borne out by the subsequent rash of popular graffiti that proclaimed: '*God is dead*, signed Nietzsche' and underneath '*Nietzsche is dead*, signed God'. It was never God that died, but who can blame the agnostic and atheistic—and even the ecclesiastical world—for coming to this conclusion when they observe the worship of the people whose final destiny and present purpose is to 'proclaim the excellencies of him who has called you out of darkness into his marvellous light'. It was so true when A. W. Tozer said, 'The church is more guilty of not being revived than the world is of not being converted.' Judgement begins at the house of God; we are those without the excuse of ignorance. There are many other lies about God which may sadly be propagated by observing some kinds of Christian 'worship'. I even hesitate to put them in print because they are such damnable lies: God is boring; God is irrelevant; God is powerless. He is none of these things and it is time that we demonstrated in our worship the truth about God, and sent the lies back to where they came from.

2

What Is Worship?

It may seem elementary to ask the question 'What is worship?' but it is surprising how little understanding there is among Christians of this most fundamental part of our humanity. Is it something religious people do on Sundays? Is it a funny internal feeling that makes you want to sing? Is it an activity for Christians of a certain emotional disposition? Is it a word to describe everything in a church service that leads up to the sermon? A pleasant corporate activity involving community singing of favourite choruses? Should it be loud or quiet, and should it be organ and choir or drums and guitars?

Opinion, it seems, will never cease to vary, along with fads, fashions and factions, as to how worship should be conducted, but it seems remarkable to me that so much of the conversation, discussion and disagreement about worship is actually concerned with our own personal preferences. One person prefers traditional hymns, another sings only new choruses. Someone else will not attend a service unless it is the 1662 prayerbook version, yet another will not come unless she is free to raise her hands and dance, while her husband won't come with her because she might! A neutral observer to these disputes might easily go away believing that worship is conducted purely for the benefit and satisfaction of the participants. Regrettably, there is often some truth in this for the question as to what we are trying to achieve through these means is rarely asked.

Worship is for God. He is our Creator, and the worship of his creatures is both his right and his pleasure. Worship is first and foremost for his benefit, not ours, though it is marvellous to discover that in giving him pleasure, we ourselves enter into what can become our richest and most wholesome experience in life. It would be quite reasonable of God to demand our worship, as a right and a duty, without any pleasure to ourselves, but it is a glorious truth about him that he wants worship to be a relationship of giving from both directions. It is surely a tragedy when the pleasure we receive, and the satisfaction of our own tastes and preferences, become the whole object of the exercise. The manner in which we worship is of course of great importance to us, but our foremost consideration must be what gives pleasure and glory to the One who is the object of our worship.

Worship is God's enjoyment of us and our enjoyment of him. In Psalm 149:2–4 we read, 'Let Israel be glad in his maker; let the people of Zion rejoice in their King. Let them praise His name with dancing; let them sing praises to Him with timbrel and lyre. For the Lord takes pleasure in His people' (NASB). It comes as a startling revelation to many of us that we are able to give God pleasure. Surely it is a most wonderful mystery that an individual human being, whoever or whatever he may be, has the potential for giving joy to the Creator of the universe! How many of us draw back from this truth into a sense of our own insignificance, disbelieving that anyone so cosmically important as God can be the least bit interested in our meagre offerings? Yet it is gloriously true, and fundamental to the whole gospel of Jesus Christ, that God's intention was not just to save us from hell and judgement (though all believers will be eternally grateful for that!) but to bear, by way of the new birth of the Spirit, children into his family: sons and daughters enjoying an intimate personal relationship with their heavenly Father.

Worth-ship

The origin in English of the word 'worship' is 'worth-ship', which expresses the value placed on someone or something. The true quality and depth of our love for God will to a very great degree be evidenced by the quality and depth of our worship. When we value somebody, we do things to demonstrate that love; we put our thanks, appreciation and adoration into words, we give gifts and show that we care in practical ways. Indeed how often do we hear the complaint, 'You say you love me, but you never show it.' Talk is cheap, but actions do speak louder than words and are a test of whether our words are genuine.

It was an important discovery for me some years ago, when I found out the full meaning of the original Greek word which is used most often in the New Testament and translated as 'worship'. In fact, there are seven Greek words: five of these occur once, another occurs three times, but the final one appears no less than fifty-nine times. This word is *proskyneo*, and its overwhelming use compared to the other words must tell us something of its importance. The basic meaning is 'to come towards to kiss (the hand)' and it denotes both the external act of prostrating oneself in worship and the corresponding inward attitude of reverence and humility (*New International Dictionary of the New Testament*, Paternoster Press 1978). This gives us a beautiful picture of worship as we approach the King of kings and Lord of lords; with open face, eye to eye, our hearts full of love and thanks, our wills set firmly to obey him, enjoying an intimacy and a mutual affection that the watching angels find astounding. Considering that in heaven's eyes we were once rebels and sworn enemies, originally made in God's perfect image yet twisted into grotesque parodies by sin, this is incredible!

Where does worship begin?

Everybody worships. Whether it is a hero, possessions, success, pleasure, a political cause, a carved idol or one-self, the way we live and behave makes evident the things we love and give ourselves to. It is in our very nature to worship, and that inner drive is God-given; the disaster is that as part of a fallen race, we have replaced the object of our worship. To be converted to faith in Jesus Christ is to return to the worship of the true God, and to dethrone all rivals to his authority. The very heart of worship is the giving, not only of our talents and goods, but of our very selves.

In Romans 12:1 the apostle Paul teaches, 'Therefore, I urge you, brothers, in view of God's mercy, to offer your bodies as living sacrifices, holy and pleasing to God—which is your spiritual worship.' Spiritual worship should not be misunderstood as something ephemeral and abstract; instead, it starts with ownership of the body. Who do I belong to? To whom should I devote my energies, muscular, mental, and spiritual?

A living sacrifice

It would be easy to pass over the term 'living sacrifice' too quickly and miss the paradox created by putting those two words side by side. To Paul's thoroughly Jewish mind, steeped in the tradition of his fathers and saturated by the Old Testament scriptures, a sacrifice was clearly one thing—it was dead. It was most likely a sheep whose throat had been cut, its life ended, offered up to God to atone for sin. Now Paul knew that in Christ full atonement had been made once and for all, but the sense of the finality of being totally offered up to God is strongly present in this picture. The animal was not a sacrifice until it was dead, so to talk of a 'living sacrifice' is on the face of it a contradiction. This is not the only place in Romans where Paul puts side by side concepts of being alive and dead at the same time. In chapter 6 verses 11–13 he says:

> Count yourselves dead to sin but alive to God in Christ Jesus.... Do not offer the parts of your body to sin, as instruments of wickedness, but rather offer yourselves to God as those who have been brought from death to life; and offer the parts of your body to him as instruments of righteousness.

Alive to God—together

This passage in Romans is at the very heart of worship, and it is the heart that God searches to see whether we are dying daily to our own selfish ways, and are therefore alive with the life and power of Jesus. If this is true of us, then every thought, action and emotion can become an act of true worship. It is evident that where a body of Christians are living like this, gatherings for worship take on a new freshness and vitality, and the problem of leadership becomes more a matter of channelling the flow, and stopping things from getting out of hand! There are things to praise *about*, answered prayers to give thanks for and be happy about, stories to relate of God's activity since the last meeting, and lessons about learning to share together. A gathering for worship is no more an act of worship than being a loving mother and housewife, or practising hospitality, or doing your job well (provided these are being done to the glory of God); it is simply a special time when we lay aside the necessary but mundane activities of life and give our whole energy and attention to *expressing* what has become fundamental to our lives. Weary minds can be refreshed and set free in thoughts about God. Our bodies, tense and tired after being hunched over a desk, a machine, the kitchen sink, or the steering wheel of a car can relax, loosen up and get ready to express our response to the presence of a loving God in every part of our lives.

A token of the whole

Meetings for corporate worship can of necessity only be engaged in occasionally; the business of life and work guarantees that. Those times, special though they are, are really just a token of the fact that all of life belongs to, and is being offered up daily in thanksgiving to, the Creator. It is like the wedding ring given as a token of the giving of one person to another in marriage, or the giving of a gift to demonstrate love and esteem.

Repentance is worship

The genuineness of our worship, however, cannot be measured in decibels of sound, and although it is vital that we express our love for God vocally, he looks to see the evidence in our lives. We do not always think of repentance as worship, but it can be much easier to sing a rousing hymn than to turn away from our favourite sin. A sinful act involves worship of the wrong kind, submitting ourselves at that moment to serve the appetites of our pride or lust, and so repentance is literally a transfer of our worship back to the One who rightfully owns it. It is significant that during Jesus' temptation in the wilderness, Satan used the word *proskyneo* (denoting a kiss of worship, as we have seen) when tempting Jesus by offering him all the kingdoms of the world and their glory if only he would bow down and worship him. Worship has been misunderstood as something that arises from a feeling which 'comes upon you', but it is vital that we understand that it is rooted in a conscious act of the will, to serve and obey the Lord Jesus Christ. The feelings, the joy of having been forgiven, follow on as a consequence of our reunion with him.

Work is worship

In Colossians 3:23–24 we are told, 'Whatever you do, work at it with all your heart, as working for the Lord, not for men.... It is the Lord Christ you are serving.' How hard it seems to vacuum the carpet for the ten thousandth time, or wash up, or lift another packing-case, or whatever it is we wish we did not have to do, for the Lord! And yet, if we relegate worship to services and meetings, we are in danger of living in a kind of spiritual schizophrenia, shutting off the greater part of our lives from being offered to the Lord who fills all of life.

Don't give up!

Worship, then, is at heart a person offered to God, claiming no rights, making no more selfish demands than a dead man does, but living fully, richly and wholly to God and by his power. To be honest, even as I write it, I know that this sometimes seems beyond reach, and yet God is able to get us there despite our kicking and struggling and running away, and I comfort myself that he has many times succeeded with far more hopeless cases than me! Even when we have begun, it doesn't happen overnight; it happens over *life*, and meanwhile our heavenly Father's patience and tenderness are inexhaustible. He takes us as we are, where we are; to be realistic, where else can we start?

Not my will—but yours

As in all things, our best example of a life of worship is Jesus, whose every breath was breathed, every meal eaten and every word spoken in natural relaxed worship of God. As a child, my concept of Jesus was a strange mixture of ideas. The Sunday School pictures didn't help much either. Most of them portrayed a golden-haired, blue-eyed man, not Jewish at all, who seemed to glow all over, particularly around the face and head, and while I understand the artist's attempt to signify the divinity of Christ in this way, the effect was to create an image of a respectable, westernized Christ who was somehow unreal, even ghostly. The image in so many minds is one of a white-robed, almost floating figure blessing people to the accompaniment of distant angelic choirs. Hollywood has a lot to answer for!

But the point is that Jesus was really human. He was really God too, but we are told that he laid aside his heavenly glory and became in all respects as a man (though never less than God), experiencing our human condition, except for committing sin, even as far as a cruel and ignominious death. What we so easily forget is his experience of humanity: his thirty years in that run-down infamous town of Nazareth; his sweated labour in the workshop; the cuts and scars of his calloused hands; the meals he ate, the washing-up, the shopping, the daily grind and no mod cons! And later on, during those three years with his disciples, the weariness such that he was not even wakened by a storm, the times of fun and laughter with his friends, their meals together and the stories they told one another. The dirt and dust, the happiness and the tears and, in the end, desertion and betrayal.

The question has often been asked, and I will ask it again: was Jesus' life more offered up to God when he was healing the sick, or when he was eating his breakfast? Was it more acceptable to his Father when he was preaching in the synagogues, or when he was enjoying a rough and tumble with his friends? Was he more holy when he was transfigured on the mountain and spoke with Moses and Elijah, or when he spat on the ground to make clay to rub on a blind man's eyes?

Worship in the mundane

The answer is that his whole life was an act of worship, including the most mundane and basic elements of being a human being, and all of it was pleasing to his Father. In fact, it was even before he had begun his three years of preaching and miracles that his Father proclaimed over him at his baptism: 'This is my beloved son in whom I am well pleased.' Surely at that time the Father must have been referring not only to his obedience in baptism, but also to the previous thirty years spent in obscurity and 'the mundane'!

The worship of the will

If, however, we were to attempt to choose an incident in Jesus' earthly life that seems most vividly to illustrate his worship of God, where might our final choice lead us? When might his heart of hearts be most exposed and revealed? The truth about us is surely never more clearly exhibited than when we are under intense pressure. It is then that our true character cannot hide because everything that overlays or embellishes it is stripped away.

I don't think that there can be much doubt as to the time of Jesus' greatest pressure. The scene in the Garden of Gethsemane shows him in such agony of spirit that he said: 'My soul is overwhelmed with sorrow to the point of death.' We read that: 'being in anguish, he prayed more earnestly, and his sweat was like drops of blood falling to the ground'. Yet despite the terrible ordeal that he knew was ahead of him, and the sorrow that itself nearly killed him, he prayed to his Father: 'yet not what I will, but what you will'.

I have heard this scene described as the greatest example of worship in the whole Bible. Obedience is worship, and without obedience to God we cannot truly worship him. However enthusiastic or 'liberated' our participation in worship may be, unless in the reality of daily living, we have offered ourselves to God, and truly belong to him, it will be no more than wasted energy and meaningless noise. Let us beware of the danger of attempting to renew our forms of worship when our daily lives are evidence that our bodies are not offered up on the altar as a 'living sacrifice'.

3

Dethroning the Gods

Worship is not just a matter of what happens between set hours on a Sunday. If we fail to realize this, we are fooling ourselves. It is not even a question of whether it is ancient or modern, staid or enthusiastic, creative or boring. What we so often fail to recognize is that worship is at the very heart of a radically different way of living. To adopt new freedoms of expression—new music, dance, drama and so on in our worship—is by no means to guarantee the reality of it or its acceptability to God, and in many places we are in serious danger of mistaking these outward developments for true worship in the sight of God. To worship implies far more than participation in a series of devotional acts at regular intervals.

Even when we talk comfortably in terms of presenting our very selves as living sacrifices, feeling that we have understood this as being true worship, I wonder whether even then we have seen its full implications. This is because of a popular tendency to 'spiritualize' our faith at the cost of 'earthing it', of abstracting it rather than seeing it right through to its practical application. Of course the worship that the Father desires is worship 'in spirit', but we must remind ourselves that the Bible sees us as whole people, and consequently a 'spiritual' act can never be separated from simultaneous actions in the body. Thus 'spiritual' activities that bear no relationship to the way in which we live our everyday lives are shown to be at best little more than sentiment, and at worst, blatant hypocrisy. (This argument is developed more fully in Chapter 9.)

Spiritual self-gratification

It is also far too easy, within the current upsurge of creative input in the realm of worship, to find ourselves chasing spiritual or aesthetic experiences, as if the highest achievement of our whole pilgrimage on earth was to enter some kind of praise-induced ecstasy! I am in fact all in favour of spiritual experiences when they are genuine, and welcome ecstasies that are gifts of God and not artificially induced, but if such things become the *aim* of our gatherings for worship, then we have turned the gospel upside down. The gospel is for the salvation of the world, and we are sometimes in danger of locking ourselves inside the rescue-shop and plundering the stock of blessings for the sole purpose of spiritual self-gratification, while millions stream empty-handed past the closed doors into eternal darkness, hearing the joyful sounds and seeing the advertisements, but never being given a chance to test the goods.

Worshipping in a fallen world

There is a desperate need to place renewed forms of worship in the wider context of what worship is, and to work through the social, economic and political implications that worshipping God inevitably creates. Worship, or rather misdirected worship, is in fact the issue at the very heart of the world's problems. It should be obvious that worship is not the exclusive property of the Christian, or of the adherents to other religious faiths. The practice of worship is an inescapable part of being human; even an atheist is a worshipper of something, because there is built into all of us the vacuum left by our loss of communion with God that took place at the Fall. We were created to worship, and having rejected the rightful worthy object of all worship, mankind has continued through his sad history, substituting every variety of false god, and serving successions of them in fear and misery.

The gods we worship

The gods of present-day Western society may not be so obvious as the gods of wood, stone and metal that sit in shrines and on mantelpieces (although it is amazing how well even they survive in a supposedly enlightened age). The subtlety of our modern gods probably makes them even more dangerous.

There is the god of affluence, to whom we sacrifice our energy, time and health in an effort to make him smile upon us and keep us in the manner to which we are determined to remain (or become!) accustomed.

There is the god of personal happiness and fulfilment, to whom we will sacrifice apparently unsuitable marriage partners and as many unpleasant and restricting duties and responsibilities as possible, and in whose honour we will chase endless fads, fantasies and quasi-religious practices (from horoscopes to transcendental meditation) in order to find the door to his elusive temple.

There is the dark foreboding god of fear, whom we attempt to appease with offerings of tranquillizers, unnaturally protective relationships and maybe even insurance policies.

There are the gods of unjust social systems to whom we

continue to permit the sacrifice of the helpless and the poor, and whose shrines we are willing to protect by the use of military force if necessary.

We could add to this abbreviated list the large-scale gods of nationalism, racism and culture and the personal gods of pride, lust, ambition and the like. It would be naïve to think that we can easily disentangle ourselves from these objects of worship, because as part of a world system that has exchanged the one true god for many 'gods', we have all been brought up, at least to some degree, to bow down and worship them. The ones that involve the most obvious sins may quickly be identified and dethroned when we become Christians, but the ones that more easily escape our attention do so because they have become so intricately woven into the whole fabric of the social, cultural and national context in which we live, that we simply cannot see them.

The renewing of the mind

It is only as we worship God intelligently and spiritually, constantly adjusting our focus to a clearer definition of his character and deeds, that the false gods are exposed for what they are, and we are more able to extricate ourselves—or rather, we find ourselves being extricated—from their destructive influence. The passage in Romans 12:1 about presenting our bodies as living sacrifices, goes on to say: 'Do not conform any longer to the pattern of this world, but be transformed by the renewing of your mind.' Each time that we set aside for praising and enjoying God we are able to shake off a little more of the conformity to the world that clings to us, not by desperately trying to shake it off (which can become a negative activity) but by absorbing our whole selves—body, mind, spirit and emotions—in God himself and adjusting our view of the world to conform to his.

Knowing how God feels

By filling our vision with him, we leave less and less room for other gods, and we are less and less deceived by them. Entering into the 'courts of God' we may also understand more of his feelings about the systems we are part of, how he views our domestic and national economies in relation to the poor, how he reacts to injustice, violence and so on. If worship can be rightly thought of as looking with unveiled face into the Lord's face, then we should expect to see his expressions as he looks at his world, and indeed as he looks into our own faces. If true worship involves knowing God as our Father, then we must expect a fatherly discipline to accompany our worship, as he lovingly but firmly corrects our attitudes and behaviour. He will also teach us to conform to his fatherly love, and put within us some of the painful feelings of a Father who watches many of his children suffer in captivity, or pain or poverty, with few prepared to help them.

Worship is a political act

How often do we blandly sing 'Jesus is Lord!' in apparent blindness to the implications of that enormous statement? To genuinely worship Jesus as Lord of all is immediately to challenge all false gods, and to pose a threat to their dark and dingy domains. Bearing in mind that the gods of this world are intricately bound into the godless political and social systems that surround us, it is absolutely true to say that worship is a political act. If Jesus is Lord, then every other 'lord' is excluded from that title and subservient to him.

For many of the early Christians, to voice the glorious

affirmation 'Jesus is Lord' was to pronounce their own sentence of death. Such a statement, linked to a life that practised Christ's lordship, was seen as an act of political treason and punished as such.

We have similar situations today under strict atheistic regimes where a denial of the 'lordship' of the state is treated as a treasonable offence because it undermines the very ideological foundations upon which the security of such states are built. It is true that, in Western 'free' society, the cry 'Jesus is Lord!' is all too often ignored by the authorities, but that should not in any way be taken as a sign that democratic states acknowledge or tolerate his lordship! Closer to the truth would be the explanation that our presence in society reflects so little of the radical challenge of the statement that we are tolerated as a peculiar but fairly harmless sect.

A rival kingdom

To give one small but down-to-earth example, the erosion of standards of honesty in Britain has taken on the proportions of a landslide, and a 'black economy' exists at every level of society involving such practices as tax evasion, petty theft, bribes and back-handers, minor and major fraud, and every kind of 'fiddling' from exaggerated statements of business expenses to the falsifying of time-sheets. By 'turning a blind eye' and compromising, a Christian employee can coexist happily with his workmates (if not with his conscience!), but the moment he acknowledges the God of truth as Lord, and refuses to join the system, the knives come out. In such a system, an honest man is an embarrassment and must be 'normalized' or disposed of! On a wider scale, a community of God's people need only to take a stand on an issue such as abortion, having come under the lordship of a God who says 'you shall not kill' and seen his anger and grief over the mass murder of the unborn, and a stream of vitriolic condemnation flies forth from the pro-abortionists and their sympathizers. To worship Jesus as Lord is not only to invite his lordship into our individual lives but to set up a rival kingdom in the middle of the old one, which inevitably invites the wrath of the 'gods' down upon our heads.

A vision of Christ

It seems that the church has often veered from one emphasis to the other, from an almost exclusive concern for its own health and 'spirituality' to a neglect of personal experience of God and his power for the sake of social and political activism. In the first case the result has often been a separatist 'ghetto' mentality, with the church falling inwards on itself, and in the second case the genuine power and experience of God has been abandoned for something that in practice is only marginally discernible from humanism or socialism. Where both these 'camps' exist, neither seems to make much impact upon the world. What we need is not a compromise, or even a union of the best of both, but a constantly renewed vision and experience of Christ. From all our activities, battles and campaigns, we need constantly to return to worship the greatest Champion of the poor and oppressed, of truth and justice, Christ himself. In him we discover the true motive for changing society, which is not our own idealism, despair, frustration or self-image as would-be 'liberators', but the God who says 'Be holy because I, the Lord your God, am holy' (Lev 19:2). It is in worship that we concentrate our attention upon the One who laid down his life for the world, and trusted neither in the power of political activism, nor in mystical escapism under the title of 'spirituality'.

We Christians are in the business of building the kingdom of God on earth, in expectation of its culmination in
an eternal kingdom; but if this kingdom does not have its
roots in heaven right now, it will turn out to be little
different from the world's kingdom which will not survive
the 'shaking of all things'. Only that which cannot be
shaken will remain, and surely anything that does not
have its roots in heaven, and in the worship of heaven, will
not continue into eternity.

Joy in the midst of sorrow

There are those who claim that they cannot with a clear
conscience worship God in joy and celebration while
there is misery and injustice in the world, and though it is
easy to understand their emotions, we must remember
that Jesus lived in the middle of a suffering world and was
spoken of prophetically in the following way: 'Your
throne, O God, will last for ever and ever; a sceptre of
justice will be the sceptre of your kingdom. You love
righteousness and hate wickedness; therefore God, your
God, has set you above your companions by anointing
you with the oil of joy' (Ps 45:6–7). There is here a direct
connection between the rule of justice, the love of righteousness and hatred of wickedness, and being outstanding
in the experience of joy! Joy is an authentic expression of
worship and this passage shows us that the King of this
new kingdom is living in a unity of spiritual and social
activity.

Because we love the King

Many of us are worshipping the King in apparent ignorance
or disregard of the justice and righteousness of his
kingdom, while others are trying to build the kingdom

while neglecting to worship the King. The King and his kingdom are inseparable, the kingdom being no less than a practical extension of his character, and we must not forget that it is built for his glory anyway! We should build the kingdom because we love and worship the King, or we may discover too late that we have been building not *his* kingdom, but ours.

The implications of worshipping God in a world of false gods are numerous and costly. Worship is a new way of living, and we inevitably feel the violence of its pull as we turn against the tide. Yet in the very act of worship—from the setting of the will to obey in a small matter of truth or honesty, to the exercise of the spirit and voice in corporate praise—there are tremendous resources of strength, healing and inspiration to be found.

It is 'Christ in us' who is the 'hope of glory', our hope and the world's hope, and it is in lifting him up that those without hope are drawn to him. There is no doubt that our forms of worship can be used to misdirect us into a false spirituality that cuts us off from the outside world, and many may have become disillusioned or critical of it for that very reason.

Worship, however—that is, an encounter with the living, caring, suffering Christ—will always send us out into the world to be more like him. Our motive for changing the world must be Jesus himself; his example, his teaching, his sacrificial giving of himself, and his presence inside us by the Holy Spirit. It is only his love in us that can possibly bear the crushing load of problems and pain that face us as we try to reach out. It is our love affair with him that gives us inspiration to love others, and his lordship in our lives that is the only power that has ever overcome the world and its gods.

4

Celebrating a New Social Order

Polishing the glass cases

The church seems to have almost an obsession with meetings, which I suppose is an occupational hazard when the nature of our faith requires the regular gathering together of its people. Yet it seems that so many of our meetings are designed to *prevent* us from actually meeting one another, beyond a polite hello and moderate physical proximity. I have often sat in services observing the way in which we scatter ourselves around the chairs or pews in an apparent attempt to keep a distance of at least six feet between each individual or bunch of friends.

At times I have found no difficulty in imagining each worshipper enclosed in a glass case, oblivious of the personal dramas, tragedies or joys of the other people around. Indeed, the introduction of such glass cases would in many cases be a more logical extension of the separatism that is habitually practised, and would make little difference to the relationships, except perhaps when it came to deciding who should keep them polished!

The armchair church

In America, the advent of the 'electronic church' now means that thousands of Christians can 'belong' to a church without ever leaving their armchairs and TV dinners, as the whole thing is piped into that shrine of isolation and privacy: the living-room. There are, however, as we all know, countless local churches where, despite small congregations, members attend services for years and years without ever finding out more than the barest details about their fellow worshippers. Individualistic attitudes to Christianity have in fact permeated so deeply into our churches that to begin to talk in practical terms about the necessity to enter into a greater depth of relationship, involving the sharing of our lives, would probably be greeted with the kind of shock you would expect if someone had suggested that we should all become Buddhists, open up a casino in the vestry or set the church organ on fire.

And yet, if one of the original apostles were to get caught in an ecclesiastical time-warp and land unexpectedly in one of our glass-case churches, what might he think? I strongly suspect that he would be shocked for quite a different reason, finding us as alien to his understanding of the body of Christ as we would be to his, and many of us able only to mutter a collection of half-baked ideas or excuses, based not upon the revelation of the kingdom of God through Christ, but upon our tastes, preferences and cultural orientation as English men and women.

Worship without frontiers

It seems that much of our worship has lost its most vital and life-giving quality, the thing that should set Christians apart as remarkably different from the fragmented society around us. That quality, which should be affirmed and celebrated whenever we meet, and should characterize our daily life, is what Paul describes in Colossians 3:11–17:

> Here there is no Greek or Jew, circumcised or uncircumcised, barbarian, Scythian, slave or free, but Christ is all, and is in all. Therefore, as God's chosen people, holy and dearly loved, clothe yourselves with compassion, kindness, humility, gentleness and patience. Bear with each other and forgive any grievances you may have against one another. Forgive as the Lord forgave you. And over all these virtues put on love, which binds them all together in perfect unity. Let the peace of God rule in your hearts, since as members of one body you were called to peace. And be thankful. Let the word of Christ dwell in you richly as you teach and admonish one another with all wisdom, and as you sing psalms, hymns and spiritual songs with gratitude in your hearts to God. And whatever you do, whether in word or deed, do it all in the name of the Lord Jesus, giving thanks to God the Father through him.

The segment of this passage that we would most readily associate with worship is probably the mention of singing 'psalms, hymns and spiritual songs'. But how many of us would be prepared to consider the whole of it as a description of the nature of true Christian worship? If worship is in any way a celebration or affirmation of the kingdom of God, then there is a sense in which the whole passage is about worship. When we choose to neglect or deliberately avoid the kind of relationships that we see described here, our singing may become in the ears of God little more than decibels and wasted energy. Worship is a celebration of the new kingdom, and the words we have just read go a long way to describe the nature of that kingdom. If we follow the passage through carefully, we will see the foundations upon which our worship should be built.

Here there are no nationalistic divisions; Jews are not better than Greeks; the British are not of more value than Asians, West Indians or Argentinians. Here there are no 'class' divisions based on different religious experiences, no exclusive and superior club for those baptized in the Holy Spirit, or caucus for the mutual protection of those who regard it with distaste or suspicion.

The rule of God's peace

Here there are no cultural prejudices but a desire to understand and accept those who are different; no divisions between the rich and the poor, the professional classes and manual labourers, but a sharing of wealth and resources. Here there is a place to belong, limitless compassion and patience, and forgiveness for one another when we make mistakes or do hurtful things. Here there is love that causes us to lay down our lives for one another. The inevitable product of all these things is the rule of peace, continued thankfulness and the growth of knowledge about God. In this context there is no lack of content or motivation for the singing of psalms, hymns and spiritual songs, as we celebrate a new order of social, economic and spiritual relationships lived to the glory of Jesus Christ. Our 'visiting apostle' would find himself completely at home in this environment while no doubt exhibiting a heartfelt sympathy and understanding for the problems of building and maintaining such a community!

A spectator sport?

It must be admitted in the light of this passage that the popular practice of worship has become tailored to individuality rather than community, and instead we have diplomatically learned to avoid anything that might upset the *status quo* of separation. We sit in rows facing the front of the building and stare at the back of each other's heads as if to watch a performance or a show, unable to see each other's faces even if we wanted to! When we enter the building how many of us search for either an empty area in which to be alone, a seat at the back near the emergency exit, or anywhere where we can avoid close contact with fellow believers we don't like or just don't know? We have loud organs playing that can be a substitute for enthusiastic singing, helping us to forget how few of us are really there! The existence of ordained professional clergymen can often create the sense of a hierarchy of spirituality, with the ordinary believer feeling that he has nothing of value to contribute, particularly if the professionals appear to run a monopoly on contributions. Hence he feels his duty is just to attend regularly in the privacy of his own thoughts and feelings.

New converts are frequently left to their own devices rather than being drawn into new friendships and a structure of teaching and pastoral care; it often seems that only those who already know how to stand on their own two feet survive. In recent times we have often been guilty of preaching an individualistic gospel, inviting people into a personal relationship with Jesus, forgetting to add that we should also be inviting them into a personal relationship with us. I suspect that we have suppressed this part of the gospel because of a niggling doubt that they might become disillusioned with what they would find. We have invited them to come and find 'purpose in life' or 'personal fulfilment' in Christ, neglecting to mention the call to die to self and become a servant of all, as part of a serving church.

'Being nice' to God

If we were to cut off from Christianity everything in it that challenges and offers to transform the way we treat other people, there would be almost nothing left. But in many cases this is what we have effectively done, by watering down the lifestyle described in our previous passage from Colossians to a vague philosophy of 'be nice to one another'. Watered-down relationships will always result in watered-down worship and end up in little more than 'being nice' to God. We cannot separate love for God from love for one another, or the way we relate to God (that is, worship) from the way we relate to one another. In 1 John 4:19–21 we read:

> We love because he first loved us. If anyone says, 'I love God', yet hates his brother, he is a liar. For anyone who does not love his brother, whom he has seen, cannot love God, whom he has not seen. And he has given us this command: Whoever loves God must also love his brother.

Right relationships

The importance of right relationships with one another as a prerequisite of worship is highlighted by Jesus himself in Matthew 5:23 and 24: 'if you are offering your gift at the altar and there remember that your brother has something against you, leave the gift there in front of the altar. First go and be reconciled to your brother; then come and offer your gift.' It is clear from these words that worship cannot be compartmentalized and detached from the way in which we treat people. These verses come in the context of three whole chapters of Jesus' teaching on relationships, beginning in chapter 5 with the Beatitudes, and the sheer volume of such teaching should encourage us to take verses 23 and 24 particularly seriously.

Who makes the first move?

Looking at these verses more closely, it might be easy to miss the fact that the situation cited by Jesus is one in which someone has something 'against you'. This must include situations where we ourselves may be in the right, quite innocent of sin against our brother, yet nevertheless an onus is put on the innocent party to 'go and be reconciled'. How much more then, one might ask, should the guilty party take heed of this command?

To me, this teaching suggests a refreshingly different attitude to blame, namely that as members of Christ's body, the innocent member cannot detach himself from the guilty member just because of the rights and wrongs of a situation, but shares a responsibility to make the move towards reconciliation in order that the body should be whole in every part. It is the same principle that resulted in Jesus, the only perfectly innocent man to have ever lived, making the first move towards guilty men, and even going as far as to take responsibility for our sins by dying on the cross. We must also remind ourselves that he did not come condemning, but with humility!

Right relationships release worship

How often, I wonder, do we struggle to get our worship 'off the ground' when the real reason for the absence of a sense of joy and freedom is that too many people are bringing their gifts of praise, or money, or service, to the 'altar' while making no effort to be reconciled with their fellow worshippers. When we consider that our 'altar' speaks of the place where the innocent blood of the Lamb of God was shed for the forgiveness of the guilty, then we should take special care to check that we are not coming in blatant contradiction of what that shed blood signifies. Rather, we should be reminded of Jesus' command to:

'Love one another *as I have loved you*' (my italics).

The practice of these teachings has been a transforming influence in many churches, and in opening the sluice-gates as far as worship is concerned. I have frequently witnessed meetings where the Spirit has moved the leaders to encourage reconciliation 'on the spot', often as a prelude to sharing the bread and wine of the Eucharist together. At the small cost of sacrificing natural reservedness, and the higher cost of sacrificing pride and fear, such breaking of barriers and healing of rifts has often come to the extent that it seemed like a dark cloud had been blown away between earth and heaven. It must be said that these were often 'crisis' occasions, and would not have been necessary had the practice of reconciliation been a normal part of the daily life of the fellowships concerned. I sometimes wonder what freedom there might be in a fellowship where everybody had learned to get right with each other as a regular personal discipline, such that they always came together united; worshipping, as it were, under a clear sky rather than under a cloud.

An eternal triangle

Reconciliation is of course a positive solution for those times when the negative side of our fallen humanity has reared its ugly head, and because of our weaknesses it will continue to be a regular necessity this side of heaven. However, we are not meant to become absorbed exclusively in corrective measures and if we can learn to worship as the body of Christ in positive, creative ways, then a whole new realm of mutual encouragement and spiritual power will open up for us. Whereas the popular practice of worship tends towards the vertical, that is, the individual to God, the New Testament clearly shows us two directions: vertical and horizontal, towards God and towards one another. In Ephesians 5:19 we read: 'Speak to one another with psalms, hymns and spiritual songs. Sing and make music in your heart to the Lord.' As we meet together we should find ourselves in a kind of invisible triangle, joined by the Spirit and relating together in a common experience of worship yet focused upon the Lord. As we move from the horizontal plane closer to the apex of the triangle, we find ourselves moving closer together.

Singing to one another

In the light of this, we would do well to question the standard poses we adopt of closed eyes, or gazing into the middle distance, and serried ranks facing the hats and hairstyles in front. How many of us conduct conversations in this manner, even with strangers! In normal life it would be regarded as quite rude! There must be a case here for our times of worship to involve at least in part the opportunity for eye-to-eye contact, and the use of psalms, hymns and spiritual songs as direct exhortations to one another. It is curious how we regularly sing words that are clearly designed for encouraging others, as if they were for the Lord! How ridiculous it is when we lift our eyes and our hands heavenward and sing, 'Seek ye first the kingdom of God and his righteousness'—as if it is *God* who needs reminding!

Strengthening one another

In 1 Corinthians 14 Paul is dealing with matters of order in corporate worship, and it is clear that the pattern was not one of a majority of passive observers seeking personal spiritual enrichment from a select group of 'performers' at the front. In verse 26 we read:

> What then shall we say, brothers? When you come together, everyone has a hymn, or a word of instruction, a revelation, a tongue or an interpretation. All of these must be done for the strengthening of the church.

This must of course be seen in the context of Paul's teaching elsewhere on authority and leadership, and not mistaken as a licence for anybody to 'do their thing' without being accountable. The list of contributions is obviously a short list, a sample, and elsewhere in the New Testament numerous additional ways of contributing are mentioned. The contributions that may be brought are clearly for a specific purpose: 'the strengthening of the church'.

Coming to give

We see here a very different attitude towards our coming together, that of coming to *give*, rather than coming to *get*. In fact, the overriding difficulty for those who fill the pews rather than the pulpit is that they are rarely given an alternative to 'taking' because of the way our services are normally structured, and it requires a considerable degree of self-discipline, initiative and imagination to give to others in these circumstances. We should not, however, use such a situation as an excuse to 'cop out' but, despite the *status quo*, use self-discipline, initiative and imagination in order to find ways to build each other up. More of that, however, in Chapter 15.

'Free' worship is not cheap

There is a great deal of fear and reticence among many church leaders when it comes to putting participation into practice, and it is understandable when you have experienced the mish-mash of good, bad and indifferent contributions that can emerge when a congregation is let loose! What about the danger of certain dominant personalities trying to take over; misguided or unbalanced persons leading the meeting off into confusion; 'super-spiritual' members mistaking a vivid imagination for visions or prophecies, an individual with an 'axe to grind' using the gathering as a platform for his or her own opinions, grievances or heresies? There is no escaping the realities of these dangers, but surely it is no answer deliberately to repress such problems or pretend they are not there. Could it not be seen as facing the reality of where people are 'at', instead of running away from it? If we are scared of what our brothers and sisters might do if given the freedom to express themselves, then would it not be better to venture on to the dangerous road towards reality, renewal and change, than to go on pretending we are functioning as the many membered body of Christ?

A foundation of love and trust

Do we love and trust one another enough to be honest when your or my contribution is not helpful, or badly timed, or insensitive to the feelings of others? The answer may well be 'no', but if it is, can we not commit ourselves to loving honesty, and agree to be real with each other for the sake of the health of the whole body? Paul says in his letter to the Romans, 15:5–7:

> May the God who gives endurance and encouragement give you a spirit of unity among yourselves as you follow Christ Jesus, so that with one heart and mouth you may glorify the God and Father of our Lord Jesus Christ. Accept one another, then, just as Christ accepted you, in order to bring praise to God.

The heart behind the song

It is not the noise of our songs that brings praise and glory
to the Lord. Besides, he already has an infinitely superior
quality of music and song to enjoy, performed by countless
angels who are no doubt extraordinarily skilled in
heavenly melody such as would make our best anthems
sound like funeral dirges! Instead he looks for the 'spirit
of unity', the 'one heart', the attitude of accepting one
another, that fuels our worship and animates our voices
and bodies; he searches for the motivation of our actions
and is not fooled when we try to substitute beautiful music
for beautiful relationships. It may seem strange to our
minds to think in terms of glorifying God with our relationships, but I would suggest that this kind of praise far
exceeds the value of music, singing and dancing in the
context of wrong relationships. It would be quite correct
to announce in a meeting 'Let's praise the Lord' and then
proceed to minister to one another's needs without a note
being sung. I could guarantee, however, that if real
Christ-like love was being practised, it would not be long
before the praise became vocal as well!

Serving one another in worship

The attitude that Paul is exhorting the Roman church to
display is that of serving others, and servanthood is surely
one of the qualities most lacking in our worship. We
should come together with each individual having determined in his heart to bring something that will build up
someone else, hence in 1 Corinthians 14:26; 'everyone
has a hymn, or a word of instruction, a revelation, a
tongue or an interpretation'. We are so conditioned to
meeting together for selfish benefit that even when we do
make a contribution, many of us (and I freely confess to

this fault) are more likely to ask ourselves 'How did I do? Were they impressed?' than to have a genuine concern for whether someone else was helped, encouraged or enlightened! When preparing to take part in a meeting, I find I have to make a deliberate effort to pray for the people who will be there, otherwise even my prayers will centre far too much upon performing well and preventing making a fool of myself—thus losing spiritual credibility!

A cure for the insecure

We may never entirely escape from the temptation towards these ego-centred thoughts and feelings, but at least we can avoid indulging them by deliberately turning our attention to the well-being of others. It is also worth remembering that such self-centredness is usually based upon insecurity—in other words, we don't feel safe with one another and are scared of rejection, failure or censure. The antidote to fear is love and I doubt if any of us will ever rid ourselves totally of feelings of insecurity, and the overconcern with self that it creates, without the depth of love and acceptance among our brothers and sisters in the church that is clearly God's desire for us.

Servants for the world's sake

Chapter 15 of Romans goes on to speak of Christ's servanthood, and attaches to it an important consquence:

> For I tell you that Christ has become a servant of the Jews on behalf of God's truth, to confirm the promises made to the patriarchs so that the Gentiles may glorify God for his mercy, as it is written: 'Therefore I will praise you among the Gentiles; I will sing hymns to your name.' Again, it says, 'Rejoice, O Gentiles, with his people' (vv.8–10).

Jesus became a servant in order to lead people from every nation to worship the one true God. The picture of the suffering servant in Isaiah 52 and 53, which emerges as a prophetic foreshadowing of Christ, comes vividly to life in the New Testament as we look at the attitudes that Jesus displayed and the life that he lived.

When Jesus commanded his followers to love one another in the way that he loved them, he effectively passed on the mission of the suffering servant to the church to be continued. Why then is servanthood connected in this passage with the Gentiles, the 'outsiders', rejoicing and singing praises (v.11)? Is it solely because of the amazing example of God's love in the servant attitude of the historical Jesus? If so, how could the Gentiles be expected to see it in the first place in order to react to it, when they were geographically and culturally so far from Judea? Would they be convinced just by verbal reports, or might they need a living flesh and blood example before the smallest note of praise left their cynical lips?

As Paul is so obviously presenting the servanthood of Jesus as an example to be followed in the church as we live and worship together, could it not be concluded that it is the living, flesh and blood demonstration of servanthood in the church that brings the reality of Christ to the Gentiles, the outsiders to faith in God, such that they praise him?

The miracle of unity

There is nothing in a divided, fragmented and violent world that can impress as much as the bringing together in love, unity, joy and celebration, of people who were once bitterly divided by economic differences, class, race, colour, ideology, culture, religion and nationality. This unity is the one thing that the world cannot achieve, and it is the lack of it that threatens our peace and, in a nuclear age, our very existence. No wonder it is remarkable enough to make 'the Gentiles' praise God! It should be obvious then that it is impossible to detach servanthood in our worship together from servanthood in our lives together, and that when these two are working together, it begins to affect the world around us. There is a rare and special quality of witness in a community of servants, worshipping a God who became a man in order to serve, and reaching out in the power of that God to serve the world. Hence there is an extension of the horizontal thrust of worship out through the church into the world.

The face of the outsider

One of the most serious dangers that we encounter when we seek to enrich our worship is our capacity as human beings to turn even the most Godward activity into a selfish pursuit. I doubt if any of us would do this deliberately, but many of us have caught ourselves in the process of carving a place for ourselves and our gifts, accompanied by a diminishing regard for serving others, and a growing sense of thirst for power or success. On a corporate level, it is possible to become so caught up in the pursuit of better, freer, richer and more creative worship that we have no time or energy left for the world outside.

Worship should not only point us to God and one another, it should also point us to the millions who have never met Jesus, and whom God loves just as much as he loves us. If indeed our worship does hide us away from the faces of the 'outsiders', I question whether we are still worshipping in reality, and whether we have in fact hidden ourselves away from the face of Jesus. True worship reveals to us the 'face' of Jesus. It is an encounter with a

Person who feels, knows, speaks and reveals himself among us as we worship ('where two or three are gathered...' (Mt 18:20)). If we are encountering in the Spirit the real Jesus, and not a distorted vision of him, then we are encountering an 'outsider'

No exclusive elite

If Jesus in his incarnation had taken the attitude of an exclusive elite, one of a privileged few, then all of us would still be bound for hell. If he had shut himself away in order to pursue the unimaginable glory of his own relationship with his Father, then the whole of humanity would remain damned to this day. The grace of God is such, however, that he took on a very different attitude. We read in Philippians 2:5–7:

> Your attitude should be the same as that of Christ Jesus; Who, being in very nature God, did not consider equality with God something to be grasped, but made himself nothing, taking the very nature of a servant, being made in human likeness.

Jesus became an outsider, a human being in the lower social orders, despised and rejected for mixing with prostitutes and sinners. He became identified in every way but sin with a world of outsiders. How then can we build around him an exclusive club, even for his praise and worship?

The stranger outside the door

In the face of Jesus we should see the face of every outsider, particularly those who are shut out of enjoying the bare necessities of natural life, let alone spiritual life. There is one particular passage in the Bible that for me is probably the most sobering and disturbing of all—Matthew 25 where Jesus talks about when he will appear in glory to judge us:

> Then he will say to those on his left, 'Depart from me, you who are cursed, into the eternal fire prepared for the devil and his angels. For I was hungry and you gave me nothing to eat, I was thirsty and you gave me nothing to drink, I was a stranger and you did not invite me in, I needed clothes and you did not clothe me, I was sick and in prison and you did not look after me.' They also will answer, 'Lord, when did we see you hungry or thirsty or a stranger or needing clothes or sick or in prison, and did not help you?' He will reply, 'I tell you the truth, whatever you did not do for one of the least of these, you did not do it for me.' Then they will go away to eternal punishment, but the righteous to eternal life (vv. 41–46).

Our worship should reveal to us the Jesus who suffers with the poor, the hungry, the sick, the naked and the imprisoned, and our meeting with him in the Spirit should send us out to meet him in the flesh of the world's outsiders. It is so much easier and more attractive to spiritualize our worship to the exclusion of the world outside, but we must face the fact that by so doing we shut Jesus out as well.

Note: The subject of unity and shared lives has been written about extensively in recent times, and it will undoubtedly be easier to grasp the implications it throws up for the way we worship if we first understand something of what the Bible teaches about the body of Christ. Hence I am taking a risk by isolating a discussion of communal worship from the wider issues, but hope that those with a deep concern for worship already have studied, or will make it their business to, what has been written by others on the subject of unity out of deep and sometimes painful experience.

5

A Royal Invitation

Being an Englishman, and living in England, I have a deeply ingrained habit that has dominated an area of my life for nearly all my adult years. I drive my car on the left-hand side of the road. Although I rarely think of it as such, it happens to be a legal requirement in this country. Obedience to it, however, is really extremely easy, such that I don't even think to feel proud of myself when I pass a police car, and would never for one moment find myself smiling broadly at the occupants as if to say, 'Aren't I doing well, still on the left!' Such a law seems so right, and reasonable, and common sense, that we hardly think of it as a law at all, and the idea of it being burdensome is ridiculous. In fact laws like that add considerably to the overall pleasure, not to mention the safety, of motoring!

God's laws and principles are like that. They are for our own safety and enjoyment and are restrictive only in the sense that they restrict chaos, unhappiness and misery. Having looked at the way in which praise and worship overflow naturally from lives that are presented to God, bringing pleasure to both God and man, it would be incomplete if we did not consider the fact that it is also a 'legal requirement'.

Worship is not optional

I don't know if anybody has ever counted the number of
commands to praise and worship in the Bible, but even a
brief search will reveal so many of them that we must
conclude that God really does require it! Looking through
the Old and New Testament there are commands to praise,
glorify, sing praises, shout, bless, give thanks, bow down,
kneel before, offer, sing a new song to, rejoice, honour,
offer sacrifices, exalt, fear, adore, serve, extol, magnify
and many others too, and in such proportions that we
cannot treat the subject in any way as an optional extra.

Consider for example these words to the people of God
from 2 Kings 17:35–36:

> When the Lord made a covenant with the Israelites, he
> commanded them: 'Do not worship any other gods or bow
> down to them, serve them or sacrifice to them. But the Lord,
> who brought you up out of Egypt with mighty power and
> outstretched arm, is the one you must worship. To him you
> shall bow down and to him offer sacrifices...'

Worship is our destination

Even if we were to exhaust these direct commands, we
would still have to take notice of the way in which God's
absolute right to our worship is implicit throughout the
Bible. It in fact begins and ends in worship, and the whole
history of redemption of which it tells is the restoration of
mankind after he ruins everything by transferring his
worship away from his Creator to himself. The serpent's
temptation was that if Adam and Eve ate of the forbidden
fruit, they would be 'like God', and so they traded their
worship and obedience to him for the chance to be as
important as he is. In that instant, they set their own egos
up as objects of worship, their own wills over his will, and

exchanged the true worship of God for a lie. The final book of the Bible, the book of Revelation, describes the destruction of sin and evil, and ends the story with a great feast, fantastic celebrations and stupendous worship by men and angels that will characterize eternity. We catch a glimpse of perfection where everything that exists gives praise to God. If we wish to be a part of this cosmic plan of redemption, then we must add our voices to the song that God commands all his creatures to sing. And burdensome it is not!

Yes you will! No I won't!

Our social experience of receiving commands, however, may cause us some problems when we encounter God's commands. The problem is this: living as we do as part of a corrupt society, made up of sinful people, the orders we are given inevitably come from people with anything ranging from true integrity to deliberate evil intent. We learn to be suspicious, to question, to rebel and to be cynical. Sometimes we even have to disobey orders on moral grounds. Such is the condition of man that we find it difficult to trust completely those in authority over us.

Sadly, we unconsciously transfer many of these doubts and suspicions to God, and impose our experience of human authority figures on to him. This is understandable, and it is wonderful to be able to remind ourselves that Jesus understands this and himself pleads our case before the Father, as one who has lived in human society in all its corruption and distortion of the truth.

Did God really say so?

However, there is also a most insidious characteristic within us that makes us coldly resistant to God's commands. It is the very same attitude that the devil planted into Eve's mind in the Garden of Eden: '*Did* God really say?' The devil went on from planting doubt about what God had said, to blatantly contradicting it and implying that God had lied. In this way God's command was undermined, then disobeyed, and thereafter there has been, mixed like a dark evil poison into the heart of mankind, this attitude: 'Did God really say that?... Take no notice, his commands are restrictive.' We would do well to give no time to discuss or argue with this attitude when it rears its serpent head inside us, but to tread it instantly underfoot, in case we should in discussing lies find ourselves in conversation with the father of lies.

God's commands are good for us

Despite our natural wariness of human commands, there are many which, though they are commands, come to us more in the manner of an invitation. Commands like 'Come and sit up, dinner's ready!' or 'Go to my wallet and take twenty pounds for yourself' are most welcome! Without the command, the person receiving the order would clearly be the loser. This is, I believe, akin to the nature of God's numerous commands to praise and worship him. The weakness of these illustrations of course is the emphasis on coming to receive, rather than coming to give. We are indeed invited to come and get, but we must remember that it is a relationship that we are invited into—a relationship of reciprocal giving and receiving.

It may be appropriate to illustrate this by what happens when a husband or wife says to their partner: 'Come and give me a hug.' In giving a hug, you inevitably get one! Jesus said that there is more happiness in giving than there is in receiving, so when God invites us, or commands us, to worship him, he knows that in giving ourselves in this way we will also receive, and then much more than if we came with the sole intention of getting.

RSVP

Though I don't have much personal contact with the British Royal family (well, none at all actually), I have a pretty good idea about the nature of the invitation cards bearing the address of Buckingham Palace. If Her Majesty Queen Elizabeth II requests the pleasure of your company, you'd better be there! In fact, royal invitations historically use the term 'commands your presence', and any suggestion of it being a take-it-or-leave-it request is just not in it! Imagine this kind of invitation in the days when the monarchy ruled supreme, when heads that caused royal displeasure tended to roll! Yet we have a standing invitation from the Kings of kings, the mighty and majestic Lord of the universe, to enter into his courts with praise. How incredibly presumptuous and foolish we are if we carelessly ignore such an invitation. His invitation cards, written with a nail-pierced hand, are scattered throughout the Scriptures, and when he invites us to come, we'd better be there!

The Creator God would be perfectly within his rights to require our worship, even if he was a tyrant and not the loving Father that he is revealed to be through Christ. Indeed, the revelation of Yahweh through the Jewish nation and Christ himself shows him to be unique when compared with all human concepts of God and gods. The gods of human imagination and demonic invention appear mostly to demand worship by way of fear and threats. In primitive times and even more recent history, such abhorrent practices as child sacrifice have been regarded as necessary to appease their anger, and countless people have lived in mental, spiritual and even physical bondage trying not to anger their particular god or gods.

He is worthy of our worship

One of the marvellous truths, however, about the one true God who has been revealed to us through Jesus is this: he is totally and utterly worthy of our worship. He doesn't just invite or demand it, he is worth it, with a worthiness that will absorb our wondering minds for eternity. One of the songs in Revelation 5 concentrates on this facet of God the Son, revealed there as a Lamb looking as if it had been killed:

> You are worthy to take the scroll and to open its seals, because you were slain, and with your blood you purchased men for God from every tribe and language and people and nation. You have made them to be a kingdom and priests to serve our God, and they will reign on the earth (vv. 9–10).

The song continues:

> In a loud voice they sang 'Worthy is the Lamb, who was slain, to receive power and wealth and wisdom and strength and honour and glory and praise!' (5:12).

Praise is really quite a natural thing for us to do when we feel that someone is worthy of it. I read in a newspaper recently the following headline: 'Praise for man who saved girl from seal.' The man's action, his courage and his willingness to risk his own life to save the girl, made him worthy of praise, and no one of a healthy disposition would deny it to him.

To attempt to expand on the worthiness of God in any adequate way, would be to begin a whole book, and I am sure that my lifetime would not provide enough time to finish it. There is a very real sense in which this is the

purpose of our lives anyway, our very life and being
reading like a book about the value of our Creator.

With a God like this, how can we keep quiet?

We do see, however, in this song of heaven, a focus on
some of the reasons why he is so worthy. The first reason
is: 'because you were slain'. We may be so familiar with
the story of God's redemption of mankind that it is easy to
take for granted what is an incredible divine act of grace
and humility, namely that described so vividly by Paul in
Philippians 2:5–8:

> Your attitude should be the same as that of Christ Jesus;
> Who, being in very nature God, did not consider equality
> with God something to be grasped, but made himself nothing,
> taking the very nature of a servant, being made in human
> likeness. And being found in appearance as a man, he
> humbled himself and became obedient to death—even death
> on a cross!

Don't you think that a God like that is worth praising!

The second reason for his supreme worth is this: 'and
with your blood you purchased men for God from every
tribe and language and people and nation'. What a Saviour
he is, paying the terrible and ultimate price for our forgiveness, despite what we really deserve. An innocent
man of immeasurable worth buying back with his own
blood traitors of indescribable guilt, fit only for the grim
punishment-halls of hell.

Not only does he buy us back: there is a third reason for
this worthiness: 'You have made them to be a kingdom,
and priests to serve our God, and they will reign on the
earth.' As if it wasn't enough to take on human flesh and
offer it as a sacrifice for our forgiveness, he goes on to
elevate these rescued rebels to a lofty and noble status,

not only to be kings and priests and reign on the earth, but as such, to engage in the highest of all acts of service, to serve God himself for ever! To quote Paul E. Billheimer (*Destined for the Throne*, Christian Literature Crusade, page 37):

> As sons of God, begotten by him, incorporating into their fundamental being and nature the very 'genes' of God, they rank above all other created beings and are elevated to the most sublime height possible short of becoming members of the Trinity itself. Although Christ is the unique and only begotten Eternal Son, yet he does not retain his glory for himself alone for he has declared, 'the glory which thou gavest me, I have given them' (Jn 17:22). Therefore, the redeemed will share his glory, his rulership, and his dominion as truly responsible princes of the Realm.

These truths, when we even just begin to comprehend them, surely leave us breathless, but when we get our breath back, how can we help but fill our lungs with air and speak, sing or shout praise to the utter worthiness of this amazing Saviour! How casual and conservative we so often are in our response to such magnificent love, to such inestimable worth!

Commands for our weaknesses

In the face of this kind of grace, you could argue: 'Who needs commands to praise him? Just try to keep me quiet!' Yet God understands us far more than we sometimes give him credit for, and he knows the weakness of our faulty and flawed personalities. He understands how easily we lose sight of him and his worthiness, how suddenly we become absorbed and distracted by the worries and troubles of life. He knows how often we entertain doubts, or lose heart in the face of adversity. For these very practical reasons he *commands* us to praise him. In fact the activity most likely to bring to vibrant life our vision of a praiseworthy God, is praise itself. It is often true that until we begin to praise, our thoughts are far away and devoid of any sense of God, but as we obey the command to praise, our spirits are stirred and begin to cut through the jungle of our tangled thoughts and feelings, and before long we break out on to a highway leading into the presence of God. God commands us to praise not only because it is his right, not only because he is worth it, but also because we often need a command to get us started at all!

God is always worth praising

Commands to praise and reasons to praise usually come together, for example in the shortest psalm, number 117— 'Praise the Lord, all you nations; extol him, all you peoples. For great is his love towards us, and the faithfulness of the Lord endures for ever. Praise the Lord.' God never leaves us for one moment without a reason to praise him. Even if we were to find ourselves with no prayers apparently answered, no good things to enjoy and give thanks for, the joys of life stolen away from us, yet his unchanging character, his faithfulness and love would still provide good enough reasons to give him the best our hearts can offer. His command is an invitation, his invitation affords us entrance into his presence, and in his presence we find an infinite number of good reasons to praise him. As David asserts in Psalm 16:11—'you will fill me with joy in your presence, with eternal pleasures at your right hand.'

6

Wired for Worship

(1) Worshipping the Father

Who are the 'true worshippers'?

'Yet a time is coming and has now come when the true worshippers will worship the Father in spirit and truth, for they are the kind of worshippers the Father seeks. God is spirit, and his worshippers must worship in spirit and in truth' (Jn 4:23, 24).

This conversation between Jesus and the Samaritan woman at a hot dirty well-side by the town of Sychar contains what is probably Jesus' most important statement on what true worship is. There is no vagueness in his words, no hint that we can worship in whatever way feels right to each one of us, but rather a clear decisive statement of the three essentials that separate those whom God declares to be 'true worshippers' from everybody else.

First, then, what constitutes a 'true worshipper'? The background to Jesus' conversation in John 4 was the old religious controversy between the Jews and the Samaritans concerning where God should be worshipped. The issue was a geographical one; should God be worshipped in Jerusalem as the Jews insisted or on Mount Gerizim as the Samaritans did? The question was to do with the externals of worship, implying location, ritual, tradition and creed.

Jesus' answer swept all these considerations aside and centred on the essential heart of worship, namely *who* we are worshipping, our relationship to him and how we are able to make and sustain a real, actual and personal approach to him. According to Jesus' words, those who would be true worshippers depend on three connections being established with God: worshipping 'the Father', worshipping 'in spirit' and worshipping 'in truth'. It may be helpful to picture these as the three pins of an electrical plug. When the three pins of the plug connect to the three corresponding holes in the socket, the circuit becomes 'live' and power can flow. Likewise it is necessary for us to be 'connected' to God in these three areas before worship becomes real. In this chapter, and the two following, we shall be looking at each of these three essentials.

Worshipping the Father

If those of you who have as yet escaped the joys of parenthood will bear with me for a moment, I will briefly indulge myself in one of its most pleasant aspects. In our family (wife, three daughters and a dog at the time of writing!), we do not hesitate to express verbally our love for one another. I must admit that for some reason, probably rooted in British reserve, the first few times I told my eldest daughter this fact, even though she was barely old enough to understand, I was slightly embarrassed. Thankfully, it quickly became quite natural, and I have been rewarded on occasions when, quite spontaneously, she has suddenly jumped on my lap and put her arms round my neck or run and hugged my leg and said, 'Daddy, I love you.' The added joy of this has been that it has always been unrelated to a request for sweets, a ride on the swing or anything else that suggests a mixed motive!

It is hard to explain exactly the effect this has on fathers, but it tends to evoke a certain melting of the insides and a dampness around the eyes, plus perhaps a lump in the throat. It is a deeply rewarding thing to be told, with unaffected simplicity and spontaneity, that your child loves you.

An astounding revelation

Surely this must be a small reflection of how God feels when we, his children, tell him the same thing. It was Jesus who revealed this marvellous truth about the fatherly nature of God to the world, and when we begin to appreciate what this means in terms of our relationship with him, it can have a transforming effect upon worship. In his conversation with the Samaritan woman in John 4:22, Jesus tells her that the Samaritans: 'worship what [they] do not know'. He then goes on to say something that must have sounded strange, if not preposterous, to her ears: 'Yet a time is coming and has now come when the true worshippers will worship the *Father...*' (my italics). Being a Samaritan, with Jewish blood in her veins and early Jewish history and teaching in her head, the idea of God as an intimate, personal Father could even have sounded blasphemous. Throughout his ministry, however, Jesus talked to his Father and about his Father, and when the scribes and Pharisees suspected that he was talking of Yahweh, the obvious implication that he was literally claiming to be Yahweh's Son offended their deepest sense of reverence, and constituted in their minds the capital crime of blasphemy. As scholars of the Scriptures, however, they must have had some idea of this concept, as there is a strong foreshadowing of it in the Old Testament, but a personal relationship with God such as this term suggests would have been unthinkable.

'Our Father...'

My interest in this led me to look in my concordance to
discover how much the term Father, as a specific name for
God, occurred in both the Old and New Testaments. In
the Old Testament there are fourteen examples of God
being referred to by the name of 'Father', and then not so
much in the sense of a personal relationship but that of a
father to the nation of Israel, but in the New Testament
there are 228 examples, plus three occasions when 'Abba'
is used—this being the word a child would use like our
'Dadda' or 'Daddy'. There are over one hundred occasions
in the Gospel of John alone when the use of the word
'Father' appears. It was Jesus who taught his disciples to
pray 'Our Father'. He himself, however, always said: 'My
Father', indicating his special unique relationship as *the*
Son of God. This we can understand, but to be invited
into a similar personal relationship ourselves is nothing
short of astounding!

'Abba Father'

It is worth looking a little more closely at this word 'Abba'.
Although there are only a handful of occasions when the
Aramaic word 'Abba' is directly transcribed, for example
in the Garden of Gethsemane account in Mark, scholars
tell us that the way in which the Greek for 'Father' or 'my
Father' is used elsewhere suggests quite clearly that it was
Jesus' normal practice to use 'Abba' when he spoke of or
to God. It is to our minds, however, a little strange to
think of Jesus calling God 'Dadda' or 'Daddy', because in
our culture we generally grow out of 'childish terms' and
replace them with adult ones. In Jewish homes, however,
what started as a 'baby word' was not discarded when the
children grew up. It would still be used even when the
children had families of their own. It was very specifically

a domestic and intimate term, used in the context of close family relationships, and the idea of addressing God in this way was totally out of the question.

Just imagine the wonder of those early disciples when they too were invited into the close family relationship of Jesus and his 'Abba', having heard Jesus use the term continually! The awesome, terrifying, even distant God that their ancestors had known was being reintroduced as something more. What Jesus revealed was certainly not *less* than, or other than, the Old Testament scriptures revealed, but rather a further dimension that completed the picture. The picture was of a God with a heart just like the heart of a father, when it is at its most tender, its most sensitive, its most generous, its most protective and its most forgiving.

'Family' love is at the heart of the universe

Our supreme and indeed original model of a loving relationship is that which can be glimpsed within the three Persons of the Godhead: Father, Son and Holy Spirit. It is quite correct in fact to understand the one true God as a type of family or, to put it the other way round, a family is a 'type', a model, of what God is like. In Genesis 1:26 and 27 (NASB) we read: 'Then God said, "Let Us make man in Our image, according to Our likeness".... And God created man in his own image, in the image of God he created him, male and female he created them.' When Adam alone had been created, God asserted that: 'It is not good for the man to be alone.'

My task here is not to attempt an exposition on the intrinsic nature of the triune God, but these verses should, I hope, begin to open up our understanding to the fact that God is not in his undivided self solitary and alone. Indeed it can be argued that a God who expresses himself by creating a society of people whose very nature it is to live in relationship, must have within his own nature that quality.

Altered images

We have to bear in mind of course that although we are made in the image of God, and set in families, we have fallen far from being a true reflection of God's nature and, for some, the mention of family relationships reawakes painful memories. Yet most of us have at least some concept of what they can and should be, and if we can picture for a moment the ideal of a loving, giving relationship, the joy of simply being together, the peace of perfect harmony, then we are some way towards putting our finger on the pulse of God's heartbeat.

Where did it all begin?

There is a fascinating chapter in Proverbs (8:29–31) that gives us some insight into this divine relationship, where wisdom, commonly understood as a personification of Jesus, speaks these words: 'when he marked out the foundations of the earth. Then I was the craftsman at his side. I was filled with delight day after day, rejoicing always in his presence, rejoicing in his whole world and delighting in mankind.' It is refreshing and exhilarating to discover that the source of delight and joy, praise and worship, is right in the very heart of God himself, and to marvel at the fact that we are invited into the 'family home'.

Worship is the response to a relationship

Within the circle of a truly loving family you will always find an increasing flow of thanks and praise and worship, as the worth of each member is affirmed by both words and deeds.

At the instant we put our trust in Jesus, and offered up our lives as a living sacrifice to God, we were adopted into God's family. We were introduced, not to a moody, selfish or mean tyrant, but to a perfectly loving, understanding and forgiving Father. It is as our relationship with him grows and develops, as we discover his love among our brothers and sisters, as we encounter his limitless grace and mercy, that praise and worship become an inevitable and glorious response. Worship, then, is a response to a relationship, and supremely the relationship is that of father and child.

Knowing God as Father changes us

I remember some years ago witnessing a most remarkable transformation in a particular person's life through the revelation of this very truth. This person, a young woman engaged in evangelistic work, had finally decided to be honest. We were at a conference, and the devotional atmosphere seemed to have brought her face to face with the fact that, unknown to anyone else, her life had become a complete contradiction. She privately confessed to a number of quite serious, habitual sins, which she just could not seem to shake. As a result, she had turned in on herself in guilt and confusion, and her life was devoid of any peace or joy, let alone praise and worship. There were three particular sins that gripped her. First of all, she was telling lies. If, for example, she was sitting opposite a stranger in a railway carriage and they engaged in conversation, she would begin to invent stories about herself. She would let it drop that she was the daugher of a millionaire or in some similar way attach a mystique to herself, and relate adventures that had no foundation whatsoever in her quite unremarkable background. Secondly, she had begun to steal. This generally took the form of shoplifting, and more than once she had slipped out of a record shop with an album under her coat. Thirdly, she was becoming embroiled in a romantic relationship with a married man, one of whose main attractions being that he said wonderful things about her! As she confessed these things, my mind was trying hard to identify what I felt sure must be there: some kind of root cause. Yet it was not clear what this was, and after talking for some time, and encouraging her to confess her sins and ask for forgiveness, I still had that 'unfinished feeling'. I prayed for her that God would reveal any root cause, and left it at that. As she went away I had the uncanny feeling that even the act of confession had some kind of ulterior motive.

The next day, the whole conference spent a long period in prayer and worship. All of a sudden, during a time of silence, she gasped. For all we knew at the time, she might have remembered that she'd left the gas on at home! Later on, however, she explained the interruption. Quite unexpectedly, she had had a vision. Call it a mental picture, a visual inspiration or whatever you like, but suddenly, vivid in her mind's eye, she had seen something amazing. She described the scene to me. God was enthroned in glory, and she was quite close to him and looking up into his face. He was smiling down at her in obvious delight, and she was returning a wondering gaze. The relationship represented was obvious; it was Father and daughter. Looking on, in open-mouthed wonder at this scene of mutual delight, was a crowd of people, marvelling at what they saw, remarking to one another in amazement. That was it; obviously God had decided to deal with this girl in his own way.

Six months later I happened to bump into her again, and she told me with delight that the vision had marked the end of her lies, her stealing, and her illicit relationship. How, you may wonder (if you haven't worked it out already!) did a revelation of that nature change her so much? The answer is that her real problem was to do with self-esteem. Various influences from her past had convinced her that she was worthless, a reject in spite of her many gifts and talents. Gnawing away for years at her insides, this was now playing havoc with her behaviour. In order to be 'somebody', she had invented tall stories involving noble origins and remarkable achievements. To draw attention to herself she stole, knowing that were she to be caught the scandal would make her somebody, if only in terms of infamy! Scandal was also a feature of her third sin, the illicit relationship, but probably more to the point was the fact that she found herself to be putty in the hands of somebody who flattered her. She wanted so much to be assured of her value and worth that she was prepared to enter into blatant sin upon false hopes of finding it. This was no excuse for her sins, but God in his mercy broke the fear of rejection by showing her his fatherly love, and illustrating so vividly her status as his child.

Filled with the Spirit of sonship

It is clear from Scripture that one of the specific activities of the Holy Spirit within the believer is to reveal to us the fatherhood of God. We read in Romans 8:15–16—'For you did not receive a spirit of fear that makes you a slave again to fear, but you received the Spirit of sonship. And by him we cry "*Abba*, Father". The Spirit himself testifies with our spirit that we are God's children.' Also in Galatians 4:6—'Because you are sons, God sent the Spirit of his Son into our hearts, the Spirit who calls out "*Abba*, Father".' The well-spring of worship is in relationship, and through the death, resurrection and ascension of Jesus we are qualified by faith to a relationship with God as Father. Furthermore, by the gift of the Holy Spirit planted within us, we are stirred to cry out to him like Jesus did: 'Abba, Father... not what I will, but what you will.'

Personal knowledge

How then does this knowledge of God as our Father affect our worship of him? There is of course a vast chasm between knowing about God, and knowing him in the sense of a relationship. Merely to know *about* God's fatherly nature will make very little difference at all to our worship of him, except possibly to enhance our aesthetic appreciation as we look on from a distance. It is only when we *know* him as Father, in terms of a living vital relationship, that our hearts are profoundly stirred by what we discover *about* him.

Our manner of approach to another person is determined largely by who we think they are, what we think they are like and how we think they might react to us. Similarly, our approach to God is conditioned by our concept of him, whether accurate or distorted. If we suspect that he is too busy with more important matters, as if we think there is a great queue in front of us, we won't want to bother him. If we see him as a tyrant, watching us sternly for any false moves, ready with a big stick to wallop us, we will come very warily! If, on the other hand, we see him as a soft and indulgent 'super-daddy', we may come presumptuously, blundering carelessly onto holy ground.

If, however, we know him by the revelation of the Holy Spirit and in our daily experience of him as a personal loving heavenly Father, and are acquainted with both his gentleness and his awesome holiness, we will run to him as children with open arms and yet deepest respect. The most important Person that ever existed loves you and me! The Creator of the universe has revealed himself as having the tender heart of a loving father, and has by his Spirit made us his true-born children. He knows your name, he knows my name, he laughs and weeps with us! In him we have discovered that we are valued infinitely far above our worth. How can we keep quiet about such a God?

7

Wired for Worship

(2) Worshipping in Spirit

John 4:24 'God is spirit, and his worshippers must worship in spirit....'

The meeting was not going at all well. There was an atmosphere of suspicion accompanied by a creeping paralysis of the arms, legs and jaws as I attempted to lead the people into a time of enthusiastic praise and worship. The harder I tried, the more my enthusiasm and jollity grew thin and unconvincing, and little signs of annoyance began to creep into my tone of voice. I encouraged, I explained, I joked, I gently cajoled and then finally handed over to the preacher to see how he would manage. As I sat at the front trying to adjust my facial expression to something more positive than my true feelings were suggesting, I was feeling sorely tempted to dwell on thoughts like 'pearls before swine' and 'why did I accept this invitation anyway?' Having dipped into my considerable resources of self-justification for a while, I began to be a little more objective and, I hope, compassionate towards the people who had just been subjected to my exhortations. What I decided I had been grappling with was not at heart a resistance to praising and worshipping, or even to my style of leading it, but something more basic.

Running on empty

I had been trying to draw out something that was not there, or at least present in such small quantities as to be almost negligible. They were running on 'empty'. The wells were dry and all I got was the hollow clanking of the bucket as it rattled in dry hearts. I say this not to judge them—they were probably living out of what they had been taught—but 'living waters' obviously did not feature much! I learned a lesson through this kind of experience: that praise and worship are the overflow of a way of life, of a *life* of worship, and that no amount of encouragement, enthusiasm, methodology or threats can draw true praise out of spiritually parched lives. In Matthew 12:34 Jesus is reported as saying: 'For out of the overflow of the heart the mouth speaks.' Although Jesus was at the time talking specifically about good and bad words and deeds, the principle still applies. It is the overflow of our hearts that provides the fuel for worship.

The overflow pipe

Years ago, when I lived at home with my parents, one of the houses we lived in (we lived in them one at a time I hasten to add!) had what is a common feature of many houses. On an outside wall, about twelve feet up and projecting over a concrete path, was a pipe. Attached to this pipe on the inside of the house was a bath, and this particular pipe was connected to a little hole just beneath the taps, called an overflow. This overflow hole and its connecting pipe were a dead giveaway if any of us children had, in the pursuit of swimming experience, overfilled the bath, and our guilt was yet more explicitly revealed should one of our parents or a visitor walk on the path beneath the pipe just as somebody was practising a belly-flop! Praise and worship are the overflow of a life that is filled with God, and to carry the illustration over to our bodies for a moment, our overflow hole is situated just under the nose!

It is obvious from John 4:4 that true worship can only be offered when, by the power of the Holy Spirit, our own spirit worships him. God is spirit, and we must be brought into his dimension to worship him as he requires. It was the presence of the Holy Spirit in the lives of Paul and Silas that inspired them, though badly beaten up, flogged and imprisoned in the stocks of the Philippian jail, to pray and sing hymns late into the night. This was not bravado, defiance or 'whistling in the dark', but a powerful stirring of the Spirit within them, eventually resulting in a violent earthquake and the conversion of the jailer! It is also clear from Luke 10:21 that Jesus' source of joy in worship was the Holy Spirit: 'At that time Jesus, full of joy through the Holy Spirit, said, "I praise you, Father..."'. It is wonderful to consider that the same Spirit that caused Jesus to be filled with joy as he praised and thanked his heavenly Father is in us as well.

Where the Spirit is—things happen

Wherever the Holy Spirit is mentioned in the Bible, it seems that something is happening. From the creation of the earth to the resurrection of Jesus, Pentecost and the Acts of the Apostles, he is powerfully active. If we think that all he does is to create a nice atmosphere at a meeting, we are guilty of the deepest underestimation. The Hebrew word for 'Spirit' in the Old Testament could also mean 'wind' or 'breath', but if we are thinking of soft summer breezes, we must remember that the commonest sort of wind in the Middle East was fierce, hot and often frighteningly forceful. Neither is the word for 'breath' referring to restful breathing; it was used for the fast breathing of someone in great exertion. When we enter into worship in the dimension of the spirit, we must not expect always to be wafted gently like model sailboats on a quiet pond; there is power there to blow a hurricane or send the spiritual equivalent of any number of ocean-going schooners slicing through the waves!

The dynamic behind corporate worship

Possibly the most detailed set of instructions about how Christians ought to worship is found in 1 Corinthians 12 and 14, chapters that are rich in references to, and content about, the Spirit and his workings in the gathered body of believers. We read of speaking by the Spirit of God, the manifestation of his Spirit, people being given messages through the Spirit, faith by the same Spirit, healing by that one Spirit, gifts being given to each one as the Spirit determines and so on. In chapter 14 there are numerous references to the activity of the believer's own spirit in praise, proclamation and the edification of the church. A reading of these passages makes it perfectly clear that while there were to be leaders, an exercise of self-control by all, and order as opposed to confusion, the real dynamic of the meeting was the unseen presence of the Holy Spirit pouring out the love and grace of God through the faith and love of the believers as they met to glorify him and bless one another.

Worship in the fourth dimension

What Jesus described to the woman at the well was a dimension of worship about which she had no concept. To her, worship was conducted by professionals in a certain place, at certain times, and the 'hot' issue of the day was should it be in the temple at Jerusalem or on Mount Gerizim. Jesus was announcing a new dimension and a new location. The new dimension was to be that of the spirit: 'Jesus answered, "Everyone who drinks this water will be thirsty again, but whoever drinks the water I give him will never thirst. Indeed, the water I give him will become in him a spring of water welling up to eternal life"' (Jn 4:13–14). The fresh bubbling spring water that Jesus spoke of is, of course, the Holy Spirit.

Announcing the Portatemple!

Concerning the new location of worship, Paul declares in 1 Corinthians 6:19, 'Do you not know that your body is a temple of the Holy Spirit, who is in you, whom you have received from God?' When we first trust in Christ for our salvation, we are born again by the Spirit into the dimension of the Spirit, and he takes up residence inside our bodies. True worship is a supernatural activity in a natural body. Paul speaks, in Philippians 3:3 of, 'we who worship by the Spirit of God', and again in 1 Corinthians 2:14, 'The man without the Spirit does not accept the things that come from the Spirit of God...because they are spiritually discerned.'

Until the divine Source of worship dwells within us, we cannot be the true worshippers that the Father seeks, and until that Source bubbles up and becomes a well of 'living water', we will find ourselves dry and thirsty, looking inwards at the empty void rather than upwards at the Giver. But why is it that so many Christians have been born again by the Spirit for many years and yet never known the experience of this inexhaustible supply of living waters overflowing into praise and worship?

Another unremarkable Sunday afternoon

We sat in my parents' lounge, eyes closed, praying occasionally. It was one of our prayer times, and 'we' were the five members of a musical singing group, formed for the purpose of evangelizing in church-based coffee bars. I was about seventeen or eighteen years old and, according to the spiritual *status quo* of the times, regarded as reasonably mature for my age and certainly zealous. However, we knew almost nothing about praise and worship, and the 'freest' we ever got was when in the Young People's Fellowship we would have a sing-song. This consisted of calling out the numbers of our favourite songs in the songbook and singing them one after the other, with little regard for anything except each person getting his or her favourite in before someone else suggested a song that you hated!

But back to the prayer meeting. I remember sitting there, eyes shut tight, concentrating my mind on God, thinking of some of the good things that are good to think about God! As I did, I experienced a pleasant sensation of being about ten feet tall, almost a floating feeling, such as you might get after a large Sunday dinner, sitting replete and relaxed in an armchair, drifting into a doze. You might be right in thinking that was a quite unremarkable experience. The only reason I remember it, is because at the time it was the most I had ever 'felt' in the context of praying and worshipping, and I was excited about it. It was, however, just a mental experience, on the same level as nearly all my devotional practices at that time. We knew of nothing more, and tended to assume that because our experience (or lack of it) was the 'norm', there was in fact nothing more that we could reasonably expect.

A comparatively normal Christian

If somebody was to refer to Jesus' words in John 4:24 about worshipping 'in spirit', I would assume that because I was a sound Bible-believing Christian, conformed to the norm of non-conformism, then whatever it was, I must be doing it anyway! The truth of the matter was that, though I had indeed been 'born again' by the Holy Spirit (I was five years old at the time and still remember it!), I had never been led into any kind of release of the spirit such as would create an overflow of praise and worship.

Faith comes by hearing

I have often thought about this in the light of Romans 10:17, 'faith comes from hearing, and hearing by the word of Christ'. Although I had been familiar with the story of Jesus and the Samaritan woman since my childhood, it was not until I met people who clearly experienced a new quality of life in the Spirit, and seemed to have discovered this inner source of joy and spiritual power, that I realized there was something tangible to be experienced. I was suddenly aware that, by comparison, my well was dusty and dry. When somebody preaches about or witnesses to a biblical truth that has become a dynamic part of their lives, faith seems to be generated in the listener in a special way, and this is what happened to me. I was faced with the possibility that I might have to ask God for the experience of the doctrine I knew so well.

Theory is safer

It is sad but true of so many of us that we think we have the fullness of all that the Bible teaches simply because the doctrines are familiar to us. Could it also be true that we prefer the theory to the reality, especially when the reality might involve trusting ourselves to God in areas beyond the control of the intellect, or taking the risk of being let down? The doctrines are vital, but they are there to explain, to interpret, to preserve from corruption and *to lead us into* the experience of God's promised gift of the Holy Spirit.

You mean... just ask?

God, in his grace and mercy, never demands anything from us that he does not at the same time offer to us. The passage that clinched the matter for me was Luke 11:13 where Jesus says after so clearly illustrating his point to his listeners: 'If you then, though you are evil, know how to give good gifts to your children, how much more will your Father in heaven give the Holy Spirit to those who *ask* him!' It is worth relating my experiences here, not in any way to suggest a norm (in fact it should be the opposite!), but possibly to illustrate the 'ordinariness' of something that has become in some people's minds over-dramatized, 'scary', or seemingly out of reach.

I walked down the quiet suburban street, counting off the numbers until I reached the one that corresponded to the address that I had been given. It was early summer and I had recently returned from college for the vacation; I was feeling a little melancholy. Still fresh in my mind was the disappointment of the previous few months, which had been dominated by a lengthy spiritual crisis, or rather the closest that my placid personality ever got to one! I could clearly remember standing under the stars on the college campus after a Christian meeting, so depressed by the apparent spiritual poverty I had just been an unwilling part of, that I seriously wondered whether I was just fooling myself about God.

I had started to be honest with myself, which usually brings you to the conclusion that you haven't been honest before! I had been 'witnessing' to unbelievers, but mainly on the basis of what God was doing in other people's lives. The racy Christian paperbacks of the day provided a great resource of stories and experiences, but they were not mine. I was ashamed of myself, and ashamed of my fellow Christians for the sham we seemed to be perpetuating, and yet somehow, intuitively, I felt that there must be more to Christianity than we knew. The decision I made out there under the stars (most of these type of things happen under the stars!) was that either I had to carry this new honesty about my disappointment with God to a practical withdrawal from 'hypocritical' Christian activities, or find what was missing.

I decided to find what was missing and proceeded to search the Scriptures and search for Christians who seemed to possess what I lacked. Three months later, having obtained the said address from a friend (whose life had been somewhat revolutionized through contact with the people living there), I gingerly opened the garden gate and proceeded to ring the doorbell of this strange house, wherein I had been told, a group of Spirit-filled Christians met on this particular evening, every week, and who for all I knew at that very moment might be setting up the chandeliers ready for a swinging-session! To cut a long meeting short, I ended up asking for prayer to be filled with the Spirit, and with understanding and wisdom they explained certain scriptures to me and, in a separate room, two of them laid hands on me and together we simply asked our heavenly Father for his gift.

Nothing happened. I waited for the tongues of fire, the mighty rushing wind, and every time a car rushed by the window my heart jumped an inch or two as I thought, 'Here it comes!' As the minutes ticked by my temptation was to react with thoughts like 'You see, it's true, nothing will ever happen to me', and 'I guess I'm not spiritual enough yet'. But I hung on to the scriptures: '... how much more will your Father in heaven give the Holy Spirit to those who *ask* him!' I had asked. It was all I could do, except now, having asked, to trust. It was out of my hands, and into his. I went home subdued but fairly peaceful. God has a sense of humour. He also knows us inside out, and knows how sometimes our very trying, our striving too hard for experience of him makes it difficult for us to receive his gifts. Back home, everybody else had gone to bed and it was late (these charismatics have no sense of time!), and so I proceeded to the bathroom to clean my teeth and get ready for bed.

I was half-way through cleaning my teeth, quietly thanking God for hearing my prayer, but no more, when quite unexpectedly I found myself smiling. Where the smile came from I wasn't sure but there was suddenly a lot more of whatever was causing it, welling up inside! I quickly finished my teeth (still smiling and almost laughing) and adopted a more 'spiritual' pose, kneeling by the bath, but it wasn't the bath that was filling up, it was me! This was totally new, I'd never felt like this before; I was so full up with joy and peace that I spent the next hour right there, *enjoying* God for the first time in my life. I wasn't generating it, in myself I had been calm, almost melancholy, and now it was almost as if my dubious doubtful mind was looking on and saying: 'Hey, what's this! What's going on? Stop it!' But my spirit had been liberated, and I remember lying at last in my bed, the fixed grin still on my face, praising and thanking God, and gingerly trying out a new spiritual language that had presented itself to my tongue with no regard at all for the objections thrown up by my incredulous brain!

My rusty tap had at last been turned on, and what came

out was a stream of praise and worship, originating in my spirit where the Holy Spirit had found at least an open channel of faith through which to glorify my heavenly Father. Though my progress was slow, and my mistakes many, something began over that sink, toothbrush in hand, that has changed, and will continue to change, my whole life. A well of praise was opened that has never failed to satisfy my thirst when I have dipped into it.

I don't recommend *my* experience to others, because through the same truths and promises God has something special and unique for each individual. But one thing remains identical, and that is his desire that all of us should experience and enjoy everything that Jesus paid for with his blood, and one of the greatest of these things is the promise of the Holy Spirit in all his fullness, power and glory.

To worship 'in spirit' is to tap into the very source of worship himself, the inexhaustible, endlessly praising Spirit of God, and to allow him liberty to join with our own spirit in expressing through our mind and body the worth of our saviour Jesus, and the love of our heavenly Father.

'If you knew the gift of God, and who it is who says to you: "Give me a drink", you would have asked him, and he would have given you living water.'

8

Wired for Worship

(3) Worshipping in Truth

The third pin of our 'electrical plug' illustrating the essential characteristics of a true worshipper, is the pin of truth. We have seen that true worship is an actual, real approach to God. It is not dependent on being in a certain place, but on being in a certain relationship with God, that of Father and child, and being brought by faith into a certain dimension, namely that of the spirit. The third pin is equally vital despite the fact that many electrical appliances work without the earth wire connected! This would be a weakness in the illustration except for the fact that the earth connection is the one that both protects the user from harm and, in the case of radio receivers, cuts down interference from other sources. There are some parallels here that I trust will be self-evident.

Truth originates in God himself; it is an intrinsic part of his character, and therefore all his words and deeds bear the divine hallmark of truth. If our worship is to make a real live connection with this God of truth, then our lives, thought patterns and beliefs must conform to the truth about him. Any other 'pin' will not fit.

Reality versus ritual

In his conversation with the Samaritan woman, Jesus was announcing the arrival of a new age in which worship would no longer be seen to depend on buildings, holy places, ceremonies, rituals and sacrifices, but on a personal relationship with God. All those things had been symbols of what was to come, and now Jesus himself was announcing the reality of the fulfilment of all that Judaistic worship had foreshadowed. The holy of holies was no longer shut off from the common man or woman, but open to all who come by way of Jesus. Yet more astounding, he was introducing God as a personal, loving Father, and one who actively seeks worshippers.

In order to worship, this relationship with God our Father must be a reality in our lives, so that our worship is not dependent on the things that can be seen—the buildings, ceremonies, rituals and trappings of religion that can so easily become a substitute for a personal knowledge of God. Worship that depends on the externals for its existence is not real worship at all; true worship is what you have left when the externals are taken away. This does not mean that certain aids to worship are not valid and useful, but they are useless without the internal reality.

Worship in truth is worship that arises out of an actual encounter with God, a response to the experience of knowing God's real presence and activity in our daily lives. This has nothing to do with sentiment, thinking religious thoughts or having aesthetic experiences in church buildings; any religion can give you that sort of thing.

Worship in sincerity

On one occasion Jesus was challenged by some Pharisees and scribes about his disciples' failure to obey the religious traditions of the day. He answered them first by exposing the way in which they used tradition to invalidate the word of God, and then by quoting some words of Isaiah chapter 29:

> These people... honour me with their lips, but their hearts are far from me. They worship me in vain; their teachings are but rules taught by men.

This leaves no doubt that true worship must be a sincere expression of the heart if it is to be acceptable to God. In David's song of confession, Psalm 51:6, he declares: 'Surely you desire truth in the inner parts.'

Just as the lettering in sticks of seaside 'rock' goes right through from top to bottom, our lives must be internally imprinted with the character of Jesus, and not just decorated on the outside with a sticky label saying 'Christian'.

The Pharisees and scribes were concerned about conformity to external rules, by which they kept people in bondage. Jesus was concerned with the hidden places of the heart and what comes out from deep within us. Heart and lips must be in harmony if we are to worship in truth.

Worship in the light of revealed truth

Having begun by focusing on the reality of our relationship with God, and the sincerity of our hearts, we must also recognize the need for our worship to be guided by objective truth.

In the holy place of the tabernacle there was a seven-branched candlestick that was the only source of light for the priests as they worshipped. It was not natural light from the sun, but from a flame fuelled by oil. In the same way, we need to worship according to the truth revealed in the Scriptures, as it is illuminated in our hearts and minds by the supernatural light of the Holy Spirit: 'Your word is a lamp to my feet and a light for my path' (Ps 119:105). God has revealed the truth about himself in the Scriptures, culminating in the most vivid revelation of all, the person of Jesus Christ. We read in John 1:18—'No-one has ever seen God, but God the only Son, who is at the Father's side, has made him known.'

To worship in truth means to worship according to God's own revelation of himself and his purposes for mankind, and not according to the religions, philosophies, ideas and inventions of man. So we worship according to the truth about Jesus, that he is our Saviour, Prophet, Priest and King—our supreme example of manhood, and an undistorted image of the Creator. Without the knowledge and application of these and other marvellous truths about Jesus, our worship would be shrouded by mists of ignorance and uncertainty.

If reality and sincerity in worship can be likened to the love relationship at the heart of a marriage, the objective truth of the Scriptures can be likened to the legal contract of the social institution of marriage that keeps it within the right boundaries.

To this end we have the priceless gift of the Holy Spirit, whom Jesus promised in John 16:13, 'will guide you into all truth'. This truth is not a doctrinal formula to be learned, but the living word of God to be obeyed. Worship that is not illuminated, refreshed and invigorated by the truth about Jesus very soon becomes either jaded and wearisome, or frothy and unreal. Both extremes can open the door to the elevation of subjective experience above the revealed truths of the Scriptures, and lead into error.

Worship in integrity

I believe that many of us unconsciously think of worship as something we 'do' to God, a kind of broadcast we send out over the distance between earth and heaven. If we think in this way, we may go on to detach ourselves and our morality from our worship. This separation of the 'spiritual' and the 'rest' will always draw worship into unreality. The prophet Amos delivered some very hard words from the Lord to people who tried to detach their worship from their behaviour:

> I hate, I despise your religious feasts; I cannot stand your assemblies.... Away with the noise of your songs! I will not listen to the music of your harps. But let justice roll on like a river, righteousness like a never-failing stream! (5:21–24)

The absence of justice and righteousness and the presence of idolatry in their lives cancelled out the validity of their worship, reducing it to a meaningless noise in the ears of God. There was no doubt that they were continuing the outward form of religion, probably with enthusiasm and cultural richness, but because of its lack of moral integrity it brought God's judgement not his blessing. I wonder how many of us have stood up with the congregation to sing, give thanks and worship, and then gone back to our family relationships, our business practices and social lives and failed to purge out our own injustices, sins and idolatries. To worship in truth is to stand before God with the words on our lips matching the actions in our lives, living a life in which belief and behaviour are integrated.

Anyone who is foolish and careless with live electrical wiring runs the risk of death or injury. Similarly, we must remember that 'our God is a consuming fire' (Heb 12:29) and we disregard his call to worship with integrity at our peril.

Truth in character

I began this chapter by reminding us that truth originates in the character of God, and all his words of truth and deeds of truth flow out from who he is. In his grace, he is redeeming us back from the moral corruption, lies and distortions of a fallen world, to make us into 'true' people, accurately reflecting his character. Truth in character bears the hallmarks of honesty, reliability, faithfulness, consistency and, above all, love, and these qualities are surely ones that God desires to see flowing out in the way we worship him.

9

Worship and Wholeness

The body in question

Under the orange and blue striped canvas of the enormous
marquee, another celebration and teaching evening was
in full swing. The sense of God's presence was giving rise
to praise of a very enthusiastic nature, there were smiles
everywhere, voices rang out, arms were raised, hands
were clapped and even some legs got liberated and danced
for joy. In the midst of one such group of worshippers sat
a severely disabled Christian man in an invalid 'buggy'. No
one would have blamed him for feeling depressed or
resentful at those around him who were praising God with
agile and healthy bodies, while he could not even stand
up. No one would have blamed him for excusing himself
from the meeting and trundling off in his electric buggy
out into the windy night and back to his room. Apparently
nothing of the kind even entered his head, because as the
spirit of praise grew stronger those nearby were treated to
a lovely example of selfless praise. The buggy was well
equipped for street use, and there he sat, flashing head-
lights, stop lights, indicator lights, warning lights, in fact
anything that flashed, moved or made a sound was in use
as he gave all he had got in praise to the Lord he loved! I

would not be at all surprised if, as God received and enjoyed his gift of worship that night, this man's expression was the most precious offering. Like the widow's mite, he had very little in human terms to give, but he gave more than anybody else because it was everything he had.

What a rebuke this was to those of us with healthy bodies knowing that we often give so little to God in praise, acting as observers rather than participants, neglecting to employ our whole being to show how much we reckon him to be worth. But how far should we go in physical expressions of worship? Is hand-raising and dancing just a passing fad, is it not irreverent and disorderly, or just something for those of us with extrovert personalities? In fact, these kind of questions are part of a much bigger issue, and many of them get answered when we understand something of the influences that have formed our thinking.

Plato rules OK!

Sadly it is true that in every age, including our own, the church has imbibed much of the world's philosophy, even when it directly contradicts the teaching of its Hebrew-Christian roots, and so it is important to see how our own thinking may have been distorted in this respect.

Plato, the Greek philosopher, headed a school of thought that preached that human beings were a unity of two parts, soul and body, but that the soul was superior to the body. This is generally termed 'Platonic dualism', and led to religious attitudes and practices that would attempt to subserve and negate the body in favour of the soul, and regard the body as evil—or at least a serious danger to religious purity. However, if we look right back to the roots of the Christian view of man, namely to the revelation that came through the Hebrew race from its earliest days, we will see quite a different view. In historic Hebrew belief and culture there is no false division made between the spiritual and the physical, no dividing up into different parts of differing values, no 'disembodying' of belief; in fact, quite the reverse is nearer to the truth.

A human trinity

The Bible's teaching is that we are tripartite beings, comprised of spirit, soul and body. (See 1 Thess 5:23; Lk 1:46; Heb 4:12.) We can identify our component parts, but for the purposes of our earthly existence we are clearly a unity of inextricably interwoven parts, evidenced by the fact that any attempt to separate mind from body, or spirit from mind, would be to pronounce a literal sentence of death! Yet living as we do in a world divided and distorted by sin, where the truth about the nature of being human has in many respects been replaced by lies or half-truths, we often find within ourselves unhealthy tensions that work against true peace of body, mind and spirit, and against peace between these members of our human trinity. If we are to worship with our whole being we must recover an understanding of God's perspective on what constitutes a whole human being.

It is highly significant that in the Hebrew language words that we translate and popularly interpret as representing something exclusively 'spiritual' nearly always carry a parallel physical meaning. For example, the various words that we translate as 'worship' indicate also a variety of physical attitudes. In John 4:16–24 the word repeatedly used for worship carries the various meaning of to kiss, bow down, and prostrate oneself. Elsewhere the word is literally 'to serve' or 'to minister', indicating actions that involve the unified commitment of the whole person, body, mind and spirit.

The division of sacred and secular

There has continued into recent times a popular but
insidious belief that life can be successfully compartmentalized, particularly into the religious and the secular.
This has been, for millions of nominal Christians, a
convenient way of escaping the practical demands of
Christ's teaching. To achieve this, one simply labels
religion as 'private' and 'too personal to be talked about',
and concentrates on preserving the traditional, cultural
and artistic heritage of the church, not as a good and
proper way of enriching living faith and worship but as a
means of keeping open the door to private aesthetic
experiences in church buildings. Meanwhile one's
business, social and domestic life carries on according to
the world's *status quo*, and avoids any challenge that
'beliefs' may present to our behaviour. In this way, an
attempt is made to separate the 'sacred' and the 'secular'
in a way that the Bible never does.

Here again we see the influence of Greek thought,
namely the very idea that 'belief' can be detached from
daily life and practice. In Hebrew understanding, the
word 'belief' itself suggests not an abstract set of ideas
about the way one should or might live, but rather a code
of life in practice. Hence, for example, the popular statement 'I believe in God' must be critically examined in the
light of the 'believer's' manner of life, and further
questions asked regarding the kind of God he or she
claims to believe in. A *genuine* belief in a God of judgement, for example, will result in the believer measuring
his life constantly against God's standards, and adjusting
it accordingly! How many of us in these terms *really*
believe in a God of judgement?

Salvation is not just 'spiritual!

It has been said, and I believe quite rightly, that the only truly secular thing in the world is sin. It is of course a stark fact of this fallen world that sin has thoroughly corrupted God's perfect handiwork, but a correct reading of Scripture will show us that the gospel is a plan of redemption not only of the spiritual side of a man, but of his body and of the whole of creation. Paul instructs us in Romans 8:19–23:

> The creation waits in eager expectation for the sons of God to be revealed. For the creation was subjected to frustration, not by its own choice, but by the will of the one who subjected it, in hope that the creation itself will be liberated from the bondage to decay and brought into glorious freedom of the children of God.... Not only so, but we ourselves, who have the firstfruits of the Spirit, groan inwardly as we wait for our adoption as sons, the redemption of our bodies.

Jesus came announcing the arrival of the kingdom of God, and demonstrating the power of that kingdom over the sickness, disease, death and decay in people's bodies. Not only that, but he exercised power over the physical elements, commanding a storm at sea to cease, a fig tree to wither and the molecules in a few loaves and fishes to multiply enough to feed 5,000 hungry people. Within this cosmic plan of liberation, salvation is available to the whole person, body, mind and spirit, and we will eventually see the redemption from decay even of the planet that supports our physical existence.

A suspicion of the body

The Scriptures, consistently and refreshingly, present us with a view of man as a complete unity, with no internal ruptures between thought and action, spiritual experience and social behaviour, inward emotions and bodily expression. Where these are seen as divided in Scripture, it is usually as the result of sin. The gospel is a gospel of wholeness, where all things come together and find their unity in Christ, and not least of these is the bringing towards wholeness of the torn and scarred human personality. I believe that if we were to adopt a more biblical view (that is, God's perspective) of ourselves then we would enjoy far more not only the experience of praising God, but also the whole experience of living. The infiltration of Platonic dualism into English culture, and consequently into the church, has tended to create a suspicion of, and even a fear of, using our bodies in worship, and a subtle denial that Christianity has anything much to do with them in practice. In the majority of our churches it is still an unwritten law that for the congregation the only physical gestures permitted in worship are sitting, standing and sometimes kneeling. Any departure from this ecclesiastical protocol is likely to be the cause of quite another set of physical gestures, namely expressions of disapproval, embarrassment and shock—in fact, a most eloquent set of statements delivered in 'body language' from the rest of the congregation!

We all use body language

The fact of the matter is that in normal everyday life we speak with our bodies as much if not more than we do with our tongues. This is perfectly natural and is a part of the whole business of communication. When we are sad or upset, we want to bury our faces and weep. When we are joyful and happy, we want to dance and sing. When we are angry we become animated and agitated. The very word 'agitated' is used to describe both inward feelings and outward gestures, because they happen at the same time.

It has been known and understood for a long time, both in the commonsense teachings of most cultures and in contemporary psychiatry, that the repression of emotions, feelings and inward convictions can cause stress and tension, neurosis and even mental illness. But the wholeness that comes through Christ first heals us and then begins to release us into a worship that wells up in the spirit, is informed by the mind, and expressed through the body. It could be argued that there is no moment of more perfect unity of personality than that which comes when a person worships the Father in spirit and in truth, when the spirit is exhilarated, the mind and imagination stimulated, and the body freely expressing 'all that is within'. In King David's exhortation to himself in Psalm 103:1, he cries: 'all that is within me, bless his holy name' (AV). It is unnatural to feel deep convictions and emotions within and not to show them. Why then do we limit 'body language' to God to the equivalent of the verbal vocabulary of a parrot?

Like a little child

Much of the delightfulness of children is their naturalness and spontaneity, their lack of inhibitions and sophistication. They let you know how they feel, frequently to the embarrassment of their parents when in public places! Sometimes it seems that 'growing up' is a process of hiding our feelings, of adopting behaviour patterns that are not really comfortable but are expected of us. We develop a fear of being different, of being rejected by the majority; we force ourselves into a harness that cuts and chafes, and so, gritting our teeth, we pull our burdens of conformity throughout our lives. It is nevertheless true that for those outside the grace of God, it is better to chafe under the law than to break free into what would quickly become anarchy—everyone expressing their inward feelings of hatred, lust and covetousness without restraint! However, under the 'law of the spirit of life in Christ Jesus', the perfect law of liberty, the rule of love, would we not be vastly richer towards God and each other were we to express ourselves in the natural way that children do, as unified personalities bubbling with life and vitality? Of course, if the inward life is not there, then any attempt at rich outward expression would be meaningless and hypocritical. But if it is there, then the expression of it would confirm it, strengthen it and encourage its permeation into the whole personality. Lamentations 3:41 says: 'Let us lift up our hearts and our hands to God in heaven.' The spiritual, mental and physical are designed to function in harmony.

'Glorify God in your body'

It is worth saying a little more about the body, simply because it is mostly with our body that we have difficulties as Christian worshippers. Paul exhorts in 1 Corinthians 6:20—'Glorify God in your body' (AV). He doesn't say that we should glorify God *despite* our bodies, but *in* them. He goes on to explain why in verse 20—'For you have been bought with a price.' In some parts of the church it needs to be shouted from the rooftops that Jesus paid the ultimate price not only for our 'souls' but also for our bodies. Salvation is a complete package; it is to do with the redemption of the whole person, in fact, the whole of creation, of heaven and earth, of things spiritual and of things physical. It is not solely a spiritual salvation—it is also to do with molecules and cells!

Centuries ago, Tertullian wrote in his treatise *On The Flesh of Christ* the following words: 'Our birth he reforms from death by a heavenly regeneration; our flesh he restores from every harassing malady; when leprous, he cleanses it of stain; when blind, he rekindles its light; when palsied, he renews its strength; when possessed by devils, he exorcises it; when dead, he reanimates it—then shall we blush to own it?' (*De Carne Christi* 4). Somewhere alongside Platonic dualism there has crept into popular theology the idea that heaven is an ethereal existence of floating spirits and eery music. The Bible speaks of no such thing. Heaven is presented to us as solid and tangible, peopled by perfected saints in real spiritual bodies. Jesus was the first to be clothed in such a 'resurrection' body when he rose from the dead, and he was solid. He even ate a piece of fish to prove that he was not a ghost! He was at the same time able to enter the room without the inconvenience of doors or windows, demonstrating a fundamental development in his new material make-up! When will we get used to the idea that we are destined not for an eternity without one, but with a new one! Without our bodies, we are dead and no longer have any earthly use for our spirits and minds; it is *in* our bodies that we should glorify God, and therefore *with* our bodies that we most naturally should worship him. We look forward to a bodily resurrection, but meanwhile we enjoy the gift of a body here and now, without which we would have no touch, taste, sight, smell or hearing; no way to sense or interpret reality. In gratitude we offer it back to God as a means of serving and worshipping him, while experiencing the healing and wholeness that he brings to it as an integral part of a complete salvation.

By giving so much attention to bodily expression, I would not like to give the impression that all praise and worship meetings should be the ecclesiastical equivalent of a cup final crowd at Wembley! It is nevertheless curious how on a Saturday afternoon, many clergymen and laymen can happily function in an extraordinarily liberated physical manner on the terraces, celebrating their team's victory over another team, and then on Sunday adopt a sombre, parsonic and restrained manner when celebrating Christ's victory over the world, the flesh and the devil! Of course there should be a profound reverence in the presence of God, particularly when we remember the price of that victory, but there is also 'fullness of joy'! Although it may be true that one of our greatest needs is for richer, louder and more expressive praise, the Bible does not back up those who would swing either to an exclusive preference for silence and sobriety, or for wild enthusiasm. The fact of the matter is that the Bible makes room for everything that legitimately expresses the life and salvation God has put within us. We see there a broad spectrum from silence to dancing, from the prostration that expresses humble submission to the bold approach to the throne of God with upturned face and raised hands.

Spectator Christianity

I suspect that much of the unreality that so easily creeps into our worship is due to the neglect of this variety of biblically endorsed poses. An action literally puts flesh on to the skeleton of an inward attitude, and fixes it in space and time. Just as the act of putting our thoughts into words clarifies, tests and fixes them, the act of putting our convictions, feelings and spiritual 'stirrings' into physical actions clarifies, tests and fixes them also. It is often far too easy to drift through a service of worship unchallenged and unmoved, simply because nothing demands *acts* of commitment. To act is to test the reality of belief and not to act is often to suspend belief. I wonder how many of us would be forced towards greater honesty towards God and one another in worship and in general, were we to be deprived of the passive 'spectator' roles that encourage us to hold our beliefs in a kind of suspended animation.

It has been proved of course that it is possible to adopt a comprehensive set of devotional actions, a wholesome and rich liturgy of worship, and still to be without the power of God that authenticates true worship. What we need is both the genuine spiritual life within, the teaching of doctrine to enliven and enlighten our minds, and the richness of appropriate modes of bodily expression. Each feeds and stimulates the other, and helps us move towards integrity as human beings. Integrity is a key word here, because God is in the business of making us like Jesus, within whom there was a perfect integrity, not only in the popular sense of the word—that is, truth and honesty—but in the sense of a perfect integration of body, mind and spirit, directed to a simple purpose of pleasing his Father.

Worship and the five senses

If we genuinely believe that salvation is for the whole person, then we must cater for the whole person in worship, allowing the truth about God to be encountered by all our senses as well as by our spirit. The more help we give our senses, the more of the truth about God we may expect to encounter. The very taste and smell of bread and wine can be powerful signs by way of the associations they call up. The waters of baptism are an experience involving all the senses (though this can depend on the amount of water used!) and it could be argued that there is no more powerful a symbol of passing through death and up into life, than one that literally plunges the five senses under gallons of water and then out again! It is a significant and memorable experience not only because of what it speaks of, but because of what it is to our bodies at the time. In everyday life, our eyes are constantly bombarded with images and symbols representing the material paraphernalia of a consumer society, and the seductive art of the advertisers has never been so carefully studied or massively exploited. We would do well to limit where possible what we absorb of all this because it undoubtedly conditions us accordingly, but we cannot go about with our eyes closed! Surely it would go some way to counter-acting the effect of all this if we 'fed' our eyes, and the 'reference library' of our visual imaginations, with images that spoke of Christ.

Much of the artistic heritage of the church originated in the days when only the rich were literate, and the poor were educated by way of picture stories in stained glass windows, symbols and ceremonies. Although now most people can read the stories themselves without the pic-tures, it is still pictures that have the edge on the other senses in terms of making a lasting impression upon us. As I have already mentioned, many churches have revived the art of banner-making, where themes or Scripture verses are illustrated pictorially on large banners, which are hung in the church at appropriate times according to the current theme of the worship. Such illustrations can preach sermons all by themselves when created skilfully and lovingly under the inspiration of the Holy Spirit. They are a magnet to wandering eyes, and their symbolic content (if portrayed successfully!) can be a powerful stimulus to the worshippers. As further aids to the senses in worship there is the oil of anointing, the laying on of hands, the kiss of peace and so on, all of which help to locate our faith in the context of a material world, and can become a means through which we 'touch' the spiritual world.

Learning to live from the spirit

I believe that it is in those times during which we concentrate ourselves exclusively upon worshipping God, that we can actually learn integrated Christ-like behaviour as a habit of bodily life. We all come to Christ in the first place with a complete set of behaviour patterns, most of which have been built without reference to the living presence of God. This is why for many people conversion is so traumatic, even if at first there is great excitement. The problem is that we are not used to having God inside us! His presence upsets everything, and so it should! We suddenly have a different moral and spiritual frame of reference; we have his voice speaking into unblocked spiritual 'ears'. Our conscience is sensitized and instructed by Scripture, and we enter a state of violent tension between the old long-established regime of sinful habit, and the incoming kingdom. Having lived according to the dictates of the mind, will and bodily instincts, we find ourselves required to live according to the gentle but firm instructions of the Holy Spirit. It is true that it is in the humdrum of everyday life that we must work out our obedience to our new Master, but it is there also that we have the added pressure of a world-system that demands conformity, trying to squeeze us back into its mould.

Just as a dancer needs the private disciplines of the rehearsal studio in order to become a natural and spontaneous performer, Christians need the practice room of worship to learn behaviour that flows from the spirit out into bodily action. Regular withdrawals into private and corporate worship, where the personality is given over entirely to practising a sensitive response to the Holy Spirit will, among countless other benefits, help to establish new habits for the whole of life, and send us out into the world as reformers, not conformers.

Breaking old patterns

When I was first filled to overflowing with the Spirit, I found my mind and body completely unprepared for the experience. As a fairly reserved and conservative person, I winced at my own attempts to give even the most primitive physical or even verbal expression to it. I remember gradually having to break down the old patterns, and I believe that much of this was done in times of private devotion when I felt most free to vent all my feelings with impunity! I would determine to express what was inside and must have gone through the whole repertoire, dancing, kneeling, prostrating myself, raising my hands, walking up and down gesticulating, speaking and singing both with the mind and the spirit! I'm sure that in this way I began to establish new patterns derived from a new source, and partly as a result of this I began to enjoy a new 'spiritual naturalness' in everyday life, even to feel more 'myself'.

Discovering a new identity in God

We live in a society that is obsessed with self-expression, and that's exactly what it gets—self*ish* expression in all kinds of destructive ways. Nevertheless it is the legitimate cry of each human heart to be a unique individual who enjoys life in a rich, spontaneous way, and surely the Creator made us that way. Sadly but predictably, his presence is the missing ingredient in most recipes designed to help you 'be yourself', and it can be a disappointing experience without him. The cake never rises! But with the living God firmly enthroned within us, far from being reduced to subservient nobodies, we become truly ourselves, and 'filled out' to a complete humanity. Through the practice of worship, the glorious by-product of losing

ourselves in the wonder of God is that we find ourselves
and steadily grow to be the unique characters God always
intended us to be.

This by-product must not become the reason why we
worship, as there is a danger that over-emphasis of this
could tend to reduce worship to the level of a kind of
therapy or spiritual health-cure. Worship undoubtedly
does us good, and is a health-promoting exercise, particularly in terms of mental health, but if this ever became the
reason for doing it then it would no longer be real worship,
but more akin to self-idolatry—self having become the
central object. Whereas in fact such benefits are just part
of the glorious spin-off from a life of obedience to God;
this is logical when we remember that in the first place it
was *dis*obedience that caused all our ills! We derive the
most personal wholeness from worship when we completely forget ourselves in the act of it; and when we forget
ourselves we can be sure that God is remembering all our
needs—'Seek first his kingdom and his righteousness, and
all these things will be given to you as well' (Mt 6:33).

The renewing of the mind

Worship helps us to break out of the thought patterns of a
fallen world. In Romans 12:1, after Paul exhorts us to
worship God by presenting our bodies to him as a living
sacrifice, he goes on to say, 'Do not conform any longer to
the pattern of this world, but be transformed by the
renewing of your mind. Then you will be able to test and
approve what God's will is—his good, pleasing and perfect
will.' One simple rule that we can identify concerning the
content of our minds is this: what goes in must come out.
What we absorb, good, bad or indifferent, is bound to
affect our thoughts and behaviour. In Philippians 4:8 Paul
says, 'Finally, brothers, whatever is true, whatever is

noble, whatever is right, whatever is pure, whatever is lovely, whatever is admirable—if anything is excellent or praiseworthy—think about such things.'

Praise and worship involves concentrating our whole attention upon the Lord: his person, his deeds, his promises, his truth, his purity, his loveliness, his grace and excellence. Worship is not compatible with evil thoughts, and we cannot go very far before seeing our need for cleansing (or freedom from Satan's accusations, whichever the source might be). But having moved into worship, our minds and imaginations will be fed with truth and beauty. (See Chapter 14 for more on this subject.)

Jesus' manifesto of the kingdom

In the little synagogue of Nazareth, before a disbelieving congregation, Jesus took the scroll of the prophet Isaiah, and applied the prophecies in chapter 61 to himself:

> The Spirit of the Sovereign Lord is on me, because the Lord has anointed me to preach good news to the poor. He has sent me to bind up the broken-hearted, to proclaim freedom for the captives and release for the prisoners, to proclaim the year of the Lord's favour and the day of vengeance of our God, to comfort all who mourn, and provide for those who grieve in Zion—to bestow on them a crown of beauty instead of ashes, the oil of gladness instead of mourning, and a garment of praise instead of a spirit of despair. They will be called oaks of righteousness, a planting of the Lord for the display of his splendour (61:1–3).

He then went out and began his ministry of making people whole, planting them in the rich soil of his kingdom as 'oaks of righteousness', strong, secure, fruitful people, able to withstand the strongest storm, not just for their own completeness, but for the 'display of his splendour'.

Shall we dance?

It is impossible to talk about the expression of a unified personality without being drawn inevitably to the subject of dance. It is a big subject, however, and I will not attempt any more than a brief look at it, and leave the rest to the experts, confessing also that my own lack of muscular co-ordination can present a health hazard to unwary bystanders!

Dance as an expression of worship to the Lord is no new thing, as it characterized the religious culture of the Hebrews right from the moment of their spiritual birth as a nation. It was on the far bank of the Red Sea that Miriam led a joyful celebration of God's victory over the Egyptians, whose army had just disappeared beneath the waves. 'Then Miriam the prophetess, Aaron's sister, took a tambourine in her hand, and all the women followed her, with tambourines and dancing' (Ex 15:20). Hundreds of years later it was written in Psalm 149: 'Let Israel be glad in his Maker, let the sons of Zion rejoice in their King! Let them praise his name with dancing, making melody to him with timbrel and lyre' (RSV). We read in 2 Samuel 6:14 that David 'danced before the Lord with all his might'.

A no-go area?

It has, however, at various periods of history, and certainly in evangelical circles in England until comparatively recent times, been regarded as exclusively 'of the world' and a 'no-go area' for Christians. This is probably the result of a whole series of influences. There was the Platonic dualism mentioned earlier, and more recent philosophies that similarly elevated the value of the mind above the body. There was the Puritan distaste for sports and leisure activities, the Protestant work ethic that looked suspiciously upon bodily recreation, and the Victorian dislike for individuality and self-expression with its consequent obsession with 'respectability'. Then of course there is the ever-present association of dance with sensuality and sexual flirtation, such that many find it impossible to conceive of dance without such overtones. The residue of these attitudes in our minds makes it difficult for many of us to think clearly and objectively about the use of dance in worship. Added to that; so many of us feel physically awkward, self-conscious or embarrassed at the prospect of it that we would rather avoid the subject altogether!

It is surely a strange contradiction if a church that derives its whole existence from an incarnation, the 'enfleshing' of the eternal Word, Jesus, goes on to negate, fear and even despise its own human flesh that Jesus came to redeem. There are undoubtedly great dangers lurking within the 'flesh', but these are most likely to leap into gear when our bodies are sitting passively in 'neutral' and are not engaged by the engine of the Spirit in serving God! The old saying 'the devil finds work for idle hands to do' may apply here. A body trained and active in glorifying God will not adapt quite so easily to fleshly sins as one that is inactive.

Evidence of dance in church history

In the written records of the church's history there is evidence that dance has in the past been seen as a legitimate and commendable expression of worship. Jerome, for example, who was known as quite a sober fellow, wrote: 'In the church the joy of the Spirit finds expression in bodily gesture and her children shall say with David as they dance the solemn step: "I will dance and play before the face of the Lord".' The 'solemn step' should not be of course misunderstood as meaning 'gloomy', particularly in the context of the 'joy of the Spirit'. There is no lack of evidence either in the Old Testament, or in church history (though there have also been objections to it!), to support the view that dancing, as a genuine expression of worship, is a worthy Christian activity.

The silence of the New Testament

Some people are naturally concerned when they find no direct mention of it in the New Testament, and read into this 'silence' an implication that it was not part of New Testament worship at all. However, it can be counter-argued that if dancing was *un*acceptable, then a direct instruction *against* it would surely have been necessary. This is reasonable to suppose, because the context in which the first Christians worshipped was Hebrew culture and, we have already seen, this included dancing in worship from its earliest history. We often forget that Christianity grew first *within* Hebrew culture, and as an extension of the religious heritage of the Jews. If we are going to speculate, is it not easier to imagine that there was dancing on the day of Pentecost (when by the way, the disciples were considered by their behaviour to be drunk), than a ban on dancing?

Leaping for joy

A short time later, Peter and John did not complain when the lame man who was healed at the Gate Beautiful proceeded into the temple walking and leaping and praising God. Peter and John seemed to accept this extreme physical expression as a legitimate response to a miracle, and when all the people came running to them, astonished at seeing a previously lame man leaping, they took the opportunity to preach the gospel, and 'many who heard the message believed, and the number of men grew to about five thousand' (Acts 4:4). It would not be unreasonable to argue that such exhilarating experiences of the early Christians must have time and time again spontaneously spilled over into dancing, this being one of the most natural responses available to match the events around them! It could also be argued that a decline in joyful physical expression may reflect a decline in the kind of raw faith with which Peter and John 'pulled the trigger' of that amazing episode, when they encountered the lame man in the first place.

The redemption of dance

Forms of dance have in fact always reflected current prevailing attitudes to other people and the spirit of the age, so it is significant to note how in the last twenty years or so popular dancing such as is practised in discos, parties, clubs and so on, has become an increasingly individualistic activity with everybody 'doing his or her own thing' with a minimum of verbal communication. Such dancing is almost totally self-orientated and tends to reinforce a lifestyle dedicated to personal gratification and regarding other people, particularly the opposite sex, as a means to one's own ends. However, it is easy for Christians to condemn the dances of the world out of hand, and to forget that for many people this individualistic dancing offers them the only experience they know of feeling like a whole person; of expressing their emotions; of 'working off' their tensions and frustrations.

Lucian of Samosata said of dance, 'It brings the souls of men into the right rhythm and shows forth in visible fashions what the inner beauty of the soul has in common with the outer beauty of the body, because it makes manifest the point where the two flow into one another.' If it is true that dancing is a God-given (though frequently misdirected and corrupted) way in which to enjoy being a whole person, of expressing in a liberated form a oneness of spirit, mind and body, then rather than negatively condemning the world's dance forms, we should be attempting to offer our dancing to him in worship. In contrast to the world, surely Christians have vastly more reason to as well as a wholeness to celebrate that dance, does not evaporate when the music stops—unlike much secular dance. Many Christian parents fear the effect that dancing to rock or disco music may have upon their children; I believe that they would have much less to fear if their children were brought up to use their bodies in worship as a natural part of family and church life, because then there would be no vacuum in this area of their lives that the world would rush to fill. I wonder how many young people have been lost to the false glitter of the world simply because there was no room in the church for their exuberance and *joie de vivre*. It should be the Christians who show the world how to enjoy life as we celebrate the genuine wholeness that comes from being made complete in Christ. Should not the redemption of a dancer include the redemption of their dancing?

Interestingly enough, the only direct reference to dancing in the New Testament comes when Jesus tells the parable commonly termed 'the prodigal son'. Many preachers would prefer, however, to call it, 'the parable of the elder brother' because it was his reaction to the prodigal's return that was the 'sting in the tail' and probably the main point of the story: 'Meanwhile, the older son was in the field. When he came near the house, he heard music and dancing.... [He] became angry and refused to go in' (Lk 15:25–28). We must of course be careful not to read more into this than was intended, particularly about dancing, but what is clear is that the older son was jealous of his younger brother's 'salvation', did not approve of the forgiving love of the father, and was envious of the celebrations because they were not for him but for his reprobate brother. Those of us who find it hard to accept the sight and sound of others joyfully dancing in the joy of salvation must examine the real motives behind our objections, and question whether or not we may be acting the part of the 'elder brother' ourselves. Having said that, we must not blindly accept everything that goes under the title of worship, but learn understanding and discernment so that we may help ourselves and one another to do what is pleasing to God, and not merely to conform either to the restrictive *status quo* of the past or the new ecclesiastical fashions of the present.

Note: Because the use of dance in worship is such a specialized area, I would not wish this brief examination to be regarded as any more than a stimulus to thought on the subject. As so little written material is currently available on this subject, I suggest that those who wish to look at dance in worship in more detail write for a book list to: 'The Sharing Company', P.O. Box 2224, Austin, Texas 78767, USA.

10

Creativity in Worship

Some time ago, my wife and I were given an old, but functional, colour television. Our redundant twelve-inch black and white portable was removed and we suddenly discovered the world of colour that we had been missing. For a while it even distracted our attention from the poor quality of much of the programme content! Previously we had been looking at exactly the same images, but our set had only conveyed part of the truth about what was happening in front of the cameras.

In a similar way, our manner of worship often falls short of reporting the truth about the object of our faith. Our worship comes out in black and white (sometimes still life black and white!) while the truth is in full technicolour moving pictures. If we are truly called by God to give expression to his character, to be the flesh and blood manifesto of his personality and attributes, then we must learn how to reflect accurately what we 'see' of him, in the richest possible way.

What is creative worship?

It is true of course that the human and finite will continually fall short in attempts to give true and living pictures of the divine and infinite, and I wonder whether eternity itself will ever bring us to the point where we adequately describe God's qualities. Nevertheless, we were made by him in his image, with the intention that our lives should, as it were, hold up a mirror to him. We will never find any greater purpose for our lives than this, and indeed we are promised that one day, when we see him as he is, we shall look at ourselves and discover that we have been made like him (1 Jn 3:2). We are meant to be the medium through which divine truth is made visible, so to take the TV illustration a little further, our spirits and minds should be like the camera that 'sees', and our bodies, lives and behaviour should be like the TV receiver that makes it all visible. We need to learn both how to 'see' more clearly, and to display more accurately the glory and majesty of God. Much of our worship, because of its 'monochrome' nature, leaves God unglorified, ourselves uninspired and the non-believer uninformed and unimpressed. If a sincere and honest stranger was invited to an average Christian meeting having been told that the Christian's God made himself known in such gatherings, what kind of impression might he get? Would he feel that he was attending a memorial service for a God who is dead, or a celebration of a rich and abundant life poured out by a God who is alive? Would he see the colourful living life of Christ, or be shown something more akin to an old and fading black and white photograph?

Creative worship happens when a fellowship of believers by faith skilfully employ their gifts to give expression to the words, gifts and power of the Holy Spirit within them.

Lack of creativity veils the truth

Even when a group of Christians are experiencing the adventure of God living in them, the fact sometimes remains strangely hidden in their manner of worship and thus veiled to the outsider. There can be a variety of reasons for this, but I believe that one of them is to do with the neglect of our God-given creativity. Creativity is an attribute of God, evidenced by the fact of our own existence and the infinite beauty and variety we see in the world around us. God is a creative God, and he made us in his image as creative people.

We are all creators

It is a mistake to associate creativity exclusively with artists, sculptors, musicians and such like, and by so doing we deny or devalue a large part of our own humanity as people made in the image of a creative God. We often forget that we are surrounded by the products of creative people: the chairs we sit on, the buildings we live and worship in, the words and music in our songbooks, the computers that send us our telephone bills! We are all creators, but there is endless scope for everybody to be more creative, especially when we realize that our creativity is for the glory of God. In relationships, for example, there exists a seriously neglected area of creativity: the art of love. Love for God, love for our families, for husbands and wives, for friends, strangers and enemies. As one who travels a lot and stays in many homes, I appreciate the creators of good hospitality and, in the many meetings I am involved in, the craftsmen of good organization. There is an art in the loving and wise use of words, in bringing up children, in giving gifts and so on, and we must not restrict our concept of creative people to an elite with outstanding talents in the performing arts.

The salvation of our creativity

However, our laziness, our 'busyness' and our capacity
for reducing all kinds of human activity to repetitive and
unimaginative habits, tend towards a 'monochrome' existence, and both the world and the church gravitate towards
uniformity and the false feeling of safety to be found in it.
Through sin, our creativity has often become misdirected,
used to glorify man instead of his Creator.

God's purpose in sending Jesus into the world was to
redeem the whole of our fallen humanity back to himself,
to restore in us the image of himself. We have become like
those fairground mirrors that throw back a distorted and
grotesque reflection of the person who stands before them.
God is in the business of renewing our personalities so that
we begin to tell the truth about him once more and redeeming our creativity from selfish corruption back to its
original purpose. I have touched on the fact that creativity
is not solely to do with the arts, but is an integral part of
everybody's life and as such is a very broad subject.
Hence for the purposes of this book I will concentrate
more on creativity in the context of corporate worship,
while wishing to emphasize that as a background to this
there is also the need for a creative approach to worship in
the course of our day-to-day, mundane living, particularly
our worship of God in the way we love people.

You cannot create in a vacuum

To be creative we need at least a little of that sometimes
illusive commodity, inspiration. As a writer of words and
music I say this with feeling, remembering the frustrating
experience I often have when sitting in front of a blank
piece of paper that seems only to reflect the blankness
inside my mind! Without something to stir my creative

energies it is impossible to get much done of any value. The best creative work usually seems to arise out of the 'melting-pot' of experience, drawing upon feelings, emotions and convictions that are formed when our lives are under pressure or undergoing changes. Inspiration, in my experience, does not so much float out of a clear sky as get washed up on the beach in a storm! This is not to say that the source of all inspiration is in hard times, but it often takes an extreme of emotion or conviction to crystallize a particular truth and make it real enough to become the raw material for creativity. Bearing in mind that pressure and continual change are two hallmarks of genuine Christian experience, we should not be left for long without inspiration!

The drama of God with us

To put it another way, it is the drama of our lives that provides the resource for creative activity. The more we are faced with the unexpected, the painful, the extremes of joy and sadness, and the starker issues of life and death, and discover the grace and mercy of God as we learn to depend on him in it all, the more we find to say about his faithfulness. When our lives become predictable or boring, there seems little to say that we have not said before. We are at the centre of the greatest drama in heaven and on earth: the incarnation of the Creator God in Christ Jesus, the drama of 'God with us'. The life, death, resurrection, ascension and glorification of Jesus is surely the most amazing story of all time, and the climax of the adventure is yet to come.

Meanwhile, as individuals and as companies of believers, our personal and local dramas continue to unfold each day as God invades, changes and builds his kingdom among us. And all the time he is drawing each one of us nearer and nearer towards the glorious consummation of his purposes for all creation. This real-life drama makes anything that the theatre has to offer pale into insignificance, though it is a sad fact that while many are only partly aware of the enormity of the events in which we play a part, others prefer to stand in the wings and watch more adventurous souls take the 'risks' of living faith.

What releases creative worship?

Taking for granted the fact that there must be something inside us wanting to get out, there are forces working upon and within us that determine to what degree it is released. What we express from the heart is very personal to us, and in a very real way it is an extension of our character. The fact that something is inspired by the Spirit does not always enable us to detach ourselves emotionally from it, and every preacher I know comes off the platform feeling vulnerable, having both opened his heart and taken on the awesome responsibility of delivering God's word. It should be obvious, then, that the more assurance we have of love and acceptance, in God and in one another, the more secure we will feel and the freer we will be to make our contribution. We also need a situation where space is made for even the more timid member to contribute, a recognition that God speaks through every personality and gift, and a sense of expectation, both corporate and individual, that God will use us.

The best way in which we can help our growth in this area is simply by encouraging and affirming one another where gifts are used or spotted in potential.

Developing our skills

Whatever the level of our abilities compared with other people's, we have a clear responsibility to make the best possible use of what we have. The parable of the talents makes this point clear, as do Paul's words in Colossians 3:23—'Whatever you do, work at it with all your heart, as working for the Lord, not for men.'

There is a popular misconception around that using your creativity as a Christian should be like tuning a radio into a broadcast and instantly receiving a completed product. We sometimes hear people say, for example, 'God gave me this song', and after hearing it one is tempted to think that there was a lot of interference on the spiritual airwaves that day! Though there are undoubtedly occasions when there is a special sense of God's inspiration, and the song or whatever it is seems to take shape almost of itself, the general rule appears to be the old formula of 10% inspiration and 90% perspiration! It is interesting to note for example that Psalm 34 was originally written as an acrostic, something that involves a considerable amount of effort, time and skill to create. God has given us creative abilities, and though he may on occasions choose to bypass them, he loves to receive from us offerings on which have been lavished loving care, time and attention to detail. There is an exhortation in Psalm 33:3 to play instruments skilfully, and in 1 Chronicles 15:22 we read that 'Kenaniah the head Levite was in charge of the singing...because he was skilful at it.' In the exercise of spiritual gifts, skills are also needed. They are like a carpenter's tools which, when handled skilfully with love, wisdom and discernment, can be used to create something beautiful. When handled carelessly or inexpertly, however, they can hack, damage and destroy.

Some areas for creative development in corporate worship

Within the limits of this book it is not possible to go into great detail, and much has already been written elsewhere on most of these areas. In the brief survey that follows, there is nothing startlingly new, but I hope it will serve as a stimulus and encouragement for those who feel 'stuck in a rut'.

1. Music

Music encompasses singing, composing, arranging and instrumental skills. All these are traditionally given more attention than most other areas, but nevertheless many congregations hold untapped abilities and undeveloped potential. Even when basic talent is absent for creating a choir, singing group or small orchestra, we can do much to improve the quality of our singing! The main reason why the Welsh sing better than the English is that apart from possessing a language with a particularly rich tonal quality, they have a tradition of good singing, and a pride in doing it well, that can make excellent singers out of good ones and even average ones out of terrible ones! Where there are people, there are always some who have musical ability. How sad it is when owing to lack of imagination, fear of change, or motivation, people with music in their hearts, mouths and fingers are kept passively in the pews.

2. Dance

Obviously an area with enormous scope for development, this has been discussed in chapter 9 above.

3. The art of reading Scripture

This may sound strange to some, but it is yet another neglected art in worship. Readings need not be just 'read'. For a start they can be read with greater expression, in an attempt to re-create the atmosphere of the event, or the sense of conviction of the writer. If we really believe it is the inspired word of God, we should read it as such, with authority, conviction and compassion. Secondly, certain passages lend themselves to being dramatized using two or three readers taking character parts, or in 'question and answer' passages with one voice asking the questions and another giving the answers. Thirdly, one voice can lead followed by the whole congregation reading the responses. There are numerous other permutations and, of course, this is nothing new, but frequently in the rush and hurry of preparation, it is easier not to bother with the planning and rehearsal required to bring a passage vividly to life in these and other similar ways.

4. The gentle art of silence

In an age of noise, silence can even be something people are scared of, and it seems that fewer and fewer of us really know how to use it in life, let alone in corporate worship. Many of us feel insecure or embarrassed by silence, possibly because we have not learned to concentrate our minds on anything other than the dominant noise that happens to be in our environment at any given time. We also find it easier to talk to God, and sometimes at him, than to listen to him, being frequently more interested in what we have to say than in what he has to say. To be able to spend time sitting silently, simply enjoying the company of another person, shows a great depth of friendship and understanding, and so it can be with God once we get to know him. We must learn how to be quiet and listen, to prick up the 'ears' of our spirit, and to take a word, phrase or verse of Scripture and meditate upon it in the presence of God. Surely all of us would benefit from a course to learn the gentle art of silence before God. The practice of silent worship would, I suspect, make our noisy worship a lot more meaningful too.

5. *One in the eye is worth two in the ear*

The drabness of many church interiors would not only benefit from a coat of paint and a good colour scheme, but more to the point they would benefit greatly from various kinds of visual aids to worship. For example, many churches make their own banners displaying pictorial lessons, illustrations of divine truths, key words or Bible verses and so on. Apart from the visual stimulation that these can provide, the groups that make them often enjoy the great friendship and mutual support that their shared labour creates. It is a widely held view in educational circles that people are twice as likely to remember what they see as what they hear ('one in the eye is worth two in the ear'). I wonder how effective our communication would be if we took notice of this fact and explored ways of illustrating the subject matter of our worship.

6. *Leading worship*

Leading worship is a creative function (see Chapter 13), an art to be learned; a creative approach to planning programmes and services of worship can bring new vitality and interest to them; even the layout of the chairs (if you have them!) done imaginatively in order to set us in the best possible positions for worship together can make a tremendous difference.

7. *Drama*

Drama can be used to powerful effect in illuminating teaching points, bringing to life biblical scenes, and facing us with the challenge of the gospel to our everyday lives. Movement, dance and mime can all illustrate spiritual truths and be a means of expressing praise and worship to the Lord (see Chapter 9). For many people this provides one of the richest ways they know of showing their love and commitment to their Saviour, and many others have been moved and spiritually challenged by simply watching.

I hope that this list helps to remind us of at least some of the most obvious areas in which there is ample room for greater creativity as we ask ourselves the question: What is God doing in our lives? How can we put into words, songs, music, pictures, movements and dances, structures and patterns, signs and symbols, smells, sounds, touch and even taste, what he means to us? How can we be rich in our expression of worship, as he is rich in mercy towards us?

Testing the product

Creative worship often involves using our own words and ideas to express truths, and we must always be careful to measure and test these against the teachings of Scripture and the witness of the Spirit within. I have once or twice, for example, seen dramatizations of Scripture stories that miss the whole point of the original, and heard song lyrics that, though sung with sincerity, are peppered with doctrinal errors! It is vital we bear in mind that to varying degrees what we produce teaches the listener or viewer. We have a responsibility to test the product first, and to ensure that it does not fall short of the truth it is intended to convey. It is true, of course, that in areas of artistic creativity, our perception is to an enormous degree conditioned by our cultural background and predispositions of taste and character. It is important, therefore, that we learn both to apply the objective tests of Scripture, and the inner witness of the Spirit, particularly when our own dislikes or prejudices are aroused!

11

A Perfect Fit

In recent years, much that had been lost in the art of worship has begun to be restored, and much that had become stale and lifeless has been renewed. It would be naïve, however, to think that we had 'arrived' in terms of our understanding and practice of it—if anything, our understanding has outstripped our practice. A show of hands at any truly 'cosmopolitan' Christian gathering will demonstrate that the majority of Christians belong to churches where they still feel trapped in dead or stale forms of worship, or restricted by tradition, culture or prejudice.

'Praise bingo'

One area into which I believe we should venture a little further is that of learning to give praise and worship that is appropriate, that which fits or matches the occasion or the particular purposes of God at the time. The nature and content of our worship should not be an arbitrary thing. Too often, someone calls out: 'Let's sing number 86!' for no better reason than because it is his or her favourite chorus or hymn. Similarly, the worship leader may make arbitrary choices, though I should add that often apparently arbitrary choices turn out to have been divinely inspired! Choice of hymns and songs, however, is just one of the many areas in which we can so easily meander on without questioning why we follow certain habitual patterns of doing things. Conversely, it is possible to pack all sorts of things in just because they are new or different or because somebody wants to 'do their own thing'. We would do well to continually ask the question: 'Why are we using this particular song/reading/tune/piece of drama?' and so on. The question should not be asked with a critical or destructive attitude, but out of a desire to fit our worship into what God is doing among us, in the way that the two pieces of a carpenter's dovetail joint are made to fit perfectly into one another.

Co-operating with the Spirit

In our human relationships we are well used to fitting our words and actions to the occasion. We are not supposed to weep and wail at weddings (except perhaps the bride's mother!), or laugh and make jokes at funerals. It is not usually considered appropriate to send the funeral procession roaring off down the street covered in ribbons and trailing tin cans, or to drive the newly weds slowly away in a hearse!

With regard to the content and form of our worship, everything should be there—or be left out as the case may be—for a reason. That reason may well be no more than an inspiration in the course of advance planning that one strongly suspects has a divine origin, or an intuitive sense of what to do next during the 'flow'of worship. The reason may, for example, be in the choice of a subject by the leadership under the Spirit's directions, which then requires that the component parts are chosen very carefully around that subject. But it is important that worship should have its roots in much more than casual, thoughtless or arbitrary choices. I have previously argued that worship is a response to the activity and character of God, past, present and future. Because he is continually working in and among us in specific ways at any given time, our worship can be a specific response, as well as celebrating general themes that form a necessary backgroud to the specific.

A perfect fit for the occasion

In Matthew 21 we find the account of Jesus' triumphant entry into Jerusalem, followed by his driving out from the temple of the money-changers and pigeon-sellers, and the healing of the blind and lame people there. In verses 15 and 16 (RSV) we read:

> But when the chief priests and the scribes saw the wonderful things that he did, and the children crying out in the temple, 'Hosanna to the Son of David!' they were indignant; and they said to him, 'Do you hear what these are saying?' And Jesus said to them, 'Yes; have you never read, "out of the mouths of babes and sucklings thou hast brought perfect praise?"'

The Good News Bible puts it as: 'You have trained children and babies to offer perfect praise.'

What did Jesus mean by 'perfect praise'? Is there such a thing as perfect praise outside of heaven? Couldn't it be argued that those children did not really even know the full implications of what they were chanting, having just copied the adults and joined in the excitement of the occasion as children do, carried along by the emotion of the moment?

Whatever else Jesus meant by perfect praise, the way he reacted to the question suggests that he certainly regarded the children's praise as perfect in the sense of being appropriate, a perfect fit. It was appropriate in a number of ways.

Firstly, there was the content. He was being called the 'Son of David', which Jesus knew was a name for the Messiah and therefore appropriate despite the shocked indignation of the priests and scribes who did not agree.

Secondly, there was the manner in which the children praised him. They were 'crying out'. It was a joyful shout of proclamation that the Messiah was before their very eyes, and doing miracles of healing. Gasps of amazement and shouts of joy and praise are surely appropriate when miracles are done!

Thirdly, we must note that it was *children* who were shouting his praises. It was a cry of welcome to a Saviour with whom ordinary children could identify, a working man in simple clothes with a special love and tenderness for them in his eyes. Children are so often mistreated and exploited, and symbolize the innocent and powerless whom Jesus came to set free, so it was also appropriate that praise should come from those who represented the kind of person for whom the kingdom was intended.

Fourthly, the children were praising him in the temple. We must remind ourselves of the significane of what had just happened in the context of where they were. Jesus had just 'invaded' the temple followed by a crush of common people, along with beggars and children. He had completed an unthinkable act of treason in the eyes of the religious establishment by appearing to take over and threaten their control of the very centre and symbol of their religious and economic power, the temple itself. As Jesus literally overturned the tables of the money changers and sellers of creatures for sacrifice they knew beyond a shadow of doubt that their system of power, position, influence and money-making was at stake. It was a racket and everybody knew it (though I suspect it was vigorously justified), but it was run by the rich and powerful and normally no one dared to challenge the system; but Jesus had just done so! In the jubilation of the crowd there was probably some degree of satisfaction that justice was being upheld at last. Those normally excluded from the inner courts of the temple and all it represented for reasons of class, economic status, health, prejudice and possibly race as well, were being led in by Jesus. The joy and power of his kingdom were taking over. Compared to the indignation and joyless legalism of the representatives of the temple regime, the priests and scribes, the simple praise of the children was a perfect fit for the occasion as far as Jesus was concerned. If we compare this occasion with Isaiah 61, which Jesus read in the synagogue at Nazareth and which has been described as his 'manifesto', we may catch a little more of the significance of it, and therefore the ways in which the children's praise was indeed perfect and even prophetic for that dramatic moment.

Everything for a reason

To look at another example of appropriate worship, we can turn to 2 Chronicles 20:1–30. You will need to read the whole story in order to make full sense of my comments on it. The story of the deliverance of Jehoshaphat and the people of Judah against overwhelming odds includes, as the story progresses, many and various acts of worship. Jehoshaphat responds to the news of impending invasion by calling all the people together to seek the Lord with fasting. There are public prayers proclaiming God's power, remembering his past deeds and his covenant with Abraham including the promise of protection. There is an appeal to God's justice to prevail in the particular situation, and a declaration of trust in him alone. There followed God's response in a prophetic word through Jahaziel, bringing comfort, a promise of victory and a precise strategy. Then Jehoshaphat and the people prostrate themselves humbly before the Lord, while the Levites stood up and praised with a 'very loud voice'. The next morning after a fresh challenge to trust God they appointed singers to lead the army out to meet the enemy, in 'holy array' and with thanksgiving on their lips. As they sang and praised, the Lord confused the enemy so that they destroyed themselves. Finally, after the spoil of battle had been collected, they had a day of thanksgiving and blessing the Lord, followed by a return to Jerusalem for celebrations with 'harps, lyres and trumpets'.

A fitting response

Here we see a rich variety in their worship, from fasting to shouting, from prostration to celebration, and everything they did was for a reason. They fasted and prayed because they knew no better way in which to express the seriousness of their appeal to God. They prostrated themselves because they did not know of a more appropriate way in which to express their wonder and awe at such a merciful and powerful God. The Levites stood up to praise with a very loud voice because moderation in volume at that particular point might have seemed to be almost an insult to a God who had just promised a deliverance without moderation! Each stage of their worship was a fitting response to the progress of the life or death drama in which they found themselves, and they did nothing that was irrelevant or superfluous. The irrelevant and superfluous in worship tends to creep in when the drama of our faith recedes. I am aware of course that because the story is about a literal life or death situation the nature of the worship described here is particularly dramatic, but even so there is no reason why worship in less tense situations should not be tailored to fit as perfectly.

The need for a greater repertoire

There is one aspect of this story, however, that should not be ignored. The nation of Judah had a big advantage over many of us in that they had a background of worship culture to draw appropriate modes of worship from, and may well have intuitively known the right responses as a result. Although the religious practice of the Hebrews went through regular periods of decline, it must be remembered that their whole culture was built around the worship of Yahweh and there were established patterns concerning how to do it. While Christians in the twentieth century have had 2,000 years in which to develop a rich worship culture on top of the Hebrew heritage where our spiritual roots lie, most of us are not aware of more than a few scraps of it. It has for all kinds of reasons tended to be reduced down into a severely limited repertoire and become more akin to the surrounding secular culture than to the kingdom of God. The 'rules' sometimes seem to limit us to sitting, kneeling or standing positions only, stiff upper lip at all times please, no emotion. We're British and in church one should be especially British! We need to have our rich heritage restored to us (and it is far richer than most of us realize), to rediscover and develop a worship culture, containing many and varied patterns that will equip us to respond in a fitting way as God moves in, among and around us. (The need for sensitivity in the choice of appropriate material for worship is developed further in the next chapter.)

Building a rich worship culture from old and new

We could start not only by digging into church history and shaking the dust off the forgotten patterns of the past, but also by making a habit of asking God such questions as: 'What is a fitting way to worship you at this moment? What would please you? What would bring us most deeply into communion with you, Father? Which action might bring us closer together as your children?' and so on. We desperately need this kind of discipline if we are to blow away the cobwebs of habit and overcome the common weakness of resorting to the 'safe' and familiar, for no better reason than laziness, lack of imagination or fear of change. Sadly, much of our worship seems designed to fit what pleases the majority (to keep most of the people happy most of the time), rather than what pleases God. There are of course many different opinions about what pleases God, but he is often the last Person we think of asking!

Just as Jesus listened to the children in the temple crying out 'Hosanna to the Son of David' and considered it to be 'perfect praise', a perfect fit for the occasion, he sits invisibly enthroned among us as we worship him, listening and watching for that same perfect fit, and searching for hearts that are concerned to give him the best and most appropriate response as he patiently builds us into a living temple.

12
Leading Worship I

Leading worship—where are we leading people?

The subject of leading worship is a very large one, made yet larger by the vast number of ideas, opinions and traditions that exist concerning what should or should not be done in corporate worship. According to the *World Christian Encyclopaedia* (Oxford University Press 1982) there are 20,780 Christian denominations in the world, and probably each one has a different slant on how worship should be conducted! In the light of that sobering fact, I am not putting forward a pattern to be copied, but attempting to draw out principles that can be applied in various situations. I am concentrating, however, on the leading of open worship where, rather than keeping strictly and exclusively to a preplanned programme, all the participants are seeking to be led creatively by the Spirit into a flow of events unique to that group of people at that point in time. The first questions we must ask when considering the role of leading worship is a question that we often seem to ignore altogether: *where* are we leading people? Hence I will start by trying to locate our destination.

Within the veil

At the precise moment at which Jesus died on the cross a strange and dramatic event occurred in the temple a short distance away. In the gospel accounts of Matthew, Mark and Luke we are told that at the moment of Jesus' death the curtain of the temple was torn in two from top to bottom. To those of us with a limited knowledge of Judaism this event may seem mysterious or even meaningless, but it was in fact a supernatural event of extraordinary significance. The curtain was for the Jews an impassable barrier into the holy of holies, the place where the presence of God was. It was only passed through once a year when the high priest alone entered to make sacrifices for the nation's sin. The rest of the year, and to the rest of the world, it was as firmly shut off in spiritual terms, as Fort Knox is to burglars in physical terms. So what does this mean? The curtain in fact spoke of the sinless purity of Jesus, the perfect standard of holiness that fallen man could never pass through, the barrier which, despite the annual visits over hundreds of years to make animal sacrifices for sin, still hung there symbolizing the disqualification of every one of us from God's presence.

The holy of holies was situated at the heart of the temple, the design of the whole building being based upon the wilderness tabernacle of Moses' day. Before some of you wonder what all this has to do with leading worship, it is important to understand that the original design was given by God as a type, a shadow, a kind of historical visual aid, to help us understand spiritual truths that would find their completion in Jesus.

For over a thousand years a simple curtain had spoken of the barrier between God and man, and then suddenly it was torn in two. It was not torn by men, because it was torn from top to bottom, not from bottom to top. In an instant it became no longer a symbol of exclusion, but an entrance, as the tearing of Jesus' body on the cross and the shedding of his blood became a way into the very presence of a holy God. Jesus, the great High Priest, had made once and for all the sacrifice necessary to open the way. It is significant that in John 1:14, when we read of Jesus that 'the Word became flesh and dwelt among us', the word from which 'dwelt' is translated means 'tabernacled'. Jesus tabernacled among us, and in him all that the wilderness tabernacle signified finds its fulfilment.

We have a temple made of 'living stones'

The holy of holies was the very centre and focus of worship for the Jews, the place where God dwelt in holiness and unapproachable light. In Moses' time they had shaken with fear at his demonstrations of power and righteous anger on Mount Sinai, and his presence among them filled them with awe. But now, amazingly, through faith in Jesus, we are invited right into that holy place, in awe and reverence, to do what the Jews would have regarded as unthinkable, to meet God as 'Father'. The gathering together of Christians is now a place where we enter the holy of holies to commune with our heavenly Father. Instead of a tabernacle of animal skins or a temple of stone, we ourselves are the temple, 'living stones' built together by love and unity, and in that living temple we are invited to walk through the ever open curtain of Christ's broken body into intimate communion with God. 'As you come to him, the living Stone—rejected by men but chosen by God and precious to him—you also, like living sons, are being built into a spiritual house to be a holy priesthood, offering spiritual sacrifices acceptable to God through Jesus Christ' (1 Pet 2:4–5).

When we look around at our brothers and sisters in a

gathering of the church, we should remember that we are
all those 'living stones', and that if we are allowing God to
do his construction work among us, we can expect to be
led into the holy of holies and into an experience of God's
living presence right in the centre of our meeting together.
Using the visual aid of the tabernacle as our guide, we can
gain a most enlightening perspective on worship. I am not
putting this forward as a standard approach to a sequence
of events in worship or attempting to interpret fully the
rich and extensive symbolism of the tabernacle, but it
speaks of so many vital principles that we would definitely
be the poorer for ignoring it.

'Enter his gates with thanksgiving and his courts with praise'

Our first step is to bring ourselves, setting our faces in
God's direction, stepping for a moment out of the distractions of everyday life in order to give our attention entirely
to worship. It is a choice we make, an entrance we deliberately step through. In Psalm 100:4 we read the exhortation:
'Enter his gates with thanksgiving and his courts with
praise.' About one-third of the psalms begin with praise
or with exhortations to give thanks and praise the Lord.
Often, psalms would be used as the people processed to
the temple, and frequently there is a sense of loud, joyful
celebration, an energetic proclamation of thanks for the
goodness and greatness of God. It could be argued that
strong thanks and praise is the best way of preparing us to
draw close to God, enabling us to break free from the
burdens of life, and an overconcern with ourselves.
Thanksgiving by its very nature turns our gaze towards
the giver, and away from ourselves. It causes us to count
our blessings rather than our troubles and, most important
of all, it gives credit where credit is due—to the Lord!

Having stirred our spirits, minds and bodies into action in this way we have adopted a giving, rather than a taking attitude, forward motion rather than passivity.

Bringing gifts

A worshipper would not enter the tabernacle empty-handed but would bring an offering for sacrifice. While our offering is first and foremost ourselves, as a 'living sacrifice' (Rom 12:1), we do not come empty-handed, and as a token of the fact that we are continually offered up to God, we bring the sacrifices described in Hebrews 13:15: 'Through Jesus, therefore, let us continually offer to God a sacrifice of praise—the fruit of lips that confess his name. And do not forget to do good and to share with others, for with such sacrifices God is pleased.' A person who belongs completely to God will not cease to thank and praise, do good and share with others—his giving to God will be matched by giving to others.

Reminding ourselves of his goodness

Psalms of thanks and praise usually focus upon particular reasons for praising God, and the deeds he has done, his unchanging character and so on, and this is very practical because our hearts often need to be stirred to an awareness of him, and our minds reminded of the marvellous truths about him before we can even begin to expect a 'face to face' encounter! We cannot expect to be intimate with somebody before we have become aware of the facts about them, and their qualities of character.

Clean hands and a pure heart

In the tabernacle worship there is much that speaks about the need to prepare ourselves for God's presence. The altar of burnt offering where the sacrifice in its entirety went up in smoke to heaven, illustrates the need for total consecration of ourselves to God, as Jesus gave himself totally for us. The brass laver, where priests would wash themselves before offering service to God, speaks of our need for cleansing; we should not blunder into the Holy Place without ensuring that we are 'up to date' in cleansing from sin. Psalm 24:3 and 4 (RSV) say: 'Who shall ascend the hill of the Lord? And who shall stand in his holy place? He who has clean hands and a pure heart.'

One with each other

Behind the curtain of the ante-room to the holy of holies we see the table of shewbread. This foreshadows the Lord's Supper and reminds us that we come as members of one 'loaf', part of the same body, and that the unity which Jesus prayed for in John 17 should be maintained if we are to see God's glory.

Enlightened by the Holy Spirit

The only light in this enclosed space comes from the golden candlestick, signifying the spiritual light which the Holy Spirit sheds on the word of God (which the 'natural' man cannot perceive (1 Cor 2:14)). Our worship needs to be enlightened, informed and beautified by the word of God, which is spiritually discerned and not by the natural light of human understanding.

Intercession

In front of the veil of the holy of holies (now torn in two and wide open!) is the altar of incense, a symbol of prayer. It signifies the intercession of the risen ascended Christ before the throne of God on our behalf, and caught up as one with his prayers are the prayers of people rising like a fragrant perfume to the Lord.

Awe and wonder

Now we approach our destination, through the torn veil, the way opened to us by Christ's broken body on the cross. After the noise of joyful singing, thanksgiving and praise, we begin to sense the majesty of God and our activity quietens down to be replaced by reverence and awe. Having been 'doing' in the courts of praise, here our 'doing' turns to 'being', our action turns to stillness. In the holy of holies we find that we can do little but wonder at, and try to take in, the picture we see of God's grace. We are faced with the completed work of Christ on our behalf. First of all we see the sprinkled blood upon the mercy seat, the sign of our forgiveness, and the price paid to bring us here. We must cease now any attempt to make ourselves more acceptable to God, or to punish ourselves for our sins and failures: Christ has done it all and we are clothed in his righteousness. Our praise turns to worship and adoration as we ponder on his great mercy. Before us is the ark and its contents that speak of Christ and what we may find in him. (The ark was made of wood but covered completely inside and out with gold. Wood signifies humanity, gold divinity, therefore illustrating Christ's nature.)

Resting in his righteousness

Within were three significant objects. First, there were the tablets of stone on which were written the Mosaic law, God's standard of righteousness. In Christ the demands of the law, impossible for us to keep, are totally satisfied, and not only that, but when we are in Christ we find the law written on our hearts (Ezek 36:26 and 27). Once again, we can only wonder at a completed work on our behalf.

Resting in his provision

Secondly, there was a pot of manna, the food that sustained the Israelites through forty years of wilderness wandering. In the New Testament Jesus makes a connection between himself and the manna, and describes himself in these words from John 6:48–51:

> I am the bread of life. Your forefathers ate the manna in the desert, yet they died. But there is the bread that comes down from heaven, which a man may eat and not die. I am the living bread that came down from heaven.

In worship we feed upon Jesus, who himself is the sustenance of our spiritual lives, and in whom is the daily supply for all our needs. In the wilderness there was always enough manna to satisfy each person's appetite for the day, and so in Christ we find that the demands of each day will never exceed the sustenance that he is able to give us. Again, God's provision is a complete one.

Jesus' eternal priesthood

The third item inside the ark was Aaron's rod. It was a simple stick of dead wood cut from a tree, which in an incident described in Numbers 17 was placed overnight in the presence of God, and by morning it had simultaneously budded, flowered and borne some fruit. This is understood to be a symbol of the resurrection of Jesus from death to an eternal priesthood: 'You are a priest for ever, in the order of Melchizedek' (Heb 5:6). Also in Hewbrews 7:24 we read, 'because Jesus lives for ever, he has a permanent priesthood. Therefore he is able to save completely those who come to God through him, because he always lives to intercede for them.' Whereas in the tabernacle there was no place for the priests to sit down, because their work was never finished, we read of Jesus in Hebrews 10:12: 'But when this priest had offered for all time one sacrifice for sins, he sat down at the right hand of God.' Here again our worship reveals a completed work, and because we are 'in Christ', we partake in the power of his resurrection, his new life and fruitfulness and have ourselves become 'kings and priests' (Rev 5:10), seated with him in heavenly places (Eph 2:6), even though our feet are still firmly on the earth.

A place of communion with God

It may seem strange to apply these last three 'types' to our worship today, but I believe that there is a vital significance here for application in our current understanding of where worship should lead us. Too often our approach to God stops short of entering the 'inner sanctuary', and we hover around aimlessly wondering what to do after we have praised, thanked, prayed, sung and so on. These pictures show us that the place of communion with God is a place of rest. The 'rest' is there because in Jesus God has done everything necessary for our salvation and for the supply and sustenance of our lives. There is nothing we can add, and all our strivings and strugglings can and must cease. Hebrews 4:10 says, 'for anyone who enters God's rest also rests from his own work'.

When we enter into the awesome presence of God, his finished work can take over in our lives, and we can go out again into the world knowing afresh where the power with which he builds his kingdom comes from. Not only that but in his presence we will be *em*powered to serve him, having 'tapped into' the source of all power. In that place, we learn to gaze and to listen, to commune with the God and Father of all mankind, so surely we cannot help but come out somewhat changed!

'With angels and archangels...'

We discover also that this meeting point with God is spiritually a meeting point between heaven and earth; after all, as we have seen, Christ is now seated 'at the right hand of the Father'. The book of Hebrews, which revels so much in the heavenly priesthood of Jesus, describes our position under the new dispensation that the tabernacle foreshadowed. Hebrews 12:22, 23 states:

> But you have come to Mount Zion, to the heavenly Jerusalem, the city of the living God. You have come to thousands upon thousands of angels in joyful assembly, to the church of the first-born, whose names are written in heaven. You have come to God, the judge of all men, to the spirits of righteous men made perfect, to Jesus the mediator of a new covenant, and to the sprinkled blood that speaks of a better word than the blood of Abel.'

Here we see heaven and earth all mixed together, which is why in our worship it can sometimes seem as if we are halfway there! When we worship, we literally join in with the praises of heaven, including all the saints and all the angels, and we 'touch' the things that are eternal and unshakeable. It is only this contact with heaven that can give us a true appreciation of God's plans and purposes for his kingdom here.

I have no desire to create out of the lessons of the tabernacle a 'formula' for worship, a strict sequence of events, or a standard 'checklist' against which to measure what we do, and certainly there is no historical evidence in the early church to suggest that they conducted their worship with a plan of the tabernacle in hand! However, the principles embodied in it are put there by God for our instruction, and should serve to increase our vision of where we are going and how we get there when we are given the responsibility of leading people into the presence of God.

> Therefore, brothers, since we have confidence to enter the Most Holy Place by the blood of Jesus, by a new and living way opened for us through the curtain, that is, his body, and since we have a great priest over the house of God, let us draw near to God with a sincere heart in full assurance of faith, having our hearts sprinkled to cleanse us from a guilty conscience and having our bodies washed with pure water. (Heb 10:19–22).

Having looked briefly at the route we are taking, we go on in the next chapter to look at the equipment and skills that will help us to make the journey.

Note: There are obvious implications here for the way in which we use music at the different stages of worship, and this is developed further in Chapter 13.

13
Leading Worship II

Leading worship—nuts and bolts

It should be clear from what we have learned so far, that the task of leading people into the presence of God is a high honour and a serious responsibility. While it is good that in recent times this role has become more open to the ordinary believer, and times of 'free' worship are common in many fellowships, it must be admitted that the job is often done badly. The desire for freedom in worship has sometimes resulted in a 'free for all', ending up in chaos and disorder. Equally, the concept of being led by the Spirit has sometimes given way to a feeling that unless everything that happens is truly spontaneous, it must be man-made and not God-inspired. The kick-back from the rigid patterns of the past is all too often a suspicion of advance planning, firm leadership and efficient organization. How often, though, is the flow of 'free' worship interrupted and the atmosphere marred by musical incompetence, poor leadership or the absence of adequate planning and practical preparation?

First of all—be a worshipper

Leading worship is indeed a role that should remain open to anybody called and gifted in that direction, but it should also be seen as an art to be learned, and the learning of that art should be approached as a serious undertaking. However, probably the most important principle of all does not entail technical experience, but concerns the heart. To lead others in worship, you must be a worshipper. There is much truth in the saying that 'you cannot take anyone further than you have been yourself', and if you do not have a real desire to worship God, you will not take others very far—in fact, they will probably overtake you! In the midst of all the practical considerations of choosing songs, sensing the atmosphere, playing the right chords and so on, the overriding activity must be to stir up your own spirit towards God and give him genuine thanks, love and praise.

Be a servant

A worshipper will also display the attitude that is foundational to both the spiritual and practical aspects of Christian leadership of any kind, and that is the servant attitude. We looked at how this attitude should characterize our worship in Chapter 4, but here we are considering the *leader* as a servant. Jesus said 'For even the Son of Man did not come to be served, but to serve.' He lived and taught servanthood, and graphically illustrated this revolutionary approach to leadership when he shocked his disciples by washing their feet, a job reserved for the most menial of slaves.

Leading people in worship must be with the attitude of serving them, and not as a way of wielding power, or a means of self-elevation. A good servant is concerned above all with pleasing his master, not himself, and will take pains to do his job to the best of his ability. He will make an effort to become skilled in the practical requirements of the job, and to build up the resources necessary so that he is always prepared to fulfil the demands of his master.

Practical considerations

If the worship leader is leading with the voice or with an instrument or both, then a reasonable level of musical proficiency is necessary. It is difficult to set a rigid standard for this, because on the one hand there are many people with limited musical training and ability who seem to lead sensitively, while on the other hand there are some highly trained competent musicians who have a 'blind spot' when attempting to apply their skills to worship!

One minimum standard to set, however, is whether a person can maintain the flow of worship without constant interruptions caused by technical ineptitude. On the instrumental side of things there is a minimum standard below which the playing starts to drag the spirit of worship down, rather than lift it. If the attention of the main body of worshippers is repeatedly drawn away from worship to discord or confusion at the front, then it would probably be better to do without instruments altogether!

Be a good workman

Having mentioned a minimum standard, I do not believe that we should be content to remain there! As well as the biblical exhortations to 'make a joyful noise', there are also encouragements to 'play skilfully' (Ps 33:3)! Many of us will have experienced how the skilful playing of an instrument, under the fingers of someone who cares about giving the best to God, can lead into an atmosphere that is especially conducive to worship. However, it is a fact of life that there are not enough of these people to go round! Nevertheless, with practice and a determination to be a good workman, a musician of average ability can provide all that is necessary, and find that his or her offering is a positive help rather than a hindrance to worship.

Repertoire and common-sense preparation

There is an obvious need for a fairly comprehensive resource of songs, tunes and arrangements, and it is important that the worship leader is conversant with the best way in which to begin and end a song. The lack of positive 'intros' and 'outros' cause people to stumble into and out of songs, creating a feeling of uncertainty. It is an obvious point but people frequently forget to check in advance that the key is correct. There are few more disrupting experiences in worship that to be halfway through a song and discover that none but a handful of brave (or foolish!) souls can make it to the top note! There is usually no alternative but to stop completely and start again, by which time it may be difficult to re-create the atmosphere. Mind you, it can also have the effect of 'breaking the ice' by helping us all to laugh at ourselves, but that is no excuse for not checking in advance.

Information 'at a glance'

Another simple but frequently neglected point of preparation is for the worship leader to know the numbers of all the songs likely to be used. Even a few seconds fumbling around looking for the number can be distracting for worshippers. Obviously this is going to happen if someone starts a song spontaneously, but as such songs are usually quite well known, it is possible to be reasonably conversant with where to find them if people do need the words. I am not renowned for having a computer-like memory, so I find it necessary to prepare a list of songs complete with number and key, and position it on a clip-board in front of me. This functions not only as a reminder of the numbers —numbers stating in which book, and which keys—but also as a reminder of the breadth of choice available. As I prepare the list I prayerfully consider the choices, devise a basic plan and then add some more options in case they are needed. To this equipment I add any bits and pieces I need for my guitar playing, plus a lighted digital clock to aid my time-keeping!

Learning your stagecraft

It is important to check your physical positioning and place yourself where you can be easily seen. You also need to be close to any other musicians in order to communicate, and to other leaders if applicable. Where microphones are used, they need to be used with care to avoid the bumps, bangs and howls that mishandling produces; and particularly when a system has been put up especially for the occasion, plenty of time should be allowed to obtain a good sound, and to become familiar with its characteristics (e.g. how close to speak into the microphone).

Despite all the experience that has been gained in recent years concerning the use of public address systems, their misuse is still far too often a source of interruption during larger gatherings for worship, and the importance of using them properly cannot be underestimated. Advance setting-up on a technical level and planning on an organizational level is vital to avoid the all too familiar mistakes outlined below:

1. The OHP (overhead projector) screen is too small and not everybody can see properly.

2. There is no blackout and the words projected by the OHP cannot be seen properly.

3. The OHP acetates are not in order, and finding the right sheet is like looking for a needle in a haystack.

4. It appears the OHP acetates were written out by a dyslexic with a broken arm!

5. You stroll breezily to the microphone and it is not working.

6. There are no songbooks/there are not enough songbooks/I thought you were bringing the songbooks.

7. It's ten o'clock and the caretaker is dropping a subtle hint by flashing the lights. He doesn't know that we usually go on until eleven-thirty, and besides the preacher hasn't started yet!

8. The piano is wildly out of tune and more suitable for New Year's Eve at the Rose and Crown than anything else.

9. The piano and the organ are not tuned to each other.

10. The pianist and the organist are not tuned to each other!

To this list could be added innumerable instances where lack of organization and preparation can seriously mar a time of worship. At stake is not so much a principle of efficiency or professionalism for its own sake, but a principle of worship. This principle of worship is that we offer the best we have to God, and surely that should include practical organization of resources and equipment.

Clear communication

If a crowd of people are to be led in the same direction, then it is obvious that there must be no confusion as to what they are being asked to do. The worship leader needs to be able to communicate well, to speak with a clear voice, and to express himself with an economy of words. There must be no ambiguity or uncertainty, and great care must be taken to say things in such a way as to draw everybody into the experience of worship rather than to alienate, offend, or set up tensions between people.

The para-message

Whenever a person speaks in public, there runs alongside the spoken words what is sometimes termed the 'para-message'. This term describes all forms of communication parallel to the voice, such as 'body language', dress, appearance, mannerisms and attitudes. All of us are just as sensitive—if not more so—to the para-message as we are to the words being spoken, and although we are to some extent stuck with our para-message, in so far as it is an extension of our personalities, we must discipline ourselves to avoid behaviour that might distract or irritate. I have sometimes been told by friends that on occasions I distract people by fiddling with the microphone stand while I'm talking. Often I have been unaware of doing it, but the people were not! Such things are usually the result of nervousness and as such can communicate tension to the people and need to be controlled so as not to divert attention.

Eye-contact

It is important when speaking or singing to people to maintain 'eye-contact'. There is no better way to ensure attention than to look straight at people, moving your gaze around the audience and engaging them briefly in direct eye-to-eye contact. People then feel that you are talking to *them* and are interested in each one, and not just talking at the ceiling or the floor. It is also a great help in assessing where people are 'at' and being sensitive to them as a collection of individuals rather than as a faceless crowd.

Teaching points

The role of leading worship often includes the need to encourage, inform and teach people about worship, and this too needs to be done well. It is a good idea deliberately to develop quick, precise and sensitive ways of saying what you want to say, possibly with humour and the occasional illustration. The requirement is to use as few words as possible so that the 'flow' is not broken, and to help people relax, feel secure, and understand what is going on.

Don't pressurize

The worship leader must if possible draw everybody who is willing and able into the experience of worship and avoid 'pressure tactics' or 'partisan' attitudes that might lead people to withdraw into themselves or into divisions. People must be set free to worship or not to worship in the way you suggest and any sense of a pressure to conform must be avoided. Instead, people should be encouraged to accept and tolerate each other's differences and to turn their attention away from what everybody else is doing, and what everybody else might think about what they themselves are doing, and on to the Lord. Remember also that you can only draw out of people the potential for worship that is in them at that particular moment and the aim is not to push and pressurize, but to encourage and draw out.

Freedom from chaos

As I have already implied, advance planning and preparation for times of 'free' worship is not to be neglected, and can in fact create more freedom—at least, freedom from chaos. People's attitudes to this question are on the one hand a fear of rigidity that stifles spontaneity and following the Spirit, and on the other a fear of the proceedings getting out of control, or becoming directionless and mediocre. Both concerns are legitimate, and I believe that a balance can be found that satisfies both.

Very simply, there should be advance planning based on prayerful listening to the Lord, intelligent discussion between those in charge of the meeting, coupled with an attitude of flexibility. All those leading or taking part should know the aim of the meeting, the 'ingredients' of it, and any particular sense of direction that has been impressed upon one or other of them in their 'listening'. This may result in a precise programme being planned, but there should always be the recognition that God is sovereign and can choose to overrule even divinely inspired plans. When it comes to the actual celebration, house group or service, we must 'expect the unexpected' and be free to alter or abandon the plans we have made.

Vision

Leading worship is leading *people*, and cannot be detached from the responsibility of standing before God on their behalf seeking their health and welfare. A good shepherd will lead his flock to water and pasture, and so must find out where water and pasture are. This is a shared responsibility and the degree to which it falls upon the worship leader depends on local circumstances, but there will always be some degree of it. While the sheep are feeding, the shepherd is thinking of where to take them next, what their needs are and how those needs can be met, and even in a short time of worship the leader must be moving towards a God-inspired destination, even if he himself may see only one step ahead at a time.

It is a process of active faith to lead people by following the Spirit, but it is not 'blind faith' in the sense that the eyes of our understanding, knowledge, experience and intelligence should be open wide and assessing what is happening. If there is vision, then there will be a sense of motion and direction, and a reason to steer things one way or another. Leading worship is like sailing a ship, in the sense of setting the sails to the prevailing 'wind of the Spirit' and steering a definite course, in faith.

Expectation

If the worship is travelling somewhere, then there will be a sense of expectation, though it may not be clear exactly what is expected, just as a party of sightseers will be excited as they approach their destination yet not knowing what they will see there. In worship, expectation is on three levels. Firstly, there is the level of expectation among the people that will obviously be dependent upon many factors. Secondly, there is the level of expectation of the leaders, hopefully yet higher. Thirdly, there is God's expectation —or possibly the word 'intention' would be more appropriate. The aim of course is to rise up to the level of God's intentions for that occasion. This 'rising up' is vital or else we will get trapped in our own moods, feelings and habitual patterns of behaviour.

Talk to God before you talk to the people

For the worship leaders, the best opportunities for the raising of expectation are in advance of the meeting, when during a time of praise and prayer they can focus upon the Lord and seek to perceive his plan about what he intends to do. The leaders will then go before the people able to stimulate their faith and raise their level of expectation.

This is not, however, the exclusive prerogative of the leaders, as it may be that any one member of the congregation, having spent a similar time adjusting himself or herself to God's perspective, will be able to create a similar effect. In fact, it should be expected that if the Lord has something particular in mind, he may have 'tipped off' one or two people outside of the central leadership group!

Expect the unexpected!

However, it must again be emphasized that whatever may have been anticipated in advance, the meeting itself may not in the end fit exactly with what was expected, and we must always allow God his right to break out of our plans and to fulfil the expectations he has given us in quite a different way than we expected!

Discernment

It is important for many reasons to be spiritually prepared on a personal level in advance of leading worship, not the least of these reasons being the need for discernment. Once again this should be a shared responsibility and not just fall upon one person. Discernment is the ability to perceive clearly what is going on, and in Christian worship this is on both a spiritual and a natural level. It is not appropriate here to go into great detail about the gift of discernment of spirits, and precisely what it is, but there is certainly a need to discern between the good, bad and indifferent contributions that people bring, and the source of their 'inspiration'. Such discernment is important so that the meeting can be kept from wandering aimlessly, focusing on unhelpful things or being dominated by certain personalities moving against the 'flow' of the Spirit.

Weighing what is said and done

In 1 Corinthians 14:29, Paul makes it clear that when
contributions in the form of prophecies are given, others
should weigh carefully what is said. This, I believe, is
simply a way of taking into account our weak humanity,
because even when inspired by the Spirit, nervousness,
excess zeal, personal bias, inability to express oneself
clearly, insensitivity to others or just bad timing, can
confuse, add to, take away from or misapply a word from
the Lord. There are also rare occasions when someone
who is spiritually disturbed, even demonically affected,
slips into an open meeting and takes the opportunity to
wreak havoc! However, we are far more likely to need
discernment between that which originated in a pure form
from the Lord, and that which was added by the mind, or
emotions, or said at the wrong time and so on.

It is reasonable to argue that Paul's principle of weighing
carefully what is said need not be applied solely to prophecy, and that the role of leadership involves maintaining
a discerning approach constantly. On the spiritual level we
need to develop a sensitivity as to when something 'jars'
against the Spirit within us and disturbs our peace, and on
the mental level we need to weigh what we hear against
the standard of Scripture. There is, however, no short cut
to obtaining discernment in worship leading, as it comes
through experience and the practice of spiritual sensitivity
over a period of time.

Steering without tears (the imperfect leading the imperfect)

Skill is indeed required when there is imminent danger of a
meeting being side-tracked or damaged by unhelpful contributions, not least because any number of needs have to
be met within a short space of time. Some of the skills
needed are listed below:

1. Loving sensitivity

Sensitivity must be shown to the person who makes a faulty contribution in sincerity and good faith. It may have taken courage for them to speak up at all, so do not 'put them down' so that they never open their mouths again in public! It is sometimes wise to treat such a contribution as one of a number of alternatives, saying something like, 'We seem to be moving towards intercession here, and it is tremendously important that we pray for Mr Smith's gout, but I feel that at this moment we should be taking note of the earlier exhortation to give the Lord a rich offering of thanks and praise so let's sing...' In other words, we are being positive and saying in effect 'that is good/may be true/something we need be mindful of, but something else is better/more timely/more appropriate to the occasion'. Hence, the person will not feel rejected out of hand.

2. Loving correction

Firmness must be shown to the person who makes a contribution out of ill-will, excess emotionalism, unhealthy influences and so on, but sensitivity and understanding must still be applied. The rest of the congregation must know that they are in a situation where there is order and control within which they can feel secure, and where people will not be allowed to get away with causing confusion and error. Furthermore, they need to see that there is love for those who make mistakes or fall into error, as nobody (especially the leaders!) is immune from that possibility. A 'second opinion' is vital in such cases, and a quick consultation with another leader (whether verbally or in sign language!) creates a safeguard and sense of security for both leaders and led. If there is no necessity for an immediate confrontation with the person concerned, then it should be avoided (the person can always be invited to speak to the leader afterwards) for the sake of minimizing the interruption.

If, however, a dangerous or hurtful thing has been said, then it should be refuted and corrected immediately or else the meeting may never recover. If such things are ignored people will find it hard to leave them behind, and the conflict created by it will, if unresolved, dominate everyone's thoughts for the rest of the meeting and beyond.

3. Keeping 'on track'

More often than not, the primary skill required in applying discernment to leading worship is far less dramatic, being simply that of redirection. A lot of the time this may not even be detected by the congregation, and it is part of the job of leading worship to carry the responsibility for the direction, thereby removing any burden from the main body of worshippers. For example, the leader may choose a song, pray a prayer, or introduce an item that by its nature brings the right theme back into focus, without making any kind of verbal comment or value-judgement.

Leading by following

There is a further area where discernment needs to be applied if the worship is truly going to be a corporate expression. It should be obvious that the leaders, though in positions of authority and hopefully under a special empowering of the Spirit, will not have a monopoly on being led by the Spirit. In fact there is a strong sense in which the leaders should be led through the people. The context of Paul's instruction for order in church gatherings in 1 Corinthians 14 is clearly one in which there is no lack of participation from the people. The problem there was not how to stir them up, but how to keep their enthusiasm and sheer volume of contributions under control!

While in current practice worship leading seems most

often to be a matter of stirring people out of inactivity, I suspect that it is meant to be a role of steering and overseeing the richness of expression that emerges as everybody contributes. The idea of one or two people having an exclusive 'hot-line' to heaven and the rest being in a kind of spiritual neutral zone is, I believe, quite a dangerous one. We should expect God to speak through anyone, even a child—perhaps *especially* through a child because children are not so likely to have 'an axe to grind'.

Hence, the leaders should be watching, listening and trying to discern the 'mind of the Spirit' in people's prayers, choice of songs and so on. As they do so, they will test what is emerging against their own minds and spirits, and act to strengthen, highlight and confirm what seems to be most clearly inspired. This is a very practical way in which to be a servant of the church as the church responds to the Spirit, rather than taking the world's idea of leadership and imposing one's own will on others. Hence, the aim is to lead by following: following the direction in which the wind of the Spirit is blowing among the people, and seeking to draw everybody together in that one direction. To use the analogy of a sailing ship with many sails, such as the old ocean-going schooners, the people are like the sails, set to catch the power of the wind and make forward motion possible, while the leaders are the navigator and steersmen who plot the course and direct that forward motion to take the whole ship's company to the destination planned by the captain.

Musical sensitivity

It is vital that there is sensitivity on the part of the musicians, and most particularly those leading them, so that what the music 'says' does not contradict what our worship is saying to God, or what God is saying to us. In the early stages of worship, the music has great value as a 'stirring' influence, moving our hearts, minds, voices and bodies into action, turning our attention outwards towards God and one another. A mood of celebration can be encouraged, and fun, laughter, noise and rhythm are not inappropriate as we allow our feelings about God's goodness and grace to overflow. Songs can be addressed to one another as well as to the Lord, providing a source of encouragement and help us to 'tune in' to being part of the body. At this stage, quiet slow reflective music will probably send half the people off to sleep!

Later on, there is a crucial point at which we sense that we are being moved from thanksgiving and praise into worship. The music needs to become less dominant and to lead us into a sense of intimacy, love and adoration. Our focus has now moved on from things about God to the person of God himself, and our attitude changes to one of bowing down in his presence. Sensitive use of music can be particularly conducive to our meditation. Alternatively, the music could be stopped altogether, and just our voices joined in an appropriate song, or it may be that the praise has climaxed in loud applause to the Lord and then suddenly we find ourselves in silence. The silence may give way to the beauty of singing in tongues, or vice versa, but the overriding sense is now of being in the presence of a God who speaks to his people. There may be a word given of prophecy, knowledge, tongue and interpretation and so on that could be responded to in a number of ways, for example, a song, or time of prayer, a reading or teaching from the Scriptures. The result of this time of listening in the presence of God should be that we are spiritually fed, and enter into spiritual rest. It should be obvious that insensitive playing of instruments or inappropriate choice of songs can hinder our entering fully into each stage, and skill is needed both in the actual playing and the directing of the flow from one stage to the next.

Authority

Implicit in what I have said so far is the need for authority and this is derived from some of the following things—the kind of authority Jesus recognized was that which is derived from being *under* authority (Mt 8:9), and being submitted to one another (Eph 5:21). Jesus was under the authority of his Father. Spiritual authority is not primarily derived from title or position but as a natural outcome of a relationship, and if people sense that you are close to the Lord, open to others, and able to lead, then they will follow without great difficulty. Your own relationship with the Lord and the people provides the only valid foundation on which to stand when leading others. Out of this relationship will flow the living faith and steady trust that make the exercise of authority a liberating rather than an enslaving power.

Understanding the context

It is important to understand the nature of different kinds of Christian gatherings—for example, the Eucharist, a baptism or even a funeral. There is a lot of difference between the nature of worship in a house-group meeting and a city-wide celebration, or a prayer meeting and an evangelistic crusade. Careful thinking through of what is really appropriate in each situation is vital.

Humility

Your aim is to become a signpost to the presence of God, not a hoarding advertising your own personality or talents. A signpost needs to be in a prominent position and clearly seen, but its aim is to point away from itself. People should leave a meeting like they end a journey—engrossed by what they have seen on the way and found at their destination, not talking about the merits and attributes of the traffic signs. With all our gifts and talents we are no more the centre of attraction than the donkey that carried Jesus into Jerusalem to the adulation of the crowds. The donkey was very privileged indeed, but just there to serve!

'Ground rules'

I have already presented the role of leading worship as a shared responsibility, even though it may sometimes appear from the front that only one person is doing the steering. This continues the principle of the 'servant attitude', and the way in which right relationships are inseparable from true worship. First of all there is what might be termed the 'moral' requirement for this, which I hope is clear in earlier chapters, hence it is foolish to think that somebody can lead others into the presence of God while neglecting to put right quarrels or disagreements with either leaders or those being led. Secondly, there are some very practical reasons why a worship leader should be in real, open and trusting relationships—some of which should also be evident from the things I have already said. It helps a great deal for there to be a set of 'ground rules', understood generally by everybody and in detail by the leaders. For example, there are the questions of who acts in the event of a crisis; who deals with the 'weighing' of prophecies; can anybody stand up and speak or do they need to ask first; can other elders etc. come freely to the fore and take over; who has the final word on such matters and so on. I remember occasions when I have been leading and something has happened unexpectedly that was beyond my 'jurisdiction' or ability to cope with. It has been a great relief to myself and indeed everyone when another leader has stepped forward and dealt competently with such a situation, and it is a source of security to be regularly working within such relationships where the 'ground rules' are understood.

A caring relationship

It must always be remembered that leading people is an expression of a certain kind of relationship with them and whereas a leader may be looking out on to the sea of faces, each face is relating back to the leader almost as if it was a one-to-one encounter. Therefore the quality of relationship, and the degree of genuine caring that the leader displays, is crucial to the kind of response he gets back. That caring is also measured by the degree of care taken 'behind the scenes', developing among the leadership a quality of friendship and functional interaction that frees the people from worry, fear, uncertainty and unhelpful interruption as they worship.

Be yourself

Probably the thing most likely to inspire confidence is to be yourself. There needs to be a balance here between being natural and unaffected and being aware of behaviour patterns that are a hindrance to others. But people will forgive a tremendous amount if they sense that you are being real and not putting on a front. Naturalness comes when you feel reasonably secure and confident, and are obviously 'at home' with God, and with his people when worshipping together. It can give people comfort when you make mistakes as it helps them to realize that you are human too. It is important to be able to laugh, particularly at your own blunders, and to avoid wearing a spiritual 'mask' or putting on a special voice. Worship must not be treated as a separate compartment from your everyday self, but as an extension of it.

Of course, being yourself does not mean offloading your personal insecurities in public, and it is wiser to share your anxieties and uncertainties only with your co-leaders, rather than risk drawing too much attention to yourself by spilling out your lack of confidence or fear of failure.

If I was asked to sum up the art of leading worship in one simple sentence, I think I would say: be a worshipper, be a servant and be yourself.

14

Transformation Through Adoration

'It's time you changed!' bellowed the preacher. He was quite right. An incriminating list of failures, sins and shortcomings relating to the church had been presented. We were in the dock and the verdict of 'guilty' was hanging over our bowed heads. Once again we confessed our sins and determined that this time we really would try harder. Things would change, they really would. But they didn't. Well, they did for a while, but it did not take long for the ticking-off to wear off, and soon everything was back to normal. Or should I say back to *abnormal,* because at least we knew that our spiritual lives were not what God must regard as normal. How could we change? Surely there was more to becoming Christ-like than making New Year resolutions all the year round! We were stuck in a syndrome that went something like this: 'I've failed—I feel guilty about failing—I must try harder—having tried harder I feel much better—oh dear, failed again—I feel guilty—must try harder'. (Repeat endlessly until fed up or exhausted!) The induction of guilt as a motivation to holiness is not a scriptural principle, but it sometimes tends to be used as if it was! But there is good news for guilt-ridden Christians. The Bible shows us a much better and infinitely more successful way by which to be changed.

To worship is to be changed

It could be summed up in the statement: to worship is to be changed. In 2 Corinthians 3:18 (NASB) Paul says: 'But we all, with unveiled face beholding as in a mirror the glory of the Lord, are being transformed into the same image from glory to glory.' The idea of being transformed by looking might on the face of it seem rather a passive way to go about something that surely requires a lot of effort. But we *can* be transformed by looking. It is not only a fact of spiritual life, it is also a fact of natural life. Even a newborn baby will very soon learn to fix its gaze on the eyes of its mother, who will spend long adoring moments gazing back. Surely this is one of its first messages of love, and without that gaze one wonders how much the child would be robbed of its first and possibly most formative experience of a loving relationship. To use a different illustration, I can remember moments up on a North Wales mountainside, gazing over a vast scenario of lakes and valleys as they subtly changed colour under the setting sun. I don't know how long I sat there but it was getting dark by the time I finally tore myself away. It had a deep effect on me, not only in terms of the pleasure of visual experience and satisfaction, but also by bringing a sense of peace, order and simplicity into my heart. As I walked back down the stony path, I had been changed in some small but significant way.

After repentance—a spiritual vacuum?

Relationships grow as lovers sit looking into one another's faces, and these are often the times when the strongest emotions stir. Who can doubt that this changes people in all sorts of ways! How much more then might we be transformed by gazing with adoration and worship into the face of God? If we are changed by getting to know *people*, how much more profound must be the changes brought about by getting to know *God?* By focusing on this means of change, I am not in any way suggesting it as an alternative to repentance, but it is often true that having repented, we leave ourselves in a spiritual vacuum, having little idea how to introduce new patterns of behaviour where the old ones used to be.

I recently came across a marvellous quotation by William Temple in which he said: 'To worship is to quicken the conscience by the holiness of God, to feed the mind with the truth of God, to purge the imagination by the beauty of God, to open the heart to the love of God, to devote the will to the purpose of God.' If all five of these happen through worship, then what they add up to is not a superficial or fleeting change, but a most radical alteration of our behaviour, even of our personality. Inward changes cannot be regarded as authentic until they have been worked out in everyday life, but I would argue that they are very likely to be initiated in the times that we set aside exclusively for looking and gazing: namely, times of worship.

Transformed into the same image

For me, these thoughts add a new dimension to what might appear to be an unattainable command of God which we read in Leviticus 19:2 (RSV): 'You shall be holy; for I the Lord your God am holy.' If we put this verse alongside the one in 2 Corinthians 3:18 that we have just looked at, then we may see a practical way to be holy. By meditating upon God's character, by praising, adoring and worshipping his qualities in detail, by allowing the eyes of our spirit to gaze into his, we will begin to discover our own behaviour altering to reflect what we have seen.

Having looked at the passage in 2 Corinthians 3:18, we

must be careful not to miss the fact that Paul talks of this gaze upon the face of the Lord in the plural: 'But we all, with unveiled face...' Without wishing to duplicate the subject matter elsewhere in this book on corporate worship, it is important here to appreciate that God chooses to reveal himself in a special way when we worship together. As each of us comes with a contribution (1 Cor 14:26), it is as if God gives everyone a small piece of a jigsaw puzzle. As we each add our piece, at the right time and in the right place, the picture God wants to show us begins to take shape, and without doubt it will show us more of himself. Were we to stay at home with our little piece of jigsaw, we may catch only a small glimpse of the Lord's glory and therefore have much less of his glory to reflect.

Mirrors and diamonds

There is also the very real sense in which the glory of God is revealed, not as a vision floating somewhere in the middle distance of our spiritual perception, but actually in the faces of the people with whom we are worshipping. We know that we cannot see the physical face of Jesus, but if, as the passage says, we are all reflecting the glory of his face, then why don't we look in the mirrors all around us? As we enter together into the glory of God's presence, we become surrounded by as many unique reflections of him as there are people in the room! Our mirrors may be flawed in places but his reflection is there if we look carefully. We are all so different, and we sometimes find that we will all reflect a unique aspect of the Lord's character and of the truth he wants to reveal to us.

Alternatively, we could see ourselves as a single diamond with many facets. To appreciate fully the beauty of a diamond, you need to turn it in your fingers and study the variety of reflections within those many facets. The beauty of a diamond is in the interaction of light between the facets, just like so much of the beauty and transforming power of our worship is in the interaction between us, as we reflect the spiritual light of God in our lives.

An uninterrupted gaze of the spirit upon God

This powerful principle needs to be allowed to operate as we set aside times for corporate worship, but it need not be thought of as applicable only to such times. Surely its effect is going to have a much greater transforming influence if it is possible to practise adoration as a habit of everyday life. There are many encouragements in Scripture towards this end, but I will simply attempt to highlight one or two of them. Again, our supreme example is Jesus, who practised an uninterrupted spiritual gaze upon his Father: Jesus gave them this answer: 'I tell you the truth, the Son can do nothing by himself; he can only do what he sees his Father doing, because whatever the Father does the Son also does. For the Father loves the Son and shows him all he does'. (Jn 5:19, 20). Jesus' spiritual eyes never looked away from the loving gaze of his Father. There was only one moment when this happened, one of utter devastation when on the cross Jesus looked and saw only blackness. He cried out in agony: 'My God, my God, why have you forsaken me?' It is significant that this is the only prayer recorded when Jesus did not call God 'Father'.

He was spiritually 'focused' such that at every moment he could 'see' his Father's intentions, and act accordingly. How we love to make our own way through our everyday lives, taking pride in our wisdom and understanding as Christians yet often without even a glance at our Father's face. A child learns to read its father's face remarkably well and will look into it for approval, for a 'yes' or a 'no', and a hundred other silent but clear messages. This is in

spiritual terms what Jesus practised—is it not good enough
for us? Do we know what our heavenly Father feels about a
situation in which we happen to find ourselves? Do we find
ourselves having been prepared in advance when we unexpectedly need wisdom and insight, simply because in
the course of our habitual looking at God, he gave us that
wisdom and insight even before we knew it was going to
be necessary? Jesus never applied formulas, even scriptural
ones, to the encounters he had with people. Each conversation was different; for example, he didn't tell Nicodemus
about 'living water', or the Samaritan woman about being
'born again'; Zacchaeus wasn't told about not giving the
children's bread to the dogs, nor did he invite himself to
the Syro-Phoenician woman's house for a meal! In each
situation his uninterrupted gaze saw his Father doing
something unique and special. How could we not be
radically changed, even transformed, in our mundane
lives and indeed see transformations in the lives of those
we meet, were we to follow Jesus' example in this way.

'I have set the Lord always before me'

In Psalm 16:7, 8, David writes: 'I will praise the Lord, who
counsels me; even at night my heart instructs me. I have
set the Lord always before me.' The passage from which
this comes is quoted by Peter on the day of Pentecost as
referring prophetically to Jesus, so obviously David in his
own devotions got 'carried away' in the Spirit and found
himself writing prophetically of the Messiah. It is reasonable however to surmise that David himself was able to
say: 'I have set the Lord always before me' and we can
gather from his psalms that he spent much time in medita-
tive worship of the Lord. (The Bible does not, however,
gloss over David's lapses of obedience to God.) One
could even argue that this habit was the key to his great-

ness. It was certainly the key to his intimate relationship with God. But how do we actually practise this amid the hectic business of living? Isn't it unreasonable to expect us to do anything more than snatch a moment here or there for a quick prayer, probably an emergency 999 one, at that!

David's words imply a deliberate act of the will, a conscious focusing of his natural and spiritual faculties upon his Maker, the nurturing of a habit over many years, such that even in the unconsciousness of sleep his whole being remained in divine communion. The key to entering into this level of communion with God lies, I believe, in the exercise of a discipline of personal praise and worship, and this is dealt with in the next chapter.

15

Personal Discipline in Worship

As long as I live it shall be a rule engraved on my tongue to bring praise like fruit for an offering and my lips as a sacrificial gift. I will make skilful music with lyre and harp to serve God's glory, and the flute of my lips will I raise in praise of his rule of righteousness. Both morning and evening I shall enter into the Covenant of God: and at the end of both I shall recite his commandments, and so long as they continue to exist, these will be my frontier and my journey's end.

Therefore I will bless his name in all I do, before I move hand or foot, whenever I go out or come in, when I sit down and when I rise, even when lying on my couch, I will chant his praise.

My lips shall praise him as I sit at the table which is set for all, and before I lift my head to partake of any nourishment from the delicious fruits of the earth.

When fear and terror come, and there is only anguish and distress I will still bless and thank him for his wondrous deeds, and meditate upon his power, and lean upon his mercies all day long. For I know that in his hand is justice for all that live, and all his works are true. So when trouble comes, or salvation, I praise him just the same (Column X, 'Manual of Discipline', *Dead Sea Scrolls*).

Personal discipline in private worship

The popularity of the word 'discipline' is probably at an all-time low, calling up images of headmasters with canes, detention after school, and government establishments designed to deliver short, sharp shocks. But if we can manage to put aside for a moment emotive images of cold showers and forced runs around the football pitch, and consider what discipline for a Christian might in fact mean, we could be on the edge of a discovery that can transform our lives.

The word 'disciple' has a much warmer feel to it; a disciple is a person under the discipline of his teacher, and we as Christians should be under the loving but firm discipline of Jesus. Bearing in mind the negative connections that the word has for many of us, we must remind ourselves that the discipline of Jesus is the route into perfect liberty, and lack of his discipline is a sure way in which to become imprisoned. It follows that the most liberated worship is most likely to arise among people who practise a discipline of worship, both in their workaday lives, and in their worship together.

The will

It is impossible to separate personal discipline from a constant use of the words 'I will', and it is interesting that time and time again the psalmists of the Old Testament begin their move towards God by saying it. For example, in Psalm 57:7, 'My heart is fixed, O God, my heart is fixed; I *will* sing and give praise' (AV). This psalm is a psalm of David, and his determination to praise takes on a further significance when it turns out that at the moment of writing he was a fugitive of Saul, hiding in caves in fear of his life. His praise was clearly based on far more than circumstances and mood. It seems that there is a popular misconception around concerning worship, that is, that it 'comes over you' and before you move, you have to be moved. While it is true that worship is a response to God, it is also true that we are frequently blind to his qualities and deeds until we determine to open our spiritual eyes and step closer to him in praise and thanksgiving. The most beautiful views are seen only by those who first determine to climb the mountain. This principle is borne out by James 4:8: 'Come near to God and he will come near to you', and though there are marvellous times when we are unexpectedly caught up in a spirit of worship, these may well be too rare to sustain us for long.

But I don't feel like praising...

There is another reason why God has made room for human initiative in coming to him, and that is his desire to receive voluntary worship, worship that we freely choose to give him. It costs far less to be wafted into worship on a passing breeze, than to determine to give it because we reckon that God is worth it, however we feel. We must also be realistic and remember that we will experience times when our circumstances and feelings in themselves give us no reason to praise at all. These are times when our worship will dry up, unless we have learned to say as did Habakkuk, when he saw a terrible vision of approaching calamity, 'yet I will rejoice in the Lord, I will be joyful in God my Saviour'. Sometimes worship starts because it is felt spontaneously in the heart, sometimes it is an act of the will. Either way, God is equally worthy of our worship, and it is his worthiness that is the important thing, not our fickle and unreliable feelings.

Our part—God's part

We must not, however, be mistaken into thinking that the will to worship can by itself produce true worship. As Richard Foster says:

> It is kindled within us only when the Spirit of God touches our human spirit. . . . We can use all the right techniques and methods, we can have the best possible liturgy, but we have not worshipped the Lord until Spirit touches spirit. . . . Until God touches and frees our spirit we cannot enter this realm. Singing, praying and praising all may lead to worship, but worship is more than any of them. Our spirit must be ignited by divine fire. (*Celebration of Discipline*, Hodder & Stoughton, pp. 138–9.)

The will to worship is our part, while God's part is to supply the fire that ignites it within us.

Shaking ourselves into action

So in what areas can we apply the will to worship? If we look at Psalm 103:1 and 2, we see the psalmist applying his will to stir his whole being: 'Praise the Lord, O my soul; all my inmost being, praise his holy name. Praise the Lord, O my soul, and forget not all his benefits.' He is talking to himself, stirring himself into action on every level. He is, as it were, shaking himself by his own lapels, picking himself up out of his slumber or apathy, and demanding obedience of all his faculties. 'Inmost being' must refer to spirit and emotions, and in addition he is deliberately concentrating his mind to 'forget not all his benefits'. In stirring up his inmost being, there will inevitably be bodily expression of praise, so his whole self is brought into play. The discipline of worship requires that we stand in complete readiness for obedience to the Spirit, like a soldier preparing himself for action.

To praise or not to praise

I remember clearly an occasion on which this lesson was firmly printed on my mind. I had been invited to lead worship at a church some hours drive away from my home, so my wife and I set off early that morning in the rather ramshackle Morris 1000 van we had at the time. It was cold and icy, and the wind blew freely through the many gaps and holes in the vehicle! I was in a grumpy mood, and proceeded reluctantly, creating tension between the two of us. At the time I was spiritually dry, and had no desire or motivation to travel such a long way, let alone to lead worship! By the time we arrived, my mood was blacker, the tension tauter, and the temperature colder.

For the duration of the last five minutes prior to facing the crowd of enthusiastic would-be praisers, I knew I faced a stark choice: to get right with the Lord, my wife (and the car!) and go on in raw faith, or be honest with my hosts about my state and back out!

Probably motivated at least in part by pride, I decided on the former course of action, confessed my sin, apologized to my wife and stepped into the meeting saying to the Lord something to the effect of, 'Lord, I'm empty, I don't feel like worshipping you. I have nothing to give to you or with which to lead the people, unless you give it to me. But, sink or swim, here I go!' From the moment I began to lead the praise, my heart filled up and so we praised with freedom and joy. I did not have to pretend, or put on an act, but because I determined to praise the Lord ignited praise within me, and I genuinely overflowed.

An inconvenient lesson to have learned!

At times I would like to forget that lesson, and those times are when I am not leading but instead am part of the congregation, and feeling similarly fed up and grumpy. I would like to use my mood as a legitimate excuse not to join in, but (to the irritation of the less noble side of me!) I now know that my feelings need not rule my spirit.

The discipline of thankfulness

In 1 Thessalonians 5:18 we read: 'Give thanks in all circumstances, for this is the will of God in Christ Jesus for you' (RSV). This surely involves a discipline, if for no other reason than that we do not necessarily feel thankful about everything that happens to us! Before we can start thanking God for the difficult circumstances, however, we must make a habit of thanking him for the good ones. This is such an obvious thing, but many of us take for granted the good things of life, natural and spiritual, forgetting to thank the Giver. It is our preoccupation with 'getting' that robs God of the thanks due to him, and turns so much of our praying to selfish ends, so that we become beggars in the presence of God instead of worshippers.

For this reason Paul tells the Philippians to give thanks alongside their asking: 'Do not be anxious about anything, but in everything, by prayer and petition, *with thanksgiving,* present your requests to God' (Phil 4:6). Have you noticed how that when we say a sincere 'thank you' to somebody, we automatically look them in the face and smile? Not to do so could seem impolite, if not rude, and I suppose that the times when we do not are usually the times when we are not really grateful at all! Thankfulness is a way of turning our faces towards God, and reaffirming our warm relationship of grateful dependence upon him.

In all circumstances?

The three words 'in all circumstances' are sometimes hard to come to terms with. Often we will feel much more like placing a vigorous or bitter complaint about our circumstances before him. This is where a stronger discipline is needed, but determining to give thanks at these times is not based upon mindless conformity to an unreasonable command, neither are we required to be dishonest. We may quite understandably feel 'How can God expect me to thank him for my being made redundant/the news that so and so has cancer/my overdraft/my failure to keep control of the children, etc.'. The truth of the matter is that if our lives are offered up to God, nothing that happens to us can separate us from his love, faithfulness and mercy, or take us beyond his sovereign control over our circumstances. The problem comes when we do not really believe that! In Romans 8:28 we read, 'And we know that in all things God works for the good of those who love him.'

This does not mean that everything that happens to us comes from God, and certainly we are not being asked to thank him for evil, but we can thank him for the fact that *in* all things, *in* all circumstances, he is still working for good. (It is significant that in the story of Job, the devil had to ask permission of God before bringing troubles to him, and all that happened was allowed by the Lord as a test. At no point would the devil go beyond the limits that God set. Let us not forget, however, that the promise in Romans 8:28 is to those who love God.) God is able to overcome evil with good, turn even the bitterest experiences of life into lessons about his grace and create glorious endings to sad stories.

Turning to God in frustrations

A chance meeting with someone I had not seen for about seven or eight years recently brought vividly home to me the way God can use even the most mundane situations if we offer them up to him in a positive and thankful attitude. I first met Max and three of his friends during a mission in Birmingham when they were teenagers at school and I was in a mission team running a coffee bar and visiting schools. They travelled quite a long way one evening to the coffee bar in the centre of Birmingham, and after spending some time there needed to get home by the times stated by their respective sets of parents. Two of us decided to make the necessary detour in the team's van and set off. Being unfamiliar with the area we soon got lost, and the time by which they should have returned passed. Tension increased as the prospect of being greeted by irate parents loomed large in all our imaginations!

Although our passengers were non-Christians, we decided to stop and pray very simply to find the route and concerning the situation with regard to their parents. Max describes this as the first time he had ever heard anyone pray as if God was real, personal and interested in such matters, and it left a powerful impression on him. For us, it was fairly routine. The next day at school the four friends compared their parental reception committees with those of the night before. They were identical; each set of parents remarked on how early they were! This simple experience of God being brought into a minor crisis was the thing that clinched Max's decision to become a Christian, and he himself is now involved in evangelistic work.

It is sobering to speculate on whether or not he would now be a Christian had we succumbed to the temptation to frustration, irritation or worry in that van, and treated the situation as an annoyance to be endured rather than an opportunity for God to step in. The discipline we need is to offer up to him with thankfulness whatever comes our way, believing against emotion, sometimes against reason, against the apparent facts, that God is still working for good, and has not abandoned us.

Praise is not a 'lucky charm'

We must, however, beware of the danger of using the

words 'Thank you, Lord' as a kind of lucky charm when things go wrong; it is rather an affirmation of faith and trust in God's promises, the vocalizing of a preparedness to risk everything on God, however faltering or mixed with doubt that trust might be at first.

Stepping through the broken glass

The Bible speaks in many places of a 'sacrifice' of thanksgiving, and this makes it clear that it is sometimes costly. It costs us to abandon our self-pity, our blaming of others, our false comforts and escape routes that we have substituted for a trust in God. Romans 1:21 shows us that the consequence of unthankfulness is that thinking becomes futile and our hearts are darkened, but Colossians 1:12 shows us that giving thanks is a practice of those who share in the 'kingdom of light'. Giving thanks is a step from darkness into light, and the discipline of thankfulness means that we take that step not only when our feet are swift with joy, but also when they are heavy with weariness, doubt and fear, and it seems that the route to God is strewn with broken glass.

The discipline of continual praise

Praise and thanksgiving are closely related and similar principles apply to both, not least that both are to be practised continually. Hebrews 13:15 tells us: 'Through Jesus, therefore, let us continually offer to God a sacrifice of praise', and David writes in Psalm 34:1: 'I will extol the Lord at all times; his praise will always be on my lips.' Most of us, however, practise spasmodic praise, depending upon our feelings and circumstances, alternating between praise and grumbling. To be honest, I am often suspicious of people whose every other phrase seems to be 'praise the Lord' or 'Hallelujah', because sometimes it turns out to be just froth and bubble that blows away when things get tough. Many of us have been put off expressing praise in everyday life because of the suspicion, that it is little more than false piety or conformity to a religious 'type', and indeed it is true that many people put on a 'spiritual' front in order to impress others.

Our resistance to it, however, may sometimes have its roots in our 'self-image'. Our picture of ourselves may not include overt expressions of praise, and we know that we would feel awkward or embarrassed were we to do it. It would be 'out of character'. Sadly it is more socially acceptable to grumble and complain, than to give thanks and praise and, sadder still, many of us are more subject to social convention than the prompting of the Spirit. Here we must be open to the power of God to change us, and not regard our self-image as unchangeable or social convention as unbreakable. At the same time we must seek to be genuine and real in our praise and ready to explain our thankfulness intelligently to mystified non-believers.

Our zeal in praise needs to be tempered by a sensitivity to others and we might do well to consider the wise and realistic words of Proverbs 25:20, 'Like one who takes away a garment on a cold day, or like vinegar poured on soda, is one who sings songs to a heavy heart'! There is also the 'back-slapping' praise enthusiast referred to in Proverbs 27:14, whose *bonhomie* is not necessarily welcome or helpful: 'If a man loudly blesses his neighbour early in the morning, it will be taken as a curse.'

Is continual praise practical?

We still have the question of how we can practise 'continual praise'. It is obvious that for much of the time our minds and bodies are occupied with working, eating, sleeping etc. and our attention absorbed by the legitimate demands of living. One could reasonably conclude that continual praise is just not practical and, not only that, if we constantly punctuated our conversation, telephone calls, business letters, meals and so on with 'Hallelujahs', we might become a nonsense, and an irritation to those around us.

'Praising God with your spirit'

There is, however, a level on which our praise can be continual, and that is on the level of the spirit. Our worship is 'in spirit' (Jn 4:23, 24) as well as on a mental and bodily level. Paul says in 1 Corinthians 14:15, 'I will pray with my spirit, but I will also pray with my mind; I will sing with my spirit, but I will also sing with my mind. If you are praising God with your spirit....' Through the Holy Spirit, our own spirits have been brought to life and function, and now we are able to pray and praise with our spirit.

The marvellous thing about the operation of the spirit is that it can function in parallel with our conscious self but independently of it. A friend of mine relates the following experience: 'The day after I first spoke in tongues I was cycling to work and thinking about some shopping I had to do on the way. After a while I became aware that at the same time as my mind was concentrating on my shopping list, my spirit was concentrating on God, praising him in my new prayer language – something was going on in me on two levels at once. Suddenly I understood a little more about what Paul must have meant by continual praise. Hence I found myself thinking about a shopping list and praising God at the same time! I was so excited at this discovery that I almost fell off my bike!' As well as a conscious, deliberate focusing of our attention on God in the nitty gritty of normal, everyday living, praise is an opening of ourselves to the Spirit so that he can bypass our minds and maintain an uninterrupted communication with the Father.

Keeping the engine 'ticking over'

It is clear that the gift of tongues is primarily for the
personal edification of the believer (except when used
with the gift of interpretation), and is a very practical way
of giving continual praise to God. With practice it is
possible to get into the habit of continually praising God
on this spiritual level (silently of course in the presence of
others!) so that it can be likened to keeping an engine
'ticking over'. It is then a straightforward matter, when an
opportunity comes for vocal praise in hymns and songs
and so on in the vocabulary of the understanding, just to
'put your foot down' and off you go!

Paul implies that not everybody enjoys the benefit of
this marvellous gift, but for all of us our birth-right as
members of God's family is a reborn, enlivened and active
spirit, which under the inspiration of the Holy Spirit will
cry out 'Abba Father', and seek ceaseless communion
with him whether our bodies and minds are working or
sleeping, relaxing or worshipping.

Praise is a public witness

Praise can be a constant 'internal' activity, but the kind of
praise God wants is also vocal and audible, because he
wants other people to hear it as well as himself! Praise is a
strong public witness to others, an encouragement to
believers, and a proclamation to non-believers. Psalm
18:49 states, 'Therefore I will praise you among the
nations, O Lord; I will sing praises to your name.' Praise
can have an evangelistic effect as described in Psalm 40:3,
'He put a new song in my mouth, a hymn of praise to our
God. Many will see and fear and put their trust in the
Lord.' And in Psalm 40:9 David makes it clear that the
truth about God should not be kept secret:

I proclaim righteousness in the great assembly; I do not seal
my lips, as you know, O Lord. I do not hide your righteousness
in my heart; I speak of your faithfulness and salvation. I do
not conceal your love and your truth from the great assembly.

Praise is a way of proclaiming the reality of God in our
lives, of making known his character and his deeds to the
world.

Personal discipline in corporate worship

Being there

You look out of the window as the cold dark evening
draws in. It is raining. Not only that, but the car is in for
repairs and you will have to use the bicycle. That's if you
go at all. Last week it was a disappointment, and tonight
you're tired. The central heating is on and a warm sleepy
feeling is beginning to pervade the corner of the room
occupied by the armchair. To go or not to go, that is the
question. The meeting starts in twenty minutes and it
takes ten minutes to get there. Oh no, the bike! It will take
at least twenty. Your sense of duty wins and you rush
around looking for the bicycle clips, treading on the dog
as you head for the door, and out into that unique sense of
dampness and gloom that only an English winter can
conjure up. As you hunch yourself against the cold and
pedal furiously, your mind is a jumble of thoughts – why
didn't you put the car in a day earlier then you wouldn't
have to cycle tonight – I hope it's worth going – disappointing last week – I must get round to papering the bathroom
– that telephone bill was a bit of a shock – now is it quicker
to cut through the Grove, or is the hill steeper that way?—
that new head of department looks like a bad-tempered
type, I'll tread carefully there.

You arrive, and puff and drip your way into the hall,

late. About half an hour later, you are just beginning to
enter a moderately suitable frame of mind for worship.
Just then the worship ends and the speaker stands up to
speak. Oh no! Not him again! By the end the dampness
seems to have pervaded not only your socks but your soul,
and you just want to get back home to the warm before
anyone inquires too deeply about your inward state!

Disciplines of preparation

So many of us end up slumped in meetings in the frame of
mind described (with feeling!) above. Usually, however,
it is just not necessary, and even when the rush of our
circumstances is beyond our control, we can do a great
deal to ensure that we arrive inwardly, if not outwardly,
ready to step into God's presence. If there is an area of
discipline that can transform corporate worship more than
anything else, I believe it is that of preparing ourselves
beforehand. The background to any preparation should
of course be our efforts to cultivate a lifestyle of thankfulness and praise, so that our gathering for corporate worship
becomes an extension of, and a genuine overflowing of, a
daily walk with God. If this is not the case, we will often
find our entering into God's presence to be a violent
wrench from a state of spiritual inertia and from a mind-
set that is reluctant to adjust to worshipful activity. Rather
than stepping suddenly from the gloom into a bright light,
to find our eyes dazzled and out of focus, we should each
come with our own light already brightly burning to enjoy
the greater brightness that comes as we join our lights
together.

'Tuning-in' to God

Richard Foster says:

> The first avenue into worship is to still all humanly initiated
> activity . . . we are to live in a perpetual inward listening silence

so that our words and actions have their source in God. If we are accustomed to carrying out the business of our lives in human strength and wisdom, we will do the same in gathered worship. If however, we have cultivated the habit of allowing every conversation, every business transaction, to be divinely prompted, that same sensitivity will flow into public worship. (*Celebration of Discipline*, Hodder & Stoughton, pp.144 and 145.)

With this in mind there are also specific ways in which we can make ourselves ready in the time immediately preceding a gathering of God's people.

What did I get—how did I do?

Let us start with our attitude to corporate worship. As members of the consumer society, it is all too easy to find that our predominant attitude, even to worship, is that of the consumer. Unthinkingly we come along to view the goods on display and take what we fancy. We come away complaining, 'Well, I did not get much out of that', and over lunch or supper we evaluate the 'performance' of the pastor or leaders; 'roast preacher' is a staple Sunday diet all over the world. We are concerned with whether or not it was to our personal taste, or emphasis, and how much it met our needs. Those of us who lead often become preoccupied with how well we did or did not do, whom we pleased or displeased. We cannot of course ignore entirely these attitudes in so far as they spring out of what and who we are, but all too often we allow such selfish attitudes to dominate our experience of worship, and we let them reign unchallenged.

I'm here for God and you

First of all, it is not for our own benefit that we come, but for the benefit of our God, to honour, praise and thank him, to give him joy and pleasure in the company of his redeemed people, his beloved children. We should come asking the question, 'Lord, what will give *you* pleasure in our worship, how can I serve *you* and honour *you*?' From this springs the second reason for coming together, that we are there to build up one another. We should come asking the question, 'Lord, how can I serve my brothers and sisters here, is there an individual who needs my friendship or special encouragement or a gift of some kind?' If we come *to give,* to God and each other, we will enter a whole new experience that our selfishness would otherwise disqualify us from.

So what about ourselves? We surely should not ignore our own needs and pretend they are not there? The principle that operates here is the one presented to us by Jesus himself in Luke 6:38 (NASB): 'Give, and it will be given to you; good measure, pressed down, shaken together, running over, they will pour into your lap. For whatever measure you deal out to others, it will be dealt to you in return.' If we concern ourselves with pleasing God, and seeing to one another's needs, God clearly promises that he will look after our own needs. Give, and it will be given to you. How many of us become dry and empty in our worship, even bored with it, and never consider that it may be because we are coming as consumers rather than givers?

Limbering up

Having established our attitude as one of giving, what can we do practically to prepare ourselves? The mime artist, Geoffrey Stevenson, with whom I often work, makes a practice of spending half an hour or so limbering up before he performs. Anyone using physical skills will do the same in order to attain the level of concentration and muscular co-ordination necessary for their work. Similarly, our spiritual faculties often need a 'work-out' before they are ready to function efficiently, and the time immediately prior to corporate worship is the crucial time.

Most of us lead busy lives, and a large proportion of us are far too busy, but nevertheless we are all able, if we put our minds to it, to limber up spiritually and mentally even if it is just as we walk, cycle or drive to the meeting. It is undoubtedly better to put aside five or ten minutes at home privately for this, but 'mobile' preparation is still preferable to none at all. Here are some suggestions for a spiritual 'work-out':

1. Clear the day's debris; fears, worries, sins, irritations all need to be brought to the cross and abandoned there. We should pray that the Lord will help us with those problems that still cling to us, possibly through the fellowship we are about to enjoy. Relax for a few minutes in thankfulness for the forgiveness and acceptance there is in Christ.

2. Focus upon the Lord; even use your imagination to picture him before you, welcoming you deeper into his presence. Ask him whether there are any hindrances to your entering in fully, and then ask him what would give him joy and pleasure in the worship.

3. Stir your spirit into greater action: sing, give thanks, praise, use the gift of tongues to sing or pray. (This I find to be particularly helpful when my mind is everywhere but where I want it to be!) Songs, scriptures and inspired thoughts that could have a relevance later on in the meeting may stir in your mind at this time, so take note of them.

4. Pray for one or two other people who are coming, and offer yourself to the Lord to be his servant to meet the needs of others. Pray for those who will lead the meeting. Expect at this time to be led to pray for a specific thing as the Lord inspires you.

5. Meditate briefly on a verse of Scripture; the psalms are particularly helpful in preparing us for worship.

6. Go expecting God to make himself known, reminding yourself of his promises and his desire to pour out his love upon his people.

It helps to arrive a few minutes early and as you sit, or greet people, continue what you have begun, watching, listening and trying to sense where you can give to God and those around you. As people come in, you may spot a worried face, or remember that you forgot to thank somebody, or encourage someone for something that has recently happened. It helps the atmosphere of a meeting tremendously if, as we arrive, we take the trouble to make physical, verbal, or at least eye-contact with our fellow-worshippers, and in this way remind ourselves that we are coming together to worship as one body. Being a self-contained person, with a tendency to withdraw into my own world, I sometimes find this an effort, but it is one of the best ways to open the doors of our little glass capsules and prepare to breathe the same fresh spiritual 'air'.

As the meeting gets under way, there are certain good disciplines that all of us can practise quite easily, to the greater praise of God and the building up of one another. (For the purpose of these suggestions I have assumed a situation that is suitable for and open to contributions from the 'floor', though many points can be carried over to a more formal setting.)

1. Give yourself wholeheartedly to praise and worship. Determine 'I will bless the Lord'. If your heart is heavy, come honestly as you are, yet giving thanks for God's faithfulness and unchanging love, and being open to joy! We must learn to offer up our tears and pain as well as our joys; it is more costly but such sacrifices of praise are of tremendous value in the sight of God.
2. Keep listening to the Lord—when distractions come

internally or externally, offer them up to God in your own heart.

3. Listen to and make room for others. Sometimes we are so caught up in what we ourselves are thinking, feeling, wanting to sing, prophesy and so on, that we blot out what other people are saying.

4. 'Desire earnestly spiritual gifts' (1 Cor 14:1)—the general rule is that if we are apathetic about gifts of the Spirit (which could also mean that we are apathetic to the needs of those around us) we probably won't receive any to give.

5. Weigh what you hear (see 1 Cor 14:29; 1 Thess 5:21). The Lord does not ask us to absorb blindly everything said and done in corporate worship; that only opens the door to error and encourages confusion. We should hold up before the Lord what we hear, and measure it against the peace in our hearts, our knowledge of Scripture, and that sense of the Lord's voice inside us. The Lord will often give leaders a special discernment in these areas.

6. Share those thoughts, words, pictures, feelings, songs, etc. that you sense are: (a) brought alive in your consciousness by the Holy Spirit, and (b) meant to be shared at the time (be wise as some things may best be shared privately later). Beware of your own mental ruts, that is, songs, thoughts, verses etc. that you suspect are just 'stuck' in your brain. This often happens with songs, which may spring to mind for no better reason than that you have come to associate them with certain surroundings. However, don't be scared to make mistakes; it is better to contribute and be wrong than to clam up out of fear. We should create an atmosphere of trust and acceptance where no one is scared to wear their 'L' plates.

7. Take action. Sometimes even when it is clear that the Lord is highlighting something, for example, a particular need for prayer, it is remarkable how we quickly move on

to the next item on the agenda, when the obvious thing to do would be to stop and take action immediately! In a media-intensive society, we must be especially careful not to treat the voice of God speaking through our corporate worship as we do background music in a supermarket— impinging marginally upon our consciousness, but not to be taken seriously or acted upon. We should treat it more like listening for announcements on a railway platform; we must be ready to take action upon what we hear because we are on an important journey and cannot afford to miss the information necessary if we are to catch the right train. We should be wary of the danger of becoming unnaturally intense in all this, and remember that the presence of God is a place of rest and joy, often fun and laughter.

It's worth the hard work and pain!

All I have said about personal discipline in worship is very simple, and accessible to all whose wills are set in the direction of pleasing God and building up the body of Christ. Yet habits of laziness, selfishness, criticism and so on are so deeply ingrained in us that learning to come to give may be harder than we expected. Nevertheless the potential of a roomful of worshippers with this giving attitude is well worth the difficulty and pain of the journey there, and best of all it has the potential of moving the very heart of God to joy and pleasure and of building up his church.

16

Can You Get There From Here?

Maurice Smith relates the true story of an occasion when he and his wife were travelling by car to a wedding without having first obtained adequate directions. Sure enough, they got lost in the London one-way systems and dead-end streets, and eventually stopped to ask three elderly gentlemen seated outside a public house for assistance. After the three had debated heatedly for some minutes—the tension in the car rising steadily as each precious second ticked by—their spokesman finally announced with some authority, 'Sorry, mate, you can't get there from here!'

That situation is not dissimilar to the experience of many Christians who, having caught a vision of where they want to go in worship and having set off enthusiastically fully expecting to get there quickly, suddenly find themselves lost in an unexpected maze of problems. Sometimes the only logical conclusion seems to be that wherever you may wish to end up, you just can't get there from where you are! With your vision fresh and vibrant in your mind of what a worshipping church should be, you step through the doors of St Bede in the Marshes and your vision bursts like a bubble, as reality stares you defiantly in the face and says 'No chance, you'll never get there from here.'

But there is of course nowhere else to start from than 'here', where we are now; and whether as individuals or a congregation, we have to come to terms with where God has put us, and believe that he can show us the route to new spiritual adventures.

This chapter is an attempt to be practical, to start from where we are and begin to move in the right direction, with some simple guiding principles. There is of course no formula or method, no pattern developed in such and such a church that we should all adopt with a guarantee of success —and for that we should thank God! There is not even a clear pattern or form for worship in the New Testament that we can follow, no A–Z on 'how to become a worshipping church'. God will continue to do a unique work in each body of believers, as led by the Holy Spirit we apply the Scriptures to our own situation. It is a walk of faith into uncharted territory, not a guided tour around a museum.

To be a worshipper

First of all let us look at what any individual can do to become a worshipper. (These points are written against the broader background of previous chapters, particularly Chapter 15.)

1. Decide to worship

Because true worship is a voluntary offering of oneself, nobody else can do it for us or make us do it. Others may teach and encourage us, but in the end we either choose freely to give it or we choose not to. Whatever the state of those around us, each one of us is responsible to God for our own gift of worship to him, and we cannot excuse ourselves or give up because others are not doing it.

2. Check the source

We have already seen that the source of worship is the Holy Spirit himself, like a bubbling spring of water inside us. If you have never experienced the release of the Spirit within, then you will not know what it is to tap that divine flow, and you will soon run dry. The gift of the Holy Spirit in all his power and fullness is the birthright of every believer in Christ, so come and ask! Jesus said in Luke 11:13 (NASB), 'If you then being evil, know how to give good gifts to your children, how much more shall your heavenly Father give the Holy Spirit to those who ask him?' If you experience difficulty in receiving as I did, then go for advice and prayer. Many of us who for many years have been 'born again' have never claimed this part of our birthright, and look on baffled and uncertain at those who are obviously overflowing from the inside.

3. Go on being filled

When we are commanded in Ephesians 5:18 to 'be filled with the Spirit', the tense is the present continuous—in other words, it means 'be being filled', or 'continually be filled' with the Spirit. It is not enough to look back to an initial experience and, as it were, dip our cup into the bucket we filled some time ago. Spring water is the water of this moment, fresh and sparkling. Yesterday's water is brackish and soon runs out. We must learn to encourage a steady flow of the Spirit by obedience, love and good deeds, thanksgiving and praise.

4. Practise in private

Even if we find ourselves in churches where overt expressions of praise are frowned upon, we can make up for our public restrictions by letting rip in private! Whether we shut ourselves away in a bedroom, head for solitude in the countryside, or drive alone in the car, most of us if we try can make time alone in which we can sing, dance, pray aloud and generally express our worship without psychological damage to others! Also, it is often easier to break down personal inhibitions and to experiment with richer forms of expression in private first.

5. Worship with others

Better still, there may be opportunities in small prayer cells, house groups and so on where a number of people may share the same concern for worship and feel safe enough with one another to break new ground. Individual worship is important, but, like the footballer who practises in the backyard knows, the real thrills come when you're playing with the team.

6. Replace old habits

If on each occasion when we normally grumbled, complained or entertained negative thoughts, we decided instead to give thanks and praise, we would be well on the way to offering up our everyday lives in worship to God. Old habits usually only die when we replace them with new ones, and while the power to change comes from God, the choice to change is ours. That decision may come a hundred times a day, when we make the choice between following our old patterns or substituting new ones.

Can we get there from here—together?

If we are to make progress in our worship, there is no escaping the prospect of change. With change comes conflict, and we are often afraid of both. If, however, we want to avoid change and conflict, then we must of necessity avoid Christ as well, because his kingdom only grows as his people radically change to become like him, and the stronger it gets the more it conflicts with rival kingdoms, whether of men or of Satan. Worship of the kind I have attempted to describe in this book, which consumes our whole being, is at the same time a gentle and a dangerous thing.

True worship is bound to reveal more of the character of Jesus, and he is described in Scripture as both a Lion and a Lamb. If our worship is to become real, then this is who will walk among us, at times in gentleness and at times in fearsome grandeur. I long, and at the same time rightly fear, to hear more of the mighty roar of the Lion of Judah in our worship, for there is a need in our times to regain first-hand knowledge of the awesome majesty and power of Jesus. Judah in fact means 'praise', so Jesus is literally the Lion of praise, as well as the sacrificial lamb who was led meekly to the slaughter. Ultimately, the central issue in our decision to pursue true worship is whether or not we are willing for this Jesus to walk among us as our King. If we are indeed willing, then we have begun the journey.

Some guiding principles

Tens of thousands of Christians find themselves either becalmed in an atmosphere of apathy, or caught up in a cross-current of differing traditions, beliefs and opinions about worship; there is no doubt that when the prospect of change comes, people are divided over how it should be done and what form it should take. There are, however, certain principles that, when applied, may make the difference between getting there together or fragmenting in the process.

Worship is a response

As I have said elsewhere, it is impossible to draw rich worship from poverty-stricken hearts, and we must be careful not to change the externals before people's own experience of God is renewed. Worship should develop alongside spiritual growth, both expressing it and stimulating it, but if we merely impose new styles and methods on top of a dead situation, we will end up with nothing better than the equivalent of a beautifully decorated coffin! Changes of a deep and real kind do not come overnight; as I have often heard it said, God does not plant bombs, he plants trees!

I was speaking quite recently to a woman who prayed for eight years over the vision of her church becoming a renewed worshipping community before she could conclude that her prayers had been answered. The noisy background to our conversation was a tremendous service of joyful worship in her church, which would have been unthinkable eight years before! I am sure many have prayed for much longer and are still praying, but how many of us have given up after two years, or one year, or six months!

Another church I know endured an organist who resisted all forms of change and heartfelt worship for seven years before he finally resigned. During this time they were experiencing renewal, but decided to be loving and patient with him hoping that he would eventually become part of what God was doing. One day he stormed out and never came back, but meanwhile the Spirit had been doing a deep work in the hearts of the congregations such that when the freedom came, there was a maturity in them to make wise use of their new liberty.

The fruit of the Spirit is . . . patience

There is of course a limit to how long we should wait for a group of believers to be willing and able to worship 'in spirit and in truth', because it would appear that in some places the waiting will go on for ever! The question of how long we should wait is not one to which any of us can give a standard answer, and indeed if God worked to a published timetable in these matters, I suspect that most of us would still miss the train! We must remember that each church, though part of a much greater plan, is a unique creation in the hands of the Builder, and it is our closeness to him and our listening to his plans that will enable us to build according to his time-scale. There is no doubt that with motivation and ingenuity, even impatience and aggression, we can build something. However, though wood, hay and stubble (1 Cor 3:12) are always near to hand and easy to scratch together into something resembling a dwelling place, gold is a totally different proposition. Gold is a hidden treasure that can only be mined with commitment and patience, and it is with spiritual 'gold' that Jesus builds his church. Patience, however, should not be confused with complacency. Rather, it is a quality that overflows from the Spirit within us. It is logical then that if we are drawing upon the Lord's patience in our situation, we will naturally be in tune with what he is doing.

Be honest, what is your motive?

The right motives and attitudes are vital if change is not to cause unnecessary friction and pain, and we need to be honest with ourselves and alert to the deceit of our own hearts. In your dreams and imaginations of glorious worship in your church, do you feature as the hero, or at least the one who gets a fair slice of the credit? Do you gloat over visions of your opponents or rivals shamed and humbled before you? Or of the retreat to other fellowships of 'stick-in-the-muds' and 'traditionalists'? Do you mentally draw up plans and budgets for recording and distributing your tape of 'home-grown' worship songs that will at least put your fellowship on the ecclesiastical map? None of us is immune to these mixed motives, and such things have often featured in my daydreams! Thankfully the Lord does not wait until our motives are 100% pure or else he would have to wait for ever, but he takes us as we are, gently but firmly turning up the heat of the Refiner's fire, bringing yet more impurities to the surface to be skimmed off.

It is vital, however, that our dominant motive should be the desire to see God worshipped, because to have any other dominant motive is idolatry and therefore a contradiction of what true worship is. If we are to be agents of change, we must be sure that we are first of all instruments in his hands, not mavericks kicking up a lot of dust and dirt to nobody's advantage.

A contrite, humble spirit

Those whom God chooses to bring about change, he draws closer to himself and plants his concerns in their heart and his love in their behaviour. A place of worship is a place close to God's heart and we read in Isaiah 57:15 in the Living Bible of the kind of people who are 'at home' there: 'The high and lofty one who inhabits eternity, the Holy One, says this "I live in the high and holy place where those with contrite, humble spirits dwell."' A concern for worship in that holy place cannot be severed from the contrite humble spirit of the servant. Our attitude must be submissive, gentle and sympathetic, sensitive and loving, yet courageous and with a godly determination. We must put aside bitterness and rivalry, genuinely seeking God's glory, not fighting for position and influence. The alternative may be to discover that though our aims were commendable and our doctrine biblical, our attitude has caused us to end up wrestling with God when we thought we were wrestling with his enemies.

Don't let your concern for, or role in, worship become your 'extended ego'. While we are genuinely serving God's interests we are not nearly so likely to become personally offended, jealous or insecure. If a position of responsibility is given to you, hold it lightly as something that is on trust from God and not your own possession. A servant is also one whose ear is alert for others, so listen to God and one another.

But I couldn't possibly...

The opposite of the 'extended ego' is the 'inverted ego', and it is probable that more of us suffer from that than the former. Most churches contain people who hide their talents, often out of lack of confidence. Feeling that they have little to offer, they do not even offer the little they have, and often the 'little' is in reality a great deal! One of the most valuable ministries in the church must surely be the ability to draw out hidden gifts and to encourage people who do not realize they have anything to offer.

To pray is to change things

In our impatience, we find it easier to rush ahead and act upon our plans and impulses than to pray. We often make the mistake of regarding prayer as a way of suspending action, a hindrance to 'getting down to the nitty gritty'. In fact, real prayer does suspend a certain kind of action, and that is action that arises out of impatience, frustration,

selfish ambition, good intentions and the like. In prayer
we have to stop and listen, check our motives, and sense
the Spirit praying his concerns through ourselves and
other people. It also causes us to look for indications of
divine activity, and as we see our prayers answered we can
more easily identify the nature of the unique work of
grace that God is doing among us.

To pray is to 'tune into' what God is doing, and then we
can proceed with divinely initiated plans. It is to enter into
that rest which comes when we work according to the
power of God working in us, and the strategy which he
knows will succeed. In matters of conflict with other
people, prayer opens us up to perceive God's perspective
of them, and we will become more able to share his love,
understanding and patience. We will also be faced with
our own prejudices and faults and learn to understand the
difficulties other people have with us!

Get to know one another

To worship in truth is to open ourselves up, to be real and
honest before God and one another, and express what is
inside us. This kind of worship involves a lowering of
barriers, and making ourselves vulnerable. This is difficult
to do among strangers when there may be fear of mis-
understanding, betrayal of trust and so on. Hence it is an
essential background to the growth of worship in a fellowship that we are getting to know one another as ordinary
people, and developing an atmosphere of 'belonging'. It
also counteracts any tendency we may have to use the
forms of worship as an escape from being real with one
another. Meetings are not always suitable places for
getting to know people personally, so build friendships in
each other's homes, through pursuing common interests
and caring practically for one another's needs.

Walk together

In any group of Christians there will be those who are impatient to steam on ahead in worship, those who move at a steady pace, and those who trail or limp slowly behind. It is a mark of our love for one another that we should adjust our pace so that we can walk together. Those who wish to rush ahead must sometimes stop to encourage the stragglers, the healthy must allow the lame to lean on them, and the lazy must stir themselves to move faster. If we are to grow in worship as a united body, we have to sacrifice our independence and make the journey together.

Worship blossoms in an atmosphere of love

If you want worship to develop, do your part in causing love to grow, because worship is like the beautiful blossom on a fruitful tree and the roots of our 'tree' must be in a deep love for one another.

Encourage a 'family' atmosphere

Not only is it conducive to worship to promote a sense of the church being a large family, it is also conducive to worship to encourage family worship of a literal kind. People are much more relaxed and open and prepared to accept change and innovation when children are involved in services. It is also worth pondering that if our celebration of knowing Christ is way over the heads of children, then it is possible that we ourselves are not coming like little children, but as cool, detached, sophisticated adults.

Get under cover!

While ideas about, and practices of, leadership and authority vary enormously, the Scriptures make it clear that we should all be in an attitude of submission. In Ephesians 5:21 we read, 'Submit to one another out of reverence for Christ.' It is out of reverence for Christ because Christ lives within each one of us, both individually and corporately, and though opinions, characters and personalities differ, we must listen for his voice in one another. Christ himself was under authority, and his conversation with the Roman centurion in Matthew 8:9 indicates that true spiritual authority is only given to those who are themselves under it. God will not trust us with the authority to bring about changes and to build his kingdom if we are loners and one-man-bands, doing our own thing.

There is great safety in being under an 'umbrella' of love from other Christians whose concern it is to help, guide and protect us, and if those people are also the ones with gifts and callings of leadership, then the possibility of moving a whole fellowship further in worship is wide open. Towards leaders and among leaders there should be respect, trust, communication, friendship, humility and flexibility, and all these can be summed up in the word 'love'.

Serve the people

It is important for those who lead in worship to act as servants of the people. It is impossible in such a position to avoid putting a personal 'stamp' of style, taste and so on upon the worship, but we must be careful not to impose it. The worship should be a genuine expression of the people, and a good look at them will illustrate their variety, which in turn implies variety of taste, style and culture. To serve the people involves enabling as many of them as possible to express themselves in ways that they can relate to or can readily learn to relate to. We must serve the old as well as the young, the conservative as well as the adventurous, those brought up in the old traditions as well as those brought in on contemporary worship choruses. If a heart for worship is present among the people, then God can be worshipped equally well in a variety of cultural and stylistic settings, as long as the material chosen successfully expresses spiritual life and truth relevant to the church at the time. The choice of style, musical setting and similar considerations are as much pastoral matters as musical ones, and have a strong influence in either uniting or polarizing people in worship.

Make God central

This may seem like an obvious thing to do, because making God central is what worship is all about, but it is very easy in a climate of change for the issues surrounding the practice of worship to dominate our thoughts instead of God himself. While we need to give attention to the principles and mechanics of worship, it is only a revelation of God that causes it to flow out of thankful and wondering hearts. There is an important principle embodied in Jesus' words recorded in John 12:32—'But I, when I am lifted up from the earth, will draw all men to myself.' A divine magnetism comes into operation when we see the kind of God that we have, One who took on human flesh and was crucified for our sake.

If through the preaching that we hear, the Scriptures that we read, and the testimonies that we share, the grace of God in Christ Jesus is revealed to us, then worship will be ignited in us. If we are asking people to worship, we must give them cause to, by lifting up before them a God whose character and deeds deserve no less than the best worship we can offer.

The Believer's Guide to Worship

CHRIS BOWATER

KINGSWAY PUBLICATIONS
EASTBOURNE

Contents

This book is dedicated to my family —
Lesley, Rachel, Daniel, Mark, Hannah and Sara,
praying that God will cause us to be a 'visual aid'
of his provision and blessing — and to the family
of God here at 'New Life' in Lincoln.

Here I am,
Wholly available,
As for me
I will serve the Lord.

(*Chris A. Bowater, 1981*)

Introduction

Teaching has been a part of my life now for so many years that the temptation to operate on 'automatic' would be very real. Looking into the trusting faces of Bible college students, conference and seminar delegates, not to mention the scores of church congregations, has caused me to re-examine communication skills normally taken for granted.

In the life and teaching of Jesus one discovers the Master Communicator at work.

Information

Every word, spoken or written; every gesture or look has the power to relay *information*. There is power in words. Power to destroy, to deliver, to encourage or annihilate. Where spiritual matters are concerned, however, words are rarely sufficient. They can impress and instruct, but more is required; and that is a change of *lifestyle*. An ocean of words can flow, a torrent of truth can be delivered, but it's what happens in terms of changed lives, people being equipped for real living, that counts. Knowing truth can be academic.

'You will know the truth and the truth will set you free' (Jn 8:32). Jesus had been teaching on who he was, his Father, his death . . . there were many words, but his hearers would remain and continue in darkness while this teaching existed to provide mere head knowledge. It is the *knowing* of truth at heart level that sets us free. That truth is centred in the person of the Lord Jesus Christ and knowing him. A real, living and vital relationship with him allows us to walk in freedom.

This book has not been written to fill your head with information, and neither is it an academic treatise! May every word, though, find a hiding place in your heart, activating your will. All truth 'heard' without being 'done' only adds to our conflicts and eventual sense of condemnation. As we put it into action, we walk in liberty.

> In the multitude of your words
> Where am I? Where am I?
> In the multitude of your words
> Where am I? says the Lord.
> For your words will not deceive Me
> If your actions do not please Me,
> In the multitude of your words
> Where am I?

(*C. A. Bowater, 1987*)

And remember: 'If you love me, you will obey what I command' (Jn 14:15).

Formation

Children learn and develop not so much by the quantity of information received, but by a process of moulding and *formation*. The environment of the home, friends, encouragement and discipline — and how those of us who are parents act and react in normal as well as stressful circumstances — all contribute in forming their present and future lifestyle. Example speaks louder than words. What we are is more potent and more powerful than what we say. When Jesus said, 'Learn of me,' it was more than, 'Hear what I say.' It was, 'Do as I do.' Jesus taught by word and by demonstration. He was the servant of people. He did more than talk at people. He shared himself. He was willing to become transparent, misunderstood, vulnerable.

In this book I will endeavour to share my heart, not just my ideas and concepts, but myself. I long for all that is beautiful — righteousness itself — to be *formed* in you.

Impartation

I am becoming more acutely aware of the power of *impartation*. 'What I have, I give you' seems to me to be totally awesome. When Peter said these words (Acts 3:6), they reflected his deep insight into who Jesus was, his profound love for him and, equally relevant, his recent experience of the Holy Spirit. Fear and inadequacy, defeat and disillusionment, had been changed to power and boldness. He knew Jesus. He had been empowered by the Holy Spirit. He was in no doubt as to what he had.

The Spirit that is within us will be imparted by our words and actions. Defeat and desolation, bitterness and barrenness can all be transferred: 'What I have, I give.'

May light and life, beauty and blessing — even the fragrance of Christ — be imparted to you; in the name of Jesus.

Chris A. Bowater

Prologue

'"Not by might nor by power, but by my Spirit," says the Lord Almighty' (Zech 4:6).

Methodology scares me sick. As soon as labels are put on people and activities we suddenly become experts at knowing the right names: words like 'restoration', 'apostle', 'body ministry' readily spring to mind. They flow off the tongue so effortlessly. The problem with labels is that they don't always represent the truth. One of the young men in our Lincoln fellowship was addressing a congregation. While he was talking, he carefully opened a tin of pears with a can-opener. The label declared the contents to be luscious, fat, juicy Australian pears. He took off the lid and began to pour into a dish — baked beans! My salivary glands suddenly became disorientated.

We get obsessed with terminology. We go around sticking labels on everything in church life. God is not too interested in pinning badges to people: 'elder', 'deacon', 'chief musician', 'worship leader' and so on. Our security is not in the badge we wear. Our security is in what we are. God is concerned with men, not methods; people, not posts.

Even when it comes to worship we fall into the legalistic trap of trying to 'pigeonhole' everything.

When I was a little boy, I used to collect the little books in the *I Spy* series: *I Spy . . . cars, I Spy . . . trains, I Spy . . . in the city, I Spy . . . in the country* and so on. Many of us have an 'I Spy . . .' mentality regarding praise and worship. How about it? *I Spy . . . charismatic praise and worship*; imagine — two points for seeing people lift their hands, three points for clapping, four points for knowing the latest Dave Fellingham chorus, five points for dancing and ten points for singing in tongues!

God is not so concerned with methods of worship. He is looking for worshippers. God is looking for people who have hearts that reach out to him, lives that are open to his leading, ears that are sensitive to his voice. He is looking for children who will take time to develop a relationship with their Father.

God is looking for 'doers' not 'knowers'. It's as if in John 14:15 Jesus was saying, 'If you love me, then do what I say.' An outworking of love is more important than an understanding of it.

Prejudiced opinion will always destroy. It will destroy relationships and will act like a tourniquet on the lifeflow of the Spirit of God. God is bigger than our puny imagination. He is not restricted by our way of doing things.

I offer this book as an encouragement. It is not a text book, but hopefully a stimulus to worshipping creatively the God of all creation. It is written on the basis of two major observations: the dangers in charismatic worship and the essentials for 'flowing' in worship.

Four dangers in charismatic worship

1. Worship that is merely response to an atmosphere: 'Worship that depends on the externals for existence is not real worship at all; true worship is what you have left when the externals are taken away' (Graham Kendrick, *Worship*).
2. 'Play church' mentality: an attitude of programme filling, where there is plenty of 'form' but little 'power'.
3. Worshipping worship: into the latest songs but not taken up with God.
4. Unreality: a failure to take off the masks and be real. Worship involves the burning up of pretence.

Three essentials for 'flowing together' in worship

1. The body: church is about people; people who are living together in unity (Ps 133), who are prepared to move with God-given visions. God cannot work through rebellious unco-operative people.
2. The eyes: leadership with vision, a sense of direction, tuned in to the heart and plan of God.
3. The legs: those who help carry the vision, priests who carry the Ark, musicians and singers with a clear calling after God in their lives and hearts.

PART 1

A Prepared and Willing People

We are gathering together — why?

Why are you here?
What have you come for?
Do you just come out of habit week by week?
You hear the songs, you sing the songs,
You're happy just to sing along —
But you go away
Just knowing the songs.

(C. A. Bowater, 1982)

Well, that's an impertinent question, isn't it? It's obvious why we gather together. After all, it's because . . . well, it's obvious! Now, when we've finished muttering and stuttering and hiding behind clichés about 'forsaking not the assembling', why *do* we come together for several hours each week? What are our motives?

Habit

When I was a child I was 'programmed', with the best of intentions, to go to church three, sometimes four times on a Sunday. Don't get me wrong; I hold no resentments. My father would, and still could, organise

13

the family with military precision. Our movements and our meals were governed by the clock. We'd be dressed up in our Sunday clothes (which was hard for a little boy who was for ever falling over, stepping in puddles and generally being normal), arrive at church early, sit inevitably in the same seats. It did occur to me, even at that uninformed age, that there was some subconscious territorial security in sitting in the same place week after week. But let's be careful we do not mock the 'family pew' concept until we examine our own habits.

The service then ran its predetermined course, not quickly enough by my reckoning, even to the extent of everyone knowing who would stand up and pray and, even more predictably, what they would pray. Rascal that I was, I would mentally give a score to these public prayers, assessing them by the responses of 'Amen!', 'Hallelujah!', 'Praise the Lord!', 'That's right, brother!' and so on. I was a spectator.

We would then rush home, rush dinner, rush back to church to go through it all again, suffering among other things from indigestion. In it all I was informed of the privilege of freedom to worship. Where, I ask myself, was the freedom in this worship? Let's not be mistaken, there was a discipline instilled for which I am most thankful. Something of the regimental approach has to be put into practice now with my own family.

The question is, how much of our Christian experience and practice is built merely on habit? I know of a church which lost half its membership because the time of a meeting was changed from 11.00 am to 10.30 am. Their routine was challenged and they could not cope with it. How often too one hears of a church's AGM (annual grouse meeting) breaking up in confusion because members have reacted against some suggested structural change to the services — when the Lord's

Table should be celebrated, or when to hold the prayer meeting. (Traditionally, the Sunday 6.30 pm service was fixed to allow farmers to milk their cows!)

So much of our experience is grounded in a form of godliness with a disturbing lack of power. It has been said that the Holy Spirit could depart from many church services and programmes and would hardly be missed.

In Luke 2:41–50 we read the account of Mary and Joseph making their annual visit to Jerusalem for the Feast of the Passover. Jesus was twelve years of age and went with his parents 'according to the custom'. We read that on the homeward journey Mary and Joseph, thinking he was in their company, travelled on for a day. But Jesus wasn't with them. He was still in Jerusalem, at work on his heavenly Father's behalf. They lost him at the place of worship!

How many churches have travelled on for a day, for weeks, months and years, assuming Jesus was still with them, ignorant of the fact that he was at work building his church where his people would let him?

A spirit of habit can not only dictate our attendance at church but also our manner of worship and what we expect of God. The Spirit of God is a life-giving Spirit and our gatherings together should manifest the very life of God, whether it be in celebration gatherings or house groups. Jesus indeed is 'in the midst', at the centre of a coming together of his people who let him have his way among them.

The atmosphere

Why are you here?
What have you come for?
Is this the social highlight of your week?
You love religious atmospheres,

They sometimes even move to tears,
But you go away
Just knowing tears.

(C. A. Bowater, 1982)

I was talking to a woman some while ago who is, to put it kindly, spasmodic in her attendance, but you wouldn't know it to see her in the meetings. 'I love it whenever I come here,' she enthused. 'I always have a good cry.' Now I can think of several things quite likely to make her cry, but were these tears of repentance, tears of joy and bliss in God? No. Doubtless she would cry at weddings, funerals, birthdays, flower shows and films like *The Sound of Music*. Tears that are not a result of a deep consciousness of God or do not result in change are, at best, self-centred.

A searching question that needs to be asked is this: How much of our praise and worship is merely a response to an emotional atmosphere? Now, don't get me wrong. I am not suggesting for one moment that our emotions are not involved in our praise and worship. Whole-hearted expression of gratitude for the goodness of God must involve our emotions. The point that I am making is that, if the measure of our expression of thanks and adoration to God is determined by the song being sung, the instruments being played, the fervour being generated, then that expression is second best.

For it to be acceptable to God, our praise and worship must emanate from a heart relationship, and not arise as a response to a created atmosphere. When all that is peripheral is taken away, what is left is the measure of our praise and worship before the Lord.

Much time and energy has been devoted to the physical manifestation of so-called liberated worship: clapping, raising of hands, dancing, leaping, kneeling, bowing and so on. Now, I don't intend to spend the next few pages defending what I consider to be clearly-defined scriptural principles. However, outside of the atmosphere of your Christian gathering, away from that very special spiritual motivation that takes place when we 'gather together unto him', at home, in that quiet secret place, are we still as free in the raising of hands, dancing, bowing and kneeling?

When we come publicly before God, our lives and worship are valued according to how we are privately before God. If our private devotions are not real, then no amount of public display will compensate.

The warning note that I am sounding is that it is so easy to be swept along on a tide of enthusiasm, and yet in our hearts and in our living be genuinely desolate of blessing. Enthusiasm is not always blessing. It is even possible to be at a place where there is a real movement of God, but for our own lives to be way off the mark. Recently, at a conference attended by pastors and church leaders, I was approached by a fine-looking young man, a pastor of a small but growing fellowship. As a result of ministry, God had challenged him to the core. He revealed that for several months he had been living two lives: one, as husband and father and energetic pastor, the other in the grip of a passion for pornographic literature. He was apparently 'in blessing', but privately desolate, empty and at variance with God.

> Going through the motions,
> Acting out the part,
> Just fine on the outside
> But desolate at the heart.
>
> The words still come so easily
> Making the right sound,
> But underneath the facade
> The altar of the Lord is broken down.
>
> (C. A. Bowater, 1984)

So then, if it's not 'habit' or 'the atmosphere' or even the 'social highlight of the week', what must be the principal desire and motivation in our joining together week by week? It must be that we might know and see the manifested presence of the Lord in his glory!

Often our criterion is activity. Fill the programme: hymns and choruses, testimonies and times of sharing, special items and notices, manifestation of spiritual gifts . . . seemingly an endless Royal Command Performance! It occurs to me that it might be relevant to imagine Jesus, standing at the door of our congregation, seeking entry to impart what only his presence can bring (Rev 3:20), but we don't allow him access or even let him have a word in edgeways. 'We'll let you have your way,' we sing. 'Opportunity would be a fine thing,' replies God.

Sometimes, when we dare to let the Lord have his say, schedules and programmes have to be put away. In 2 Chronicles 5:13–14 it describes how when the glory of the Lord filled the house of God, those who were 'booked' to minister laid aside their ministry. Can you imagine it? All the work was finished. The house of the Lord was prepared. Choirs were rehearsed, trumpets were polished, the band was ready (cymbals, psalteries and harps); the sermon for the grand opening had been sweated over for months, and then somebody started a chorus: 'The Lord is good and his mercy endureth for ever.' It took off! The place resounded with their united thanksgiving, and God inhabited their praise. He joined them. His glory filled the house.

Be sure of this: when God really gets involved with the gathering of his people you may as well forget about Mrs Jones' solo, the youth item and the notices. The King must do what the King must do! He will move among the people in sovereign power, bringing salvation, healing and restoration — God in the midst of his people!

May God bring us to that condition of heart and quality of praise in which he can be enthroned.

A heart for worship

'As the deer pants for streams of water, so my soul pants for you, O God. My soul thirsts for God, for the living God. When can I go and meet with God?' (Ps 42:1–2).

A desire to know God, to meet with him. This is the key to Spirit-filled worship of God. Without this desire to stand in his presence, worship becomes a fruitless experience. Worship that is without expectation, without a tangible sense of the presence of God, is fruitless.

As we worship God in spirit and reality we receive from God. However, our motivation must always be that we worship him for *who he is*. Worship is for God. It is not in order to fulfil some self-centred desire, to make us feel good, or to obtain any other kind of benefit. Worship is for God because he's worthy. He's worth it all! None the less, because God is obedient and faithful to his own word — 'it's better to give than to receive' — because it is impossible to 'outgive' God, the One who inhabits the praises of his people does so in blessing. He comes not as a spectator. He comes bearing gifts.

We worship too because we've been *called* to worship. We've been called and chosen to be a kingdom of priests. This is man's highest calling. Not to be obsessed with activity, not *doing*, but *being* a 'Royal Priesthood, a Holy Nation, set aside for *his glory*'.

Albeit blessings are not the reason we worship God, that does not negate the fact that we receive from him as we worship.

The most important fruit of worship is God's presence. This is the very *heart of worship*.

The presence of God

God is always present. By the very nature of being eternal, he is omnipresent: 'The eyes of the Lord are everywhere, keeping watch on the wicked and the good' (Prov 15:3). 'Where can I go from your Spirit? Where can I flee from your presence? If I go up to the heavens, you are there; if I make my bed in the depths, you are there' (Ps 139:7–8).

The God who is everywhere, to make himself specifically seen and known, has to appear *somewhere*. The 'somewhere' for Moses was the burning bush; for Jacob, a personal wrestling encounter; for Paul, a pre-conversion flash of light and an audible voice. The God who is everywhere delights to reveal and manifest his presence. He desires to meet with his people and especially enjoys the environment of praise: 'But thou art holy, O thou that inhabitest the praises of Israel' (Ps 22:3, KJV); '. . . thou who art enthroned upon the praises of Israel' (NASB).

Sometimes in Scripture the manifested presence of God is referred to as 'his glory':

The trumpeters and singers joined in unison, as with one voice, to give praise and thanks to the Lord. Accompanied by trumpets, cymbals and other instruments, they raised their voices in praise to the Lord and sang: 'He is good; his love endures for ever.' Then the temple of the Lord was filled with a cloud, and the priests could not perform their service because of the cloud, for the glory of the Lord filled the temple of God (2 Chron 5:13–14).

When the priests withdrew from the Holy Place, the cloud filled the temple of the Lord. And the priests could not perform their service because of the cloud, for the glory of the Lord filled his temple. Then Solomon said, 'The Lord has said that he would dwell in a dark cloud; I have indeed built a magnificent temple for you, a place for you to dwell for ever' (1 Kings 8:10–13).

Imagine the *reality* of God's presence. How tangible and real. If God does not turn up, our services are mere 'acts of worship', futile and, at best, superficial religious indulgence.

Jack Hayford says: 'The Scriptures show that God manifested his glory in a visible sense when his order of worship was established and honoured among his people.'

It is written of Mary and Joseph that: 'Thinking he [Jesus] was in their company, they travelled on for a day' (Lk 2:44).

It's worth wondering how many days, weeks, months or even years have been 'travelled' in the lives of individuals and churches assuming the Lord's presence. Large congregations, fine preaching, accomplished musicians or successful meetings do not constitute or guarantee it. It is not a matter of style, traditional or radical. It is the heart of the people that causes God to respond. Informality can replace liturgy; songs of fellowship replace hymns. The hymn-book sidelined in favour of the overhead projector. God still cries: 'Rend your hearts and not your garments' (Joel 2:13).

There is often so much pre-occupation with external matters that the real issues are ignored. There are many more things that are needed in the church today. Let them not be however at the expense of this single priority: we need more of the life-imparting presence of God. And then, when by his grace that happens, not to become complacent or satisfied but to hunger and thirst for even more.

David was a man with a heart for God. His love for God was the mainspring, driving force and the love of his life. He loved God for himself, not just for what he did for him. He had tasted of the Lord's goodness. He had first-hand experience of God. He had delighted himself in the Lord and he desperately wanted more. His chief desire was 'to gaze upon the beauty of the Lord' (Ps 27:4).

David was a man possessed by the glory of God. His great heart for God and his presence was his greatest strength: 'I have set the Lord always before me. Because he is at my right hand, I shall not be shaken' (Ps 16:8). The deepest cry of his heart was: 'Do not cast me from your presence or take your Holy Spirit from me' (Ps 51:11).

The evidence

Surely a fair definition of 'having a meeting' is to actually meet with someone. Let our desire always be to encounter the living God. The presence of God will always be evidential. Consider these hallmarks:

Salvation: He will be present to save. The church was born in praise. On the Day of Pentecost, as the newly empowered disciples declared the glory of God *and* preached the gospel of Jesus, thousands were added to the church in a day.

Deliverance: Deliverance comes to the people of God who honour him in praise. Jehoshaphat (2 Chron 20), in obedience to the word of the Lord given prophetically, saw the enemy defeated as the singers sang praises for 'the splendour of his holiness'. Paul and Silas (Acts 16), while in the depths of prison, sang praises to God. The prison chains and gates could not withstand the shaking as God began to get excited by the song! Worship defeats the schemes and power of the evil one.

Healing: 'The power of the Lord was present . . . to heal' (Lk 5:17). The presence of the Lord brings healing. As worship ascends from an open-hearted people, the great Physician in the midst performs open-heart surgery. In his presence things have to change.

Joy: 'You will fill me with joy in your presence, with eternal pleasures at your right hand' (Ps 16:11); '. . . glad with the joy of your presence' (Ps 21:6). The church needs a baptism of joy. Not the deep down variety that needs a North Sea oil rig to get at it, nor a superficial, 'clap-happy', unreal kind, but the real thing that makes and keeps us strong. The joy of the lord is our strength.

And in his presence . . .

We are changed: This is an important principle in God — that when we see him we become like him. That is why no man could see his full glory. If we saw his full glory while in our fallen state, our bodies would 'melt like wax' and we would enter into eternity. However, if we learn to worship in spirit and truth, we are going to learn how to be more like Christ. We all become a little like one another, especially if we spend a lot of time with another person. The same thing happens when we spend time with the Lord — we are likely to become like him. The good news is that this is what God intended. Perhaps there are so few Christ-like Christians around because there are so few who have learned the secret and fulfilment of spending time in his presence. God is not poor, sick, depressed, incapable of solving problems. If we take on his likeness, we can also take on his health, joy, compassion, wealth and power. When Moses saw even the hind parts of the glory of the Lord (Ex 33–34) he had to veil his face. In Exodus 34:29–33 we see that Moses' face shone. The Hebrew word says that 'beams of light' came from his face.

Paul says: 'If that which was done away with was glorious, much more that which remains is glorious.' In other words, if Moses could see the glory of God and have his face shine, and he was under the law of God which was done away with (or fulfilled in Christ), how much more should we who know Christ be able to come into his presence and 'behold his glory', and shine for him.

We no longer have to come through the veil only once a year, but have free access to come in worship before him with unveiled face: 'Beholding as in a glass the glory of the Lord [and] are changed into the same image from [one degree of] glory to [another degree of] glory, even as by the Spirit of the Lord.' Worship changes us. We become like the One whom we worship.

If you want to be a great teacher, pastor, evangelist, prophet, apostle, businessman or housewife, then learn how to worship God: become like him. Seek him with *all your heart* and you will find him and be like him.

Flowing together

There is always going to be a fundamental problem when using words. The probability is that people will hear what they think is being said instead of what is actually being conveyed.

Many of us have failed an examination because we answered what we thought the question required. On closer scrutiny we discovered some important implication that had initially evaded our attention.

'Flowing in worship' happens to be one of the 'in' phrases in today's charismatic language: 'Are you in the flow, brother?'; 'It really flowed this morning!'

What is flowing together?

What does it mean to 'flow together'? It is not saying the same things. We can say and sing all the right words, but still not 'flow together' in worship.

I have a friend who, when he says that he is hard-up, really means that he is going to have to withdraw some money from his building society account. He's down to his last £2,000. When I'm hard-up it means that I am going through all the trouser and jacket pockets in my cloakroom hoping above all hope to find some loose change. The same words, 'hard-up', but very different in their implication.

Flowing together is not doing the same things.

There is a great deal of emphasis today on the physical manifestation in worship: clapping, dancing, leaping, the raising of hands — and rightly so.

The Hebrew word for 'high praise' is *tehillah*. It is *tehillah* praise alone that God says he will inhabit, or within which he is enthroned. It is the powerful praise of warfare and victory (2 Chron 20:22), it is the praise that is comely, becoming and appropriate (Ps 33:1), it is the realm of praise where God manifests his glory and causes us to fear (Ex 15:11). This is not gentle, casual, 'laid back' praise. The most often-used Hebrew word associated with praise is *halal*. It means 'to shine', 'to boast', 'to celebrate and commend'. The word also implies 'to sing until clamorously foolish'. Doesn't that paint some wild pictures in your imagination!

I believe that an extravagant, generous God desires and deserves both *tehillah* and *halal* praise, but a congregation that considers it is 'into' all the physical manifestations of praise is not necessarily 'flowing together' simply because it is doing the same things.

To 'flow together' is to 'see together': 'Then thou shalt see, and flow together' (Is 60:5, AV).

What do you see?

What you see of Christ will determine how you worship him. If you see him only as the baby in Bethlehem's manger, or as the One who lived a good life; or if your vision of Jesus ends at the cross or even the empty tomb — then your worship will be determined by what you see.

In the Book of Revelation, John repeatedly declares, 'and I saw . . .', and the throne of God was central to that unfurled revelation. God would have us come to an understanding of his throne, his kingship and his kingdom, to see him high and lifted up. Then, and only then, will we know an ever-growing recognition of who he is . . . and worship him. 'Flowing' is to do with 'seeing'.

How do we see?

This level of vision is not according to natural eyesight. We see with the heart. It is when hearts are united, one in love and one in purpose, not merely in words, that truly it can be said, 'We flow together.' When a congregation or fellowship moves into this realm of heart commitment, one to the other, our corporate worship will begin to 'flow'.

Can you sense the 'flow' indicated in this precious Psalm?

> How good and pleasant it is when brothers live together in unity!
> It is like precious oil poured on the head, running down on the beard, running down on Aaron's beard, down upon the collar of his robes.
> It is as if the dew of Hermon were falling on Mount Zion. For there the Lord bestows his blessing, even life for evermore (Ps 133).

Unity at heart level creates a flowing together that results in 'life for evermore'.

Relationships

> If the Lord is not the builder
> Then your labouring is vain,
> Unless the Lord unites you,

Divided you'll remain,
And that which is divided
Against itself won't stand.
How can a righteous God ignore
No thought for His command?

The problem may be someone else,
The answer may be you,
Relationships are possible
To those who dare be true,
And truth amongst the brethren
Is an attitude of heart,
Someone, somewhere, someday,
We'll pledge to make a start.

Then existing barriers,
Imagined or for real,
Can piece by piece be taken down,
Allowing God to heal
The hurts of insecurity,
The scars of battles done,
Let all things be relinquished
For the honour of the Son.

Let love be rich amongst you,
In reality and power,
Considering the time we live
Is God's selected hour.
In unity there's blessing,
There's strength in being one,
The spirit of the Lord still strives,
Beware lest He be gone!

(C. A. Bowater, 1985)

Living together in unity may be good and pleasant, but my word, isn't it difficult? We sing lustily about being heirs of the Father and joint heirs with Christ; we link hands and declare that we are family, we are one. Truth is easy to sing about. Reality needs to match our confessions. Experience and expression must match our apparent enlightenment.

Praise and worship is a lifestyle. If I am at odds with anyone — wife, child, parent or fellow church member — my thanksgivings are not acceptable to God. He does not hear them. He will not receive them. 'First . . . be reconciled to your brother' (Mt 5:24).

How often, I wonder, do Christians come to the communion table, that most sacred of feasts, with bitterness and enmity towards someone else? Failing first of all to examine their own hearts before God (1 Cor 11:28), they eat the bread and drink the wine 'without recognising the body of the Lord' (1 Cor 11:29). Small wonder then that so many individuals and churches are 'weak and sick', sleepy and approaching premature death (1 Cor 11:30).

Some while ago I was ministering at a church in the north of England. It was a mid-week meeting and I was pleasantly surprised to see a congregation of about seventy people. The period of praise and worship seemed to be 'free'. The people certainly could not be faulted for exuberance. I began to minister on Psalm 133. There was fluency of tongue and buoyancy of spirit. Those of you who preach will know the feeling of cruising along a largely premeditated route. Then God intervened. He began to hold a conversation with me while I was still in full flow of preaching. He said, 'I've got something very specific for you to say to the people.'

'Oh yes, Lord?' I enquired in my heart, while my tongue was rattling on about oil flowing down Aaron's beard. 'What is it?'

'Tell them about genetic bitterness.'

I would, I concurred, if I knew what it meant. The oil by now was reaching to Aaron's garments.

Genetic bitterness, the Lord patiently explained, was that which underscored the lives of several members of my congregation which was now being deluged with the dew of Hermon. They had imbibed attitudes from parents and unwittingly become part of an ongoing murmur of dissatisfaction. Years before, at dinner tables and times of so-called 'fellowship', they had been systematically drained of trust and respect. Their own views had become coloured. They were now the perpetrators of someone else's grudges.

Before my now long-suffering congregation could receive further rhetoric on the dew upon the mountains of Zion, God said, 'Tell them!'

'But, Lord, what about the command of blessing, and life for evermore?'

'There can be no blessing if you don't shut up.' God can be blunt at times. 'Tell them, now.'

Homiletics took a discernible nose-dive. The purposes of God, however, became apparent. I gently shared with them what God had been saying to me. If God was speaking, I explained, he was doing it in order to bring them into a release from the bondage of genetic bitterness. A simple altar call saw fifteen people — mostly young, some weeping — stand before the Lord in repentance.

What we are before God is, in part, conditional on what we are with each other. As far as God is concerned, actions speak louder than words. Our actions can in reality deny our knowledge of him (Tit 1:16).

I've always been a great listener. My home, during childhood, was always a place of hospitality for visiting pastors, missionaries and the like. Instead of banishing me to some far-away room, Father always allowed me to sit in a corner quietly. 'Listen and learn, son,' was his firm but well-intended advice.

Somehow I can't help it: I listen to conversations on the train, in lifts and wherever people meet. I don't listen out of mere curiosity — it comes from a profound interest in people. They reveal so much about themselves by the way they speak. One can discern regional accents, levels of education, perhaps even social standing, but more revealing — the spirit of the person. The tongue betrays the real heart.

I am frequently concerned and distressed by the way Christians speak to each other. The Bible says that we should be involved in encouraging one another, building each other up in the faith, and yet how often does one hear derogatory and unkind speech among those who claim to belong to the Lord. Sarcasm destroys confidence. Sarcastic humour is often even worse. Within moments the same lips will be foremost in public prayer and praise! 'Out of the same mouth come praise and cursing. My brothers, this should not be' (Jas 3:10).

My praise must flow out from a lifestyle of praise. It is not something to be switched on like some spiritual Blackpool illumination. My relationship with my wife and children is fundamental to my relationship with God. It is an awesome thought to know that God refuses to accept my worship, however fervent or extravagant, unless it comes from a clean heart and a right spirit.

> With a clean heart I'll praise You,
> With a pure heart I'll honour You
> With a right spirit within me,
> I will magnify Your Name.
>
> (*C. A. Bowater, 1984*)

Let's get things right with each other. The responsibility is on us if we are aware of a relationship problem. Most of us know when things are wrong. It doesn't need times of heavy sharing. More often than not, 'Sorry,' or, 'Will you forgive me?' brings immediate healing. It may at times have to go deeper. A critical spirit is a sign of sin and needs repentance. Let us be a 'love in action' people, for only then can we lift our hands and voices and sing, 'I love you, Lord.'

Remember Psalm 133! Where this level of relationship exists among his people, God commands his blessing. What a mighty seal of approval! Who knows, maybe you will be responsible for starting an epidemic of love in your church.

Father make us one,
That the world may see the Son,
Release through us
Streams of pure love,
Father, make us one.

(*C. A. Bowater, 1982*)

Spirit and truth

Because God is, there is worship. God is Spirit and desires spiritual worship from a spiritual people. In a sense, Jesus removed much of the need for discussion and debate about worship when he declared in John 4:24 that 'his worshippers must worship in spirit and in truth'. The options are removed. Sure, you can choose *what* you worship: money, ambition, power and position or whatever, but when Father God is the object of devotion, adoration and reverence, we no longer choose *how* we worship him. We must worship him in the way he desires. Furthermore, he is looking for those who will do just that (Jn 4:23).

What, then, is it to worship in spirit and in truth?

It appears that it is not related to a place or a tradition. The woman of Samaria, on recognising Jesus as out of the ordinary, 'a prophet' (Jn 4:19), albeit that hers was a partial revelation, immediately began to enter a Samaritan versus Jewish debate on worship: 'Our fathers . . . this mountain . . . you Jews claim . . . Jerusalem' (Jn 4:20).

Have you noticed how people become defensive of

their traditional positions when the person of Christ is under discussion? In reply to, 'What do you think of Jesus?', along with hurried barrier constructions comes, 'Well, of course, we've always been Baptists . . .' or, 'You know, we like the way the Church of England do it.' Spirit and truth worship has nothing to do with the building, liturgy or lack of it. How often though do we become astonishingly building-orientated. I've even heard someone say at a house-group fellowship, 'It's not like being at church!' We *are* the church — and God is building it. It's not made up of pews and chairs, pianos and organs, stained-glass windows and pulpits, even hymn-books and overhead projectors, beautiful or necessary though these can be. You and I are joined together, not merely in fellowship, but in a miraculous 'limb-ship', into the body of Christ, of which he is the Head. God is seeking a flow of worship that comes from his body, each member in glorious, loving harmony with each other.

One hears these days, and maybe it has always been so, certain people lamenting, 'It's not like it used to be.' What isn't? God? Has he changed? Maybe they have! Perhaps they are not so diligent, so fervent, so determined to worship the Lord as they once were. Perhaps their relationship with God is not what it used to be!

'The true worshippers will worship the Father . . .' (Jn 4:23). You see, the true worshippers are those who are living in the reality of their relationship with God. It is a now relationship. I am secure in his fatherhood but I must never become complacent in it.

Years ago, when Hannah, one of my triplets, was approaching her first birthday, she was involved in an unfortunate accident, and broke her leg. It was on a day when I was due to travel some distance to preach

at a fellowship in the north of England. My wife was
distraught, the other children were naturally also
distressed and I was faced with a most awful dilemma.
Should I try to cancel the meeting, contact the team
that was travelling with me . . . and so on? Dozens of
possibilities and permutations of them crowded into my
somewhat numbed mind. I took so long determining
alternative decisions that I made none. Such is organised
panic! My wife, Lesley, brought some semblance of
direction at last, insisting, 'You must go!'

Feeling humbled and deeply grateful to God for a
life-partner with spiritual discernment, I sped up the A1
northwards. Positively, that night God spoke into the
life of the fellowship and many came into a deeper
understanding of his purposes. I motored home through
the night, restricted not so much by the speed limit but
by the capabilities of my old car. By pre-arrangement,
on arriving at Lincoln in the early hours of the morning,
I went straight to the local hospital. I entered the ward,
somehow unusually conscious of the stillness. My
footsteps became an intrusion into the peacefulness. I
found Hannah's cot. Both legs were suspended in
traction. She was awake but had not seen me approach.
Kneeling beside her, God became so real to me. I was
just preparing to leave, as unnoticed as I had arrived,
when Hannah turned and saw me. It was as if someone
had turned on the lights . . . she smiled . . . she shone
. . . I wept. Hannah's voice, even at nearly one year
old, had always been in the 'alto profundo' category,
but the word 'Dad' was as sweet and melodious as
anything I have ever heard. The fact that she had very
few other words in her vocabulary seemed at that
moment to be beside the point. The smile was one of
recognition. There and then God dropped a pearl of a
song into my heart:

Abba Father, Abba Father, my soul delights in You,
Abba Father, Abba Father, my soul delights in You.
Hallelujah my heart has cause to sing,
I'm a spirit-born, blood-bought, child of the King.
Abba Father, Abba Father, my soul delights in You.

Worship must emanate from a current, ongoing intimate relationship with God. When was the last time your spirit shone as you whispered, 'Father, I love you, I worship and adore you'?

I am reminded of the visit Jesus made to Bethany (Jn 12). The home of Lazarus, Mary and Martha was frequently a haven of hospitality and solitude. Jesus loved these good people, and they loved him. On this particular visit, Martha had busied herself, as usual, preparing and serving supper. Mary, though, made the most significant demonstration of worship possible. She anointed the feet of Jesus with fragrant, refreshing spikenard ointment. To Mary it was the most obvious way of expressing love and gratitude to Jesus (who six days earlier had raised her brother Lazarus from the dead). Worship involved relationship, love and gratitude. It is worth commenting too that the spikenard was costly. It was so costly it brought upon her a deluge of criticism, predictably from Judas Iscariot. There is cost in worship. Certainly there is a cost of concentration.

On discovering that the Greek word for 'worship' has its origin in the verb *proskuneo*, meaning 'to kiss towards', a whole new area of understanding was opened up to me. The word implies an act of total reverence. In the Scriptures worship is often associated with people bowing down or prostrating themselves.

Kissing requires concentration. I discovered this to my embarrassment and cost at a tender age. When I was thirteen years old I had my first girlfriend. At the end of the school day I would walk with her through the nearby park to her bus-stop. And then it happened. It was a warm summer evening. I had made up my mind. I would kiss her goodbye . . . my first kiss . . . my first love. I had rehearsed the kiss a thousand times in my imagination. Every time it had been executed in a wonderfully sophisticated and mature way. Reality and dreams could not have been further from each other. I made the mistake of closing my eyes. After all, that's what happens on all the films. I aimed, lurched forward with lips protruding — and missed. The girl had moved, leaving me a feverish wreck of embarrassment. Kissing requires concentration.

How often does the Lord receive only half of our attention? Should I be invited one day to visit Her Majesty the Queen and be escorted into her throne room, I guarantee that I will not be at all bothered about the colour and texture of curtains and carpets, the flowers or the ornaments; my eyes will only be on the one who has graciously invited me to come before her throne. True worship is a throne ministry. Songs like 'Majesty', 'Jesus, we enthrone you', 'He is the King of kings' freely pour from our lips but our minds are on so much more than the One who is enthroned in the midst of the praises of his people. We get taken up with all that is peripheral. Even the songs themselves, intended to be vehicles for our own worship, become intrusions. There is a very real danger of worshipping worship — the new songs, the atmosphere. We must see the Lord, upon the throne, and concentrate on him alone.

Linked with this is the cost of our will. Praise and worship has nothing to do with our feelings. Our will, including our feelings, must be brought into subjection. Whether we feel like it or not, we will bless the Lord. Many people are governed by their feelings. Feelings must become secondary to the prime motivation of giving honour and glory to God. John the Baptist put it in another way, but he meant the same thing: 'He must become greater; I must become less' (Jn 3:30).

The Lord deserves and requires our worship and praise. We praise him because he is our God and we are his people (Ps 95:6–7), because he is worthy, great and a King (Ps 47:6–7), because we were created to praise the Lord (Ps 102:18). It is a good thing to give thanks to the Lord (Ps 92:1–4).

When we praise God, we are saying, 'Thank you for all that you have done, are doing, and will do.' We recognise God's greatness and favour at work in all of creation. It is rather like a husband and wife thanking each other for all the things that they do for each other.

When we worship God, we are also saying, 'I love you for who you are.' A husband and wife relationship is not based on the statement, 'Thank you for what you have done, are doing and will do for me,' but rather, 'I love you for who you are.' In order to be able to say this, a husband and wife must know one another. In order for us truly to worship and love God, we have to move from the realm of praise, where we are loving him for what he has done, into the place where we know him.

Reality in worship

Evangelical jargon has been perhaps the most destructive force in truly communicating the gospel. We fill our heads with phraseology that has very little relevance for the uninformed, uncommitted, and generally disinterested person. But such dearly-held statements of faith are often fiction disguised as truth. Not that what we say is not true, but it has little foundation of truth in our experience. I'm talking about being real.

At the very least God wants us to be real with him. Worship in truth depends on a recognition of who God is and an acknowledgement of who we are — in reality.

I wonder how many times we have cried to God in a prayer meeting, 'Lord, manifest yourself, reveal yourself and your power.' An excellent, commendable prayer. But what if God actually took us at our word? Would we be able to handle a manifestation of his power? In truth, God is love. He is gracious and merciful, long-suffering and kind. In truth also he is holy and righteous in all his ways. His anger and wrath are as relevant as the more attractive aspects of his character. We must not come before God wearing rose-coloured glasses, choosing not to see certain facets of his nature.

My children know that I love them. I tell them so often. They know I get pleasure from their fun and activities, and am usually patient with their child-like inconsistencies. They also know that I hate their lies and deceit and their abuse of each other. My love does not keep me silent but expresses itself in correction and, when necessary, punishment. They are getting to know me!

The more I get to know God, the more I find out about myself. My relationship with God cannot and must not be founded on self-deception.

One of the most honest prayers in the Scriptures was that of the one who cried, 'Lord, be merciful to me, a sinner.' Perhaps the most honest and relevant prayer we can pray is, 'Lord, be merciful to me, a saint.' If we needed the mercy of God when we were still unforgiven, without hope, spiritually blind and deaf, how much more, if we have experienced his grace, and have been reborn by his Spirit, do we need his mercy, knowing as we do the way we talk about other members of his family; knowing the real level of our commitment to his will in our lives; knowing how much time we really spend allowing God to speak to us through his word and through prayer; and knowing how we 'roller-coast' on our way, being spiritual, as if nothing were really wrong. We really do need to cry for mercy.

I fear that, in the same way as we can be drawn into the evangelical jargon trap, knowing what to say and when to say it, so we can also drift into a worship-orientated jargon, knowing what to do and say in order to make it appear that we are 'in the Spirit'. Sooner or later jargon-based experience leaves an aching void, emptiness and disillusionment. My plea is for reality. 'Worship . . . in truth.'

My goal is God Himself, not joy, nor peace,
Nor even blessing, but Himself, my God.

(*F. Brook*)

In order to know him we have to spend time in his presence. There is a cost of time.

Many Christians never move from praise to worship, because they love to spend time expressing their love to him. In order to worship God, we have to have a change of lifestyle, where nothing else matters except our relationship with the Lord. Many live only in the realm of constantly saying 'thank you', and do not enter into the intimacy of 'I love you', simply because to express genuine love means a surrendering of wrong lifestyles and attitudes: 'If you love me, you will obey what I command' (Jn 14:15).

We never hear of the 'sacrifice of worship' as there is no sacrifice involved. We are in a place where we know who God is, and the natural result is that we worship him. The psalmist says that we should 'enter his gates with thanksgiving and his courts with praise' (Ps 100:4). Worship is when we are able to go beyond the gates and courts into the holy and intimate place with our God. However, we cannot go into the holy place without going through the gate of thanksgiving and the courts of praise. Just as a husband and wife grow in their knowledge of each other, so too do we need to develop a life of worship. It doesn't just happen. We must be worshippers, people who are dedicated to knowing our God, not just knowing about him.

In a very real sense, also, there is a cost of our emotions. As a nation we seem to be wary of emotions, and this has overspilled into attitudes in the church. The psalmist says, 'I will praise you, O Lord, with all my heart' (Ps 9:1), and again, 'Praise the Lord. I will extol the Lord with all my heart' (Ps 111:1).

Furthermore, he speaks of delighting in the Lord (Ps 37:4), being glad and rejoicing (Ps 9:2), 'shouting for joy' (Ps 32:11, AV). Laughter, shouting, speaking, crying, calling and singing are just some of the whole-hearted attitudes of praise that consumed David's spirit. Not to mention clapping, lifting of hands, standing, bowing, dancing, kneeling, walking and being still. There are so many potential manifestations for a heart whose sole desire is to magnify the Lord. Whole-hearted worship must by implication involve a surrendering of that last bastion of our human defences, our emotions.

Could it in fact be pride that will not allow us to show what we really feel, for fear of what people will think? Worship should be Godward alone. 'Fear of man will prove to be a snare' (Prov 29:25), but living in truth always brings liberty (Jn 8:32).

I can well remember the time years ago when my brother Anthony desired the baptism in the Holy Spirit. His natural temperament made him ultra-defensive where emotion was concerned. He had great difficulty expressing his feelings and, more importantly, he would not allow his emotions to be seen. He was a rational man and all things were dealt with on the basis of deduction and logic. He deduced, however, that he needed the indwelling power and presence of the Holy Spirit. And the Holy Spirit is capable of reaching the parts that nothing or no one else can reach! Simply, and unemotionally, a friend and I prayed for Anthony. He had the wettest baptism in the Spirit that I have ever witnessed. For practically three hours he sobbed and wept, at times with astonishing force. God taught him how to cry! Now, the wells are very near the surface. Begin to mention something of the mercy and grace of God, his loving-kindness and faithfulness, and Anthony's eyes will readily fill with tears of gratitude and love.

Worship cannot flow from a heart that is hard. That is why in the middle of Psalm 95, which is an exhortation to praise and worship, beginning, 'Come, let us sing for joy to the Lord; let us shout aloud to the Rock of our salvation,' David turns aside to bring a warning, 'Today, if you hear his voice, do not harden your hearts.'

This is an interesting scripture. I had always associated it with passionate gospel sermons. It is, though, at the centre of a call to worship.

The Father's heart

Today, if you hear . . .

What does the *voice* of God sound like to you? Do you know when he is speaking to you? When our triplets, Mark, Hannah and Sara, were babies, friends who visited the home were astonished that we were capable of distinguishing one child's crying voice from the others. I do realise that yelling infants tend to sound the same unless of course you live with them. One soon learns to discern the little characteristic squeaks and gurgles. Recognition comes out of relationship. Worship must emanate from a real relationship with God our Father. A relationship of talking *and* listening.

Some years ago, I heard of a pastor who would personally interview members of his congregation entering into membership in his church. He had standard questions that he would ask, including, 'What does the voice of God sound like to you?' His own teenage son was a candidate for membership. The pastor kept to his normal format. 'What does the voice of God sound like to you, son?' he enquired. Without so much as a moment's hesitation he replied, 'Dad, he sounds just like you.' That's such a good answer. The voice of his heavenly Father was as real and as clear as his own dad's. That young man had a real relationship with God. I long for my children to hear God in the same way. It will be even better if they respond to his voice a little more readily than they do sometimes to mine!

'To hear God speak' has such grand and spiritual overtones. One at least expects an audible voice, perhaps a vision or two, fire maybe or a mighty rushing wind. How dramatic; how reassuringly *real*. Imagine musing horizontally in the doze zone between *Grandstand* and *Jim'll fix it*, and hearing the unmistakeable voice of God, calling you by name. Or even while walking through a garden to be strangely drawn towards a rhododendron bush that without warning bursts into flames and speaks. Yes, how dramatic, but not part of most people's real world. God speaks to real people who really want to hear through his word, through prayer conversations, meditation and, of course, through his church. God doesn't want to shout at his children, though to get their attention he sometimes needs to, but he wants to speak to them in the stillness. A few years ago I entitled a worship album 'In the stillness' putting new music to the beautiful words written decades ago by E. May Grimes.

Speak, Lord, in the stillness
While I wait on Thee,
Hushed my heart to listen
In expectancy.
Speak, O blessed Master
In this quiet hour,
Let me see Your face, Lord,
Feel Your touch of power.
For the words You speak, Lord,
They are life indeed,
Living bread from heaven

Now my spirit feed.
Satiate my being
With Your fullness fill,
As the dew descending
Let Your speech distil.
All to You is yielded
I am not my own,
Blissful glad surrender
I am Yours alone.
Speak, Your servant hears now,
Be not silent, Lord,
Waits my soul upon You
For the quickening word.
Fill me with the knowledge
Of Your glorious will,
All Your own good pleasure
In Your child fulfil.
Like a watered garden,
Full of fragrance rare,
Lingering in Your presence
Let my life appear.

(© *South Africa General Mission*)

Two things before I continue. First, do you want to hear from God? Then learn to linger in his presence. He does not share the secrets of his heart in hurried encounters. Secondly, do you feel that God has gone silent on you? Do you feel that he's not talking to you? Then I would ask: What was the last thing he said, and what did you do about it? *Whatever he says to you, do it.*

Close enough to hear . . .

Lesley and I have five children. Rachel is studying medicine at Leicester University. All her eventful life (another story) she's been like a caffeine overdose! Active, against many odds, creative and noisy. Life is never dull!

Daniel is eighteen and like a valium overdose. He's so laid back he's almost horizontal. I'm sure that 'the last trumpet call' will be greeted with, 'Hey that's a great riff!'

The triplets, now thirteen, are all different too. Mark Simeon is the eldest by fifteen minutes. Sport crazy in general, football and Aston Villa in particular, he spends his days acting out seasonal sporting activities, hardly ever without a ball in his hand or at his feet. Sleep is a temporary inconvenience. Sara Kate, the youngest, spent her first few weeks in the babies' IC unit. She is thirteen going on sixteen! A 'talkaholic', it seems she's taken on from where Rachel left off. Hannah Elizabeth was born with a chromosome abnormality resulting in her requiring special education. She has neither Mark's mobility nor Sara's vocabulary. Bedtime sees Mark celebrating in over-the-top fashion, 'scoring' the winning cup final goal for the Villa (he's very imaginative!), and Sara talking to herself because she's run out of willing listeners. A few years ago, when much smaller, Hannah, with noise and confusion around, would climb onto my knee for a cuddle. Her shape and mine matched. In the midst of the bedlam we were lost in each other's love. Her head buried in my chest, her breathing in unison with mine, life and time for a few precious moments stood still.

'Daddy, I can hear your heart beating. Why?'

Moved by the simplicity and yet profoundness of the question, I replied, 'Hannah, it's because you are as close to me now as it's possible to be.'

The answer must have been sufficient. We soon slipped back into our 'world without words'.

The Father's heartbeat is heard in that 'world without words'. The throb of forgiveness, acceptance and affirmation is known in the pure intimacy between Father and child.

Father . . . who?

In a generation of broken marriages, single parents and child abuse the image of wholesome fatherhood is under siege. In truth, previous generations have had similar problems but they were veiled and hidden beneath the surface of respectability. Many times in counselling I've heard the cry, 'I have no concept of a heavenly Father. I cannot worship God as Father . . . I never knew a real father.' I've seen people almost choke on singing, 'Father in heaven, how we love you.'

Two things: first to those who have been so tormented and scarred, Satan will cause you to be obsessed by the scars, the loss, the pain, the injustice. Hell will always make the scars look ugly. *Heaven can make scars beautiful*. The scars of Calvary will be features of heaven that will be seen by the numberless gathering of the redeemed and revered and adored. 'By his wounds we are healed.' Submit those scars to heavenly influences. Jesus can make all things beautiful.

Secondly, given that you are one of the many who feel robbed and cheated of enjoying a relationship with Father God because of the inadequacies of the human equivalent, may I ask, 'Who gave you the right to look at an earthly father to be a role model of your heavenly Father?' I'm not underestimating the heartache, the regrets. The question though is still valid. Who do you look at to find out what your Father is like? Jesus. You've seen him, you've seen the Father.

Turn your eyes upon Jesus. Enjoy those 'cuddles'.

Do not harden your heart

How do hearts that once responded to the gentle stirrings of the Holy Spirit become hard? It is so easy to become complacent, thoughtless and laid back in our relationship with the Lord. On the human level, when we begin to take someone for granted, the 'spark', the *joie de vivre* soon diminishes. Many a marriage has collapsed simply because thankfulness and mutual concern have been replaced with apathy. Amos warns about becoming complacent where once there was blessing (Amos 6:1). Psalm 95:2 says, 'Let us come before him with thanksgiving.' Where there is a spirit of gratitude there will be worship; where there is not you have hearts that have become hard.

> Reign in me,
> Sovereign Lord, reign in me.
> Captivate my heart
> Let Your kingdom come,
> Establish there Your throne,
> Let Your will be done.
> Reign in me,
> Sovereign Lord, reign in me.

(*C. A. Bowater, 1985*)

PART 2
Leadership

'I will enter . . .'

How often have you heard it said at your church, 'Let us now enter into a time of praise and worship'?

That word 'enter' is the key to leading worship. It implies a 'coming from' and a 'moving into' — a journey. Failure and frustration occur when we try to rush or stumble into the presence of God.

As a leader, you can take the people only where you have already been. Your ability to 'lead worship' will be proportionate to the reality of your own worship life. If you find it impossible to 'press in' on God, really to draw close to him, how can you expect to encourage those who are looking to you for leadership?

Priority

Before you stand in front of any group and say, 'Let us now enter . . .' be sure that you have already spent time with God.

Anyone (almost) can lead what is best described as a chorus medley, getting the enthusiastic whip out and driving people along at an exhausting pace. The task, however, is to lead, often enthusiastically, sometimes gently, but at all times sensitively.

What, then, is the purpose of first spending time alone with God? It is to tune one's heart and mind, through lingering in that 'secret place', with the heart and mind of God. You do, of course, realise that the Spirit of God has some real desires to fulfil at each gathering of God's people? More often than not the Spirit of God wants to move in the lives of his people but we don't give him room to get involved; we crowd him out with the never-ending chain of singing. Leaders must seek God as to the direction his Spirit desires to take. Can I hear someone saying, 'But I like to be led by the Spirit during the meeting'? That's good, but it's better to be led by the Spirit *before* the meeting. The Holy Spirit needs to be released because we all have things in our lives that need to be resolved. As your heart is before God, he will give you direction, so that you can truly lead the people into that dimension of praise and worship that is purposeful. Second Chronicles 5:11 speaks of the priests consecrating, or sanctifying, themselves before entering into the place of worship. Preparation invariably leads to a consciousness of the presence and often the power of God.

First steps

Having prepared yourself before the Lord you will probably become very conscious that the people themselves are ill-prepared. Maybe they have not personally spent time with God or lived 'practising the presence of Christ'. Some have even come from alien environments and a transition period becomes necessary.

'Who may ascend the hill of the Lord? Who may stand in his holy place? He who has clean hands and a pure heart' (Ps 24:3–4). The condition of the heart is still central to the congregation's ability to enter into praise.

In Psalm 51, David clearly indicates a process of preparation before true praise can ascend to the Lord.

1. 'Create in me a pure heart . . .' (v. 10)

If our hearts condemn us, if sin is unconfessed, God not only cannot receive our offerings of praise, he cannot even hear them.

2. 'Renew a steadfast spirit within me' (v. 10)

Our hearts can only be really clean before God if our spirits are right, and that means brothers and sisters in the Lord being right with each other.

'If you are offering your gift at the altar and there remember that your brother has something against you, leave the gift there in front of the altar. First go and be reconciled to your brother; then come and offer your gift' (Mt 5:23–24).

3. Restore to me the joy of your salvation' (v. 12)

Often in our praise there is much surface joy, but underneath the facades, there can lurk many desolate and discouraged hearts. Genuine praise will flow from hearts whose joy springs from an assurance of salvation and forgiveness. There can be no greater joy than that rooted in the knowledge and experience of forgiven sins. Then, and only then, could David cry, 'Open my lips, and my mouth will declare your praise' (v. 15). When the heart is clean, the spirit is right and the joy restored, praise can flow.

The costs

Be aware that there are costs involved in true worship. David declared, 'I will not sacrifice to the Lord my God burnt offerings that cost me nothing' (2 Sam 24:24).

I have already discussed the cost of the will, which we should use to stir ourselves to worship regardless of our feelings; the cost of time, which we need in order to let God have his way; the cost of emotions and the cost of concentration. Hearts and minds must come into subjection. 'I will sing with my spirit, but I will also sing with my mind' (1 Cor 14:15).

I have laid down certain foundations, but these have practical implications for leaders:

1. Preparation of the leader's heart is necessary.
2. The leader should seek vision or direction for the meeting.
3. Part of the task is stirring the congregation physically, vocally, emotionally, to praise.
4. A standing congregation is more likely to find full involvement.
5. The leader needs to be relaxed.
6. Move purposefully from vigorous praise to more personalised worship: moving from the 'we' to the 'I'.
7. Have an open heart concerning the flow: do not automatically follow a line and procedure that was particularly blessed last time.
8. As the worship becomes more intimate the leader will become less prominent. Mistiming a 'breaking in' at a time of intimate worship can be disastrous.
9. Realise that worship will ebb and flow; it is good to understand the variety of intensity that enhances the worship time.
10. Encourage the people to avoid 'second-hand worship': riding on someone else's experience or

inspiration. The hymns and choruses are an excellent vehicle to take us into the realm of personal worship.

Sing a new song

The Scriptures frequently implore us to sing a new song to the Lord (Ps 33:3; 40:3; 96:1; 98:1; 149:1; Is 42:10). Even heaven resounds with the strains of 'a new song' (Rev 5:9; 14:3).

The Spirit of God is one that is creative and desires to create within us songs, new songs to the Lord —

So from deep within
My spirit singeth unto Thee

(Keri Jones/David Matthew,
© 1978 Springtide/Word Music (UK))

— songs sung with the spirit and also with the understanding. So in the midst of all the known songs that we sing when we enter into worship, let us be released into singing 'new songs' to the Lord, that find their birth in the reality of our relationship with him.

Leading a worship service

Read 2 Chronicles 29:25–30 for an account of how to lead a worship service. The Lord is looking for worshippers (Jn 4:23–24) who will worship him in spirit and truth. When a body of God's people assemble to worship him, somehow the worship needs to be guided. Hezekiah himself took the lead on that occasion. Today many people, whether they feel gifted or not, find themselves in the position of guiding someone else's worship to a place of fulfilment. It is an awesome duty. Whether it is a large convention meeting, a regular local church worship service or a home-group gathering, many of the principles are the same.

A gifted worship leader is as valuable to a church as a good Bible teacher. Certain qualities are inherent in a good worship leader; others are acquired as skills by experience and a teachable spirit.

Obviously the worship leader is not acting alone and is faced with a number of influencing elements.

We are gathered together

We're together again . . . but in what condition? Varying states of readiness, willingness, spiritual and physical stamina, tradition and expectation are evident in most gatherings. Some people are there because they have to be, are told to be; some because they want to be. A hard day at the office or factory, family sickness, troublesome children, unconverted relatives all contribute to the attitudes prevalent at the start of a meeting. Recognise these factors and begin to join the hearts and minds of the people in the pursuit of praise.

The reason for gathering

The purpose and style of the meeting may dictate the intensity level of the praise and worship attempted. Is it a 'regular' or a 'special'? Your own folk or a mixed bunch? The style of meeting and reason for gathering need to be clearly understood. I happen to believe that praise and worship must be central to all activity — prayer, Bible study and, yes, evangelism. On the Day of Pentecost, when the promised Holy Spirit came upon the waiting followers of Jesus, as they declared the wonders of God (Acts 2:11), 3,000 people were added to the church. That's church growth. Imagine, 120 at the morning service and 3,120 at the evening. The manifestation of the Holy Spirit and worship are central to evangelism.

Who was it who said, 'Too much of a good thing is not good for you'? With celebration gatherings being so prominent in our Christian calendar there is a real danger of trying to cultivate a celebration-type atmosphere in every meeting. I've known some house-group meetings led with arm-waving exhilaration! The size of the gathering genuinely affects the style of praise and worship.

The celebration — probably 250 and upwards. This meeting will be centrally controlled with most initiative coming from the platform. Large gatherings lend themselves to prolonged periods of sung praise and worship. It can be sustained simply because of the number of people present and the size of the musical group.

The congregation — probably up to 200 or so people. The style of praise and worship can here be much more varied. Along with the singing, opportunity can be given for verbal participation – prayers, Bible readings, times of sharing and testimonies. The smaller the congregation becomes, the harder it is for singing to be prolonged or sustained. Greater variety of expression is required.

The cell — a home group or house fellowship. The ideal size is twelve to fifteen people. Although some singing is desirable, more emphasis will be on verbal praise, sharing and ministering.

Leadership of singing

Suddenly, it seems, a new breed of leadership has emerged: the worship leader. Some churches cannot handle any other concept than all leadership coming from a pastor or elder. Gifting often does not even come into the equation. Unless there are clearly defined areas of responsibility, confusion and disharmony can arise in a meeting. Who is leading? There are various possibilities.

1. Leadership can be left totally open. In fact, there is no leader. Everyone is a chief (as opposed to being Indians). This tends to be supported by the 'we want to be led by the Spirit' group. It sounds good, but in reality God sets up authorities in his church. Leadership is part of his plan.

2. The meeting can be started off by one person then 'left open for God to move'. This too presents problems. Abdication of leadership, or responsibility, is hardly the language of the kingdom of God.

3. The meeting is led by a group of musicians and singers. Now this is an attractive alternative. However, the problem could be that everything then in terms of praise and worship takes on a musical bias, because most of us will operate in the realm of our preference. Also, it is crucial that the meeting is not just being led by skilful musicians. The musicians and singers of David's tabernacle sang prophecies with skilled musical accompaniment. It is clear that they were trained and proficient (1 Chron 25:7). How sad when some of today's finest Christian musicians are not motivated to serve in worship. However, if it comes to a choice between the skilled or the sensitive, the professional or the prophetic, choose the one who has that prophetic anointing every time. If it is combined with musical skill, then there is potentially a dynamic ministry.

4. An alternative form of leadership is one that is clearly shared between two or three people. This works only where there is a good relationship already existing (competitive spirits cannot 'flow together'). It also works if there is a unity of vision and purpose in worship.

This team style of leadership does have some real advantages. The meeting can flow with the anointing, and there is less personal pressure to get it right, knowing that one is being 'covered' by fellow leaders.

5. The final alternative is to have only, and probably always, one person leading, supported by the musicians. This provides continuity but may not provide sufficient contrast. All leaders have their own way of doing things, but when it becomes the only way, real progress and development can be stifled.

What shall we sing?

1. Mainly hymns with choruses relegated to the pre-service sing-a-long, or
2. Almost exclusively choruses with spontaneous song, or
3. Mainly choruses with frequent hymns and spontaneous song.

Suggestions 1 and 2 tend to imply exclusivity, whereas 3 provides breadth and flexibility of expression.

Hymns — Many churches are throwing out their hymn-books. By doing so they are removing a heritage and wealth of experience that may never be replaced. Don't throw the baby out with the bath water. Rid yourselves of certain hymns that are conceptually and theologically questionable. 'Hold the fort, for I am coming' implies a 'hanging on' against all odds; a 'we'll soon be rescued from all this sin and strife' mentality. God doesn't want us to 'hold the fort' but to be a part of the building of his church. We're not 'hanging on' but 'pressing on' from victory to victory. The church of Jesus Christ is not in retreat but is reclaiming territory that our enemy has taken.

> We will reclaim the territory
> Where the enemy's been moving,
> We will fight with authority
> With the Holy Ghost and power.
> With a God like our God —
> What a God is our God!
> We cannot, we must not,
> We will not know defeat.

> *(C. A. Bowater, 1982)*

'Gentle Jesus, meek and mild' has produced a meek and mild generation. The Jesus I serve is indeed gentle and meek but he is also the One in whom God has

invested all authority. At his name devils fear and
tremble. Rather let's confess:

. . . that Jesus Christ is Lord . . .
He's omnipotent, magnificent,
All glorious, victorious . . .
I confess that Jesus Christ is Lord!

(C. A. Bowater, 1982)

And what about, 'Prone to wander, Lord I feel it'? Such
negative confession produces negative lives.

But in some of our hymnology there is a depth of
truth expressed that we must never lose. 'No more veil,
God bids me enter' (Frances Bevan) needs to be sung
from generation to generation, as must 'My Goal is God
Himself' (F. Brook), 'Love divine, all loves excelling'
(Charles Wesley) — and so many more. The objective
of hymns is to declare truth and doctrine, to teach and
release worship. Let's not rob today's generation. Let's
expose them to hymns that are foundational and
fundamental to our faith.

Choruses — The abundance of choruses today is both
a blessing and a possible blight. So many new songs . . .
so many new books . . . how does one keep up with it
all? There is a real pressure to keep up to date with the
latest songs. A fellowship that tries to keep pace with
every new song that bursts onto the scene will probably
fall into one of various traps.

There is the possibility that no song will be able
properly to filter through into the fabric of church life
or into the depths of an individual's spirit. Many of the
new songs need to be allowed time to become a part of
the expression of the church. Choruses must be allowed
to evolve; my experience is that the new songs are 'killed
off' in two or three weeks.

There are choruses that have a very short life-span

— important in their time but without a timeless quality. Others, like certain hymns, need to be retained in the church's repertoire.

It's a good exercise to collate and classify the choruses, identifying themes, styles and key for example. Also establish those choruses that have some 'increase potential'. These are songs that can develop into extended periods of 'symphonic' praise. Some songs have this quality, others don't. I defy anyone to be able to make very much of 'I will enter His gates with thanksgiving'. It's a great starter, and we have to begin somewhere, but it's not a spring-board into spontaneous song — it doesn't lend itself to too much variation of musical interpretation.

Here is a suggested classification:

1. Thanksgiving/rejoicing/praise/gathering — of restricted 'increase' potential.
2. Thanksgiving/rejoicing/praise/gathering — of useful 'increase' potential.
3. Bright, exuberant praise.
4. 'Easy' praise.
5. 'Earnest' praise.
6. 'Grand' praise which also tilts towards worship.
7. 'Grand' worship — especially Godward.
8. 'Earnest' worship — especially Godward.
9. 'Easy' worship.
10. Very basic worship — extreme simplicity.
11. Personal need/hunger/seeking/aspiration/touch/ blessing.
12. Themes — for example: relationships among saints; healing and ministry of Christ; commitment/availability; knowing him; warfare and conflict; starting songs; going-out songs.

Always make a note of choruses which 'work' and say something no other chorus you know says.

I was recently reading an article written by Donald Gee, often called the pentecostal prince of writers. He said, back in 1929:

A fault we can quickly drop into in hymn and chorus singing is the placing of far too much emphasis upon our own experiences, feelings, desires, etc. We are apt to thus, all unconsciously it may be, sing about ourselves or to ourselves, or to one another, rather than 'to the Lord'. Singing is a perfectly legitimate expression of the sweetness of Christian emotion in the same way that honey is a real article of diet in the Promised Land: but there was to be no honey in the offering brought to the Lord (Lev 2:11), and we must not confuse the expression of all our feelings of revival exhilaration with true worship in spirit and in truth. And in any case 'honey' is to be taken in moderation (Prov 26:16). Too much singing of a 'sweet' type of hymn or chorus always produces spiritual nausea in the end. Real worship never tires.

That, I believe, has real application for the early 1990s.

Mention has been made of spontaneous song, often called (misguidedly) singing 'in the spirit'. Bryn Barrett from Toowamba, Australia, in an article entitled 'Christian Worship' says:

Spiritual songs are those distinctive spontaneous outbursts of holy song. Anyone may have one. A whole company may have one. The Spirit himself prompts it. If you want to know it in public then enjoy it in private. It has nothing to do with personal musical talent . . . there is that about spiritual song that not even the world's best choirs can equal.

Preparation of your heart and spiritual life

A good leader will:

Have the heart and spirit of a worshipper. Most people really want to worship, but sometimes they have difficulty rising above the mundane aspects of their daily lives to see and experience God. Worship leaders shouldn't scold or rebuke the people of God: 'Come, stand to your feet. Don't you know he's the King of kings? He's worthy. What are you doing still sitting down in his presence . . .?' Don't do it. Most of them are doing their best to magnify the Lord out of the revelation in their own hearts. The anointed leaders, those who are in touch and in tune with the people, who know how to exercise the prophetic gift and bring encouragement, will direct people's attention to God's greatness and goodness. They will aim to create an atmosphere that is charged with inspiration and illumination. The light and truth that come into the midst of the assembly through prophetic men and women stir, encourage and motivate God's people to thank and glorify him. Then, set free and inspired, they have little difficulty lifting their voices to the Lord.

Bill Patton, in an article called 'Radical Worship' (*People of Destiny* magazine), said:

> This then is the role of worship leaders: they are to develop an environment where prophecy, praise and worship can flourish; they are to lead by example, prophesying themselves, and then to co-ordinate the blending together of musical and prophetic gifts so that God is exalted without inhibition.

Maintain freshness in spiritual life. Freshness springs from a real and relevant relationship with God, a current and consuming indwelling of the Holy Spirit, and a passion for the love of Christ 'that passes all knowledge'.

Be at one with the leadership in the church. You need their support and encouragement. The worship leader is potentially the first target. When the javelins start flying, you need to know that there are those around you who in every sense are with you. Be at one in respect to relationships and vision. Psalm 133 often gets rewritten. It becomes, '. . . when brethren *dither* together.' There must be clarity and continuity of vision. Lack of direction could mean failure to reach the correct destination.

Have good communication with the musicians. You need them, so don't take them for granted. Involve them in prayer and planning. They may just have some valuable insight into worship. Listen to them. Share with them. Flow with them.

Be sensitive in administering the anointing. Let any control be without conflict. Be prepared to move away from a pre-arranged plan. Persevere through times of 'hardness' but let any sustaining be without striving. The Spirit of God, more often than not, is a gentle spirit. He will not force his way through obstructions. But he will occupy that place where an opportunity has been made for him to move.

Be sensitive towards the people. Have a servant's heart. Many may be inwardly crying, hurting and sore. Minister the grace of God, the all-sufficient grace.

> You're crying inside, but there are no tears,
> You're trying to hide the deepest of fears.
> Tomorrow's a day you don't wish to face
> But Jesus says, 'You will know today . . .
> My grace.'
>
> (C. A. Bowater, 1985)

Have a personal sense of vision and revelation concerning spiritual and scriptural worship. You are seeking to bring the congregation 'before him' (Ps 95:2) in thanksgiving, in praise and rejoicing, and in worship.

'Bring an offering and come before him; worship the Lord in the splendour of his holiness' (1 Chron 16:29).

You are seeking to lead people to his footstool and worship (Ps 132:7); the release of the ministering Spirit of Christ; to see God genuinely honoured.

Approaching the task

You are embarking on a journey — the most meaningful adventure that people can undertake. It begins with where we are at — acknowledging the conditions we are in — and ends in the Holy of Holies with an encounter with God. The journey can be truly plotted in looking at the psalms of ascent (Ps 120–134).

They begin, 'I call on the Lord in my distress . . .' (Ps 120:1): the confession of a state of heart and mind.

They continue, 'I lift up my eyes to the hills . . .' (Ps 121:1): the confession of longing for God and commitment to move towards him.

They go on, 'I rejoiced with those who said to me, "Let us go to the house of the Lord"' (Ps 122:1): an expression of excitement, anticipation; a willingness to move.

Gradually, the songs become less person-centred and more God-centred. They move away from their own feelings to an awareness of God.

On this journey, recognise and appreciate the 'geographical features'. There are rises and falls; heights and depths; steep places and gentle undulations; shaded pastures and rocky paths. All feature in the journey. Let our times of praise and worship be free to explore all the wealth of expression available to us. There are times to linger by the still waters, and times to press on towards the heights. There will be periods of resting and moments of active pursuit.

Grasp the potential of each song that is being sung. Let it accomplish its potential. So often we give up on a song too early. Some songs need to be sung until they are more than words but become confessions of faith.

As you 'move with the Spirit', allow each 'turn' and 'ascent' to run its full course. We must learn how to press through even at times when it seems the going is hard. Learn how to 'move with the cloud'. The presence of God is an active, moving presence. The presence of the Lord will be there to heal, restore, forgive, encourage, enlighten . . . and much more.

Avoid too much talking. Once the people are truly pursuing that encounter with God let the 'voice over' involvement be minimal. The closer folk get to God the less aware they are of other people. The last thing they need is a third person dropping in on their intimate moments with the Lord.

Don't tire the people with too many ascents or climaxes. There is no need to be afraid of silence. Just let God speak in his own inimitable way during those moments. He is able to do more in those few seconds than we can with any number of words. Teach your people not to panic. Another chorus, a prayer, a Bible reading, even a prophecy may not in fact add to the reality of people's encounter with God; on the contrary, they could be major distractions.

At all times be gracious, in word and in gesture. Keep your countenance enthusiastic. Don't allow your mind to wander. Remember, you are leading.

Worshipping God brings us into one accord

This then is the ultimate motive of leading worship. True worship will bring everyone, be it a handful or several thousand, into the unity of the Spirit. This is the task.

As we worship the Lord with many other Christians, we
are brought into a unity, a oneness. Instead of concentrating
on our differences, we look at Jesus and focus on Him. As
we are caught up in the wonder of His person, those
differences pale beside Him. It is as we look together to
Jesus and worship Him that we are drawn closer to Him
and to each other.

(Roxanne Brantk, *Ministering to the Lord*)

We can never love Jesus too much. We can never spend
too much time with him. He is worthy to receive 'glory
and honour and power, for [he] created all things, and
by [his] will they were created' (Rev 4:11).

Radical prophetic praise

I had a phone call recently from a young man in the south of the country; a young man probably very well known to many of you, who is at the forefront of involvement in leading worship and praise. For about fifteen to twenty minutes he just poured out his heart to me, saying how empty and disillusioned he had become. Disillusioned, not with God, but with the level at which people were moving and operating in the realms of praise and worship. We have learned all the technology, as it were, of worship and praise. We have got all the equipment. We have learned what it is to become 'free in our worship and free in our praise'. But, as he said, underneath all that there has still been a niggling sense of disillusionment.

I don't want to write about techniques or methodology. I want to write about *radical prophetic praise and worship*. What do I mean by this phrase?

In all honesty, I am going to say a few things that maybe every one of us has felt but never dared say, because somehow it would not have sounded as if we were 'walking in faith and victory', and somehow it might have cast a cloud across our so-called spirituality. But if we are to be honest, many of us have had experiences in times of worship where we have not been fulfilled, where those moments have not been saturated with the real life of God. Oh yes, they have been good meetings. But they have not been filled with the real life of God. They have not been filled with reality. They have not been filled with relevance. John 10:10 says: 'I have come that they may have life, and have it to the full.'

I went to a church in the northwest of the country and was greeted at the car park. The pastor came along and gave me one of those charismatic, bone-crushing hugs. I said, 'How are you?' I had obviously pressed the button and for the next five minutes it was, 'Oh, brother . . . Hallelujah . . . Glory to God . . . Isn't God wonderful? . . . We are walking in faith and victory . . . We are children of the Light . . .' and so on. For five minutes it was just a flow of positive proclamation. At the end of it all I took a breath and said, 'Really?' He said, 'No, not really . . . but no one has ever asked the second question.'

I desire that, in my worship and in my praise, more than anything else I am real. I want to be real with God because God is real. I don't want to do things just because it is expected of me. I have this year withdrawn myself from seventy-five per cent of travelling commitments. A lot of people haven't understood that but I know the need in my life for seeking God and for waiting on God for more from him. And sometimes we get taken up with the whirligig of activity. We begin to operate on automatic. If we are used to working with people and leading people, we can make a meeting happen. We know how to get people on their feet, get them singing. And they can go away with a sense of having been in a good meeting.

I am becoming more and more concerned that people don't just go away having been in a 'good meeting', but that they have come into contact with God; because then people will go away changed from having had a real encounter with him. It's easy to become satisfied with the predictable patterns into which we begin to fall. Somebody once said that the only difference between a rut and a grave is the depth. It's easy to begin to get into ruts, into predictable patterns. It's easy to lose the desire to experience God in our corporate times, to lose that determination to excel in worship. But we must never, as people of God, accept mediocrity. We must never settle for second best.

Psalm 103:1 says, 'Praise the Lord, O my soul; all my inmost being, praise his holy name.' We must desire that pursuit of excellence. Anything less becomes passive. Anything less becomes superficial, and is empty religion. We can even be into the latest choruses — and I speak as a chorus-writer — but in truth we worship them, or worship 'worship'.

The fundamental problem in the Old Testament with the people of God was that other things besides God began to raise themselves up in the estimation and the attention of the people, and they fell into the sin of idolatry. I would like to suggest that today there is idolatry in the church. We have clothed our idols in all sorts of spiritual attire but I suggest that one of the idols can be the latest chorus, the latest song. We can even put people onto pedestals and allow them to become idols.

Outward expression must always reflect our inner feeling and honest gratitude before God. Anything else does not bless God. Anything else is not blessing. Half-hearted mechanical worship is a waste of time. We might just as well close our meeting down. But contrast

Psalm 28:7, 'My heart leaps for joy and I will give thanks to him in song.'

One of our congregation leaders had the courage that we all wish we had at some time. His meeting started at 6.00 pm in his area. At 6.15 pm he sent everybody home. He said, 'People, you have not come desiring to meet with God. You have not come with that attitude of expectancy. And we are not just going to go through the motions. We are not having a meeting for the sake of having a meeting. Go home.' A week later they came back and they were ready. They desired to meet with God. They had that passion, that anticipation. Hebrews 13:15 says: 'Through Jesus, therefore, let us continually offer to God a sacrifice of praise — the fruit of lips that confess his name.'

Half-hearted mechanical worship doesn't please God. It leaves us unaffected and disillusioned. I believe that when we behold him we are changed. That means that people will not be going out of our fellowships and out of our times of worship still carrying the same heaviness they came in with: 'I sought the Lord, and he answered me; he delivered me from all my fears. Those who look to him are radiant; their faces are never covered with shame' (Ps 34:4–5). They will not be going out still gripped by the same fear, or entangled and crippled by that bitterness and cynicism. If, indeed, we behold him we will be changed.

What is prophetic worship and prophetic praise? It is praise that is sustained, not by the effort of people, but by the reality of God's presence. I was in the Shetlands a few years ago in a meeting that started at 7.00 pm. At 11.30 pm no one was moving. Come midnight they were still there, most of them on their knees or on their faces before God. Why? It wasn't because I was at the piano sustaining the thing and keeping it going. No. The presence of God was so heavy upon the meeting that praise and worship began to emanate out of that atmosphere at a level which I have never ever experienced.

We must not compromise our commitment to progress in worship. I believe that what is happening to fellowships in many places is that they have been to all the seminars, they have been to all the lectures. They have learned a set of rules and principles which are good and which will bring a level of release. But they have been happy to stay at that measure of release. But that isn't progress in God. What happens if you 'plateau off' in God is that you run the risk of going backwards.

The purpose in God is to progress continually.

Worship is not a formality. It's not a preliminary activity to warm us up for the preaching, although some of us can remember when it used to be like that. The congregation got so exhausted that when they sat down they could do nothing but listen to the preaching. On the contrary, worship is central to our reason for existence. Worship is not a press-button experience on a Sunday morning or on a particular meeting night. Worship is a lifestyle.

If you think that is a new principle, then listen to Horatius Bonar, the hymn-writer of many years ago, declaring: 'Fill Thou my life, O Lord my God, in every part with praise.' What I am on Monday morning is as important to my worship life as what I appear to be on a Sunday morning. What I am with my wife and children is as fundamental to God in my worship life as how I appear before my pastors at the church. Because what I am in my home when the pastors and the elders are not there to be observing and giving marks out of ten, is what I really am.

Let me ask you a question. It's a question I have had

to ask my own heart many times. How is your worship life at home? I don't mean only your prayer life. That is part of it. Or reading the word of God. That is also an important part of our spiritual lifestyle. But how is your worship life at home? Within all the dimensions in which we move in Holy Spirit liberty within the fellowship, I wonder how often what we do is a reaction to what everyone else is doing. You must ask yourself this question: Are you ready in your own times at home to get before the Lord and lift up hands before him when there is no one else there except the Lord to see those hands lifted up? Are you as full of anticipation to lift up that voice of gladness when the only one who is listening to you is your heavenly Father? Psalm 63:3–4: 'Because your love is better than life, my lips will glorify you. I will praise you as long as I live, and in your name I will lift up my hands.' What we are at home in our worship is what we really are in our worship; when we are out of focus, out of the spotlight. Leaders — if you desire to lead your people into an area and a realm of worship, you must be a worshipper.

Jesus said the Father was seeking those who worship him (Jn 4:23). That probably implies that he is not finding them too readily. But the Father is seeking those who will worship him in spirit and in truth. You can choose what you worship, but you cannot then, on the authority of God's word, choose how you worship.

Let me illustrate this. We can all choose what we worship in our lives. To some it may be that car parked outside which is your pride and joy, and you worship it. I kick mine. But you may worship yours. People do actually pour love and devotion, time and attention into their cars. But once you have selected your car to be the object of your worship, you actually have to follow a procedure of how you must worship it. You have to buy the magazines, you have to go to the clubs and the societies which cater for those with an interest in cars; buy in-car entertainment systems; expend much energy polishing it until it gleams. You begin to follow up the object of your worship with time and money. Luke 12:34 says, 'For where your treasure is, there your heart will be also.'

Maybe the object of your worship is money. You have chosen what you worship. But when you dream, you dream in pounds and pence, and money becomes a source of obsession in your life. Once you have chosen money to be the object of your worship you then have a necessary procedure to satisfy the longing of your worship. It's going to cost in time and attention, much outlay of money in order to accumulate money. The accumulation of possessions can, in itself, be a form of idolatry. And you can go on. You choose the object of your worship, but then you have to satisfy it. 'What good is it for a man to gain the whole world, yet forfeit his soul?' (Mk 8:36). Jesus said, 'God is spirit, and his worshippers must worship in spirit and in truth' (Jn 4:24). Note that 'must' — there are no options. God is looking for a high level of truth in our lives — truth before him.

A favourite theme of mine is the restoration of the tabernacle of David. Energetic pursuit of biblical vision includes the restoration of prophetic worship. The time of restoration of the ark, temple and tabernacle was one of great spiritual development. Empty ritual gave way to new vibrant worship. There was the introduction of many and varied musical instruments (1 Chron 15). It was a period when God's people praised with a loud voice (Ps 98:4); they shouted (Ps 47:1); they sang enthusiastically (Ps 47:6); they sang with joyful noise

(Ps 63:5); and they danced (Ps 150:4). These were the things that God was bringing into the life of the people of God.

But also the restoration was led by a prophetic people in celebration and praise to God. Praise was filled with the present word of the Spirit. It was filled with revelation; it was filled with the heart of God. The Psalms reflect the richness of their times together. In the tabernacle of David priority was given to worship and because of this God poured out his wisdom, his direction and his power. He lifted the nation to heights of glory and influence, and God was pleased to rule in their midst and manifest himself and lead them from victory to victory. Doesn't that sound like the kind of church you want to belong to? Doesn't that sound like the kind of people you long to be — those on whom God is pouring out his wisdom, direction and power; those whom God is lifting to heights of influence in society; those in whose midst God rules, manifesting himself and leading from victory to victory?

Sadly, as time went on, musicians, singers and prophetic ministries disappeared. Pure worship died in the hearts of all but a remnant. How sad. Why? It died because of moral and religious compromise, starting with the leaders. It is interesting that you read about the wisest man in the Bible, Solomon, and the strongest man in the Bible, Samson, and both of them began to fall from power and authority through moral decline. But God spoke again through Amos, about the fallen ruins being rebuilt (Amos 9:11–15). The prophetic ministries that flourished during David's reign were destined to emerge again with greater intensity and with more far-reaching effect.

And that restoration is now happening. I believe we are living in days of restoration and that is not because 'restoration' is an 'in-word'; in fact in some areas it is becoming an 'out-word'. See Psalm 132:13. Zion is no longer just a geographical position but a people found in every place who are moving into freedom in worship and praise, lifting hands, clapping, dancing and singing with a proliferation of many instruments, and a prophetic spirit once again coming upon the people.

So, why *radical* prophetic worship? I believe that 'radical' really means doing what we already believe. The emphasis so often in Scripture is, 'If you hear, do it. If you love me, do it' (Jas 1:22–25; Jn 14:15). What is the problem? It is living in the light of the revelation that we say we have. We are so often full of revelation and yet a little slow on the outworking of it. Revelation, knowledge and understanding can either bring us into greater freedom and liberty or greater bondage — according to what we do with it. I believe that to be radical is to do what we already believe in God and actually to put into practice what we hear from God (Jas 1:22–25; Mt 7:24–27).

Prophetic worship is worship that is not predictable. I can remember meetings when you could actually tell the time of day by what was happening. You knew that when the elders came down to the front for the communion part of the service, it was twelve noon because that was the way it always was, ever shall be, world without end, amen! There was a predictability about our services. There was even a predictability when certain individuals stood up to pray. You knew what they were going to pray, you knew the phrases they were going to use. People would even stand up with a prophecy that they had given last week and the week before. There were tongues messages that seemed to happen every week, and you had heard them so many times you could give the same tongues messages.

I heard a story about a man who, week after week, stood up on a Sunday morning and prayed, 'Lord, take the cobwebs out of my life.' The first time that was prayed it was a pretty good prayer. But week after week went by and he was still praying, 'Lord, take the cobwebs out of my life.' At last the pastor could stand it no longer, and we know when pastors get to that point! This man stood up for his final time, 'Lord, take the cobwebs out of my life.' And the pastor, like a shot, stood up and said, 'Lord, kill the spider!'

There is a predictability in our worship. We say the same things. We do the same things. The Bible says, 'Without faith it is impossible to please God' (Heb 11:6). What is the level of faith in which we actually operate in our times of worship? We are moving always within the realms of what we know. Predictability ultimately kills.

What is prophetic worship?

By all means plan for direction. We could all come together and stay put, saying, 'I am waiting for the Spirit to move.' God would probably say, 'I am waiting for you to move first.'

Let me tell you the way we do it in Lincoln. We meet as a team every week and we look back on the previous Sunday. You probably do it in your fellowship with your pastors. 'How did it go? Where did we want to go? Why didn't we get there?' We begin to think, and maybe John Shelbourne, one of the pastoral team, will ask, 'If we could have changed anything, what would we have changed?' Should that prophecy have been allowed at that particular time in the meeting? Did we sing too much? Did we really give full opportunity for the people to worship? Many questions. Occasionally we simply say that we wouldn't have changed anything! But then we begin to project ourselves to the next Sunday morning's worship. The preachers among us quite reasonably expect that if they are asked to speak and bring the word of the Lord, they are given time to do that. They would not like a five-minute warning before the meeting of, 'Oh, brother! You are bringing the word of the Lord today.' But five minutes before a meeting is often all the warning a worship leader will get.

I believe that God has things he wants to do in times of worship. I believe it's a relevant question to ask God, 'Lord, what is it you want to do among your people during the worship time? What are the needs of your people? What are the needs of your Spirit among your people this morning?' That is a fundamental question I ask of God. There is nothing worse than a situation where the people are needing to be stirred in God, they are needing that dimension of faith, and someone comes with a soft voice across the microphone to say, 'Let's be still in the presence of the Lord. Let's know that he is God.' You see, that person is saying the right things but at the wrong time. But it works the other way round too. There are times when the people do need to know what it is to linger in the presence of God and be still. Generally speaking we are very afraid of silence. We get the spiritual Polyfilla out and we try to block the silences and fill them up. Somebody thinks of a chorus. There are times when we don't need any more choruses. There are times when we don't need someone to stand up and pray. There are times when we don't need a 'word from the Lord'. I sometimes feel there are prophecies saying: 'Thus saith the Lord . . .' and God is shaking his head and saying, 'No, I haven't said it. Don't blame me.'

Somebody said in the office recently that the devil and hormones get blamed for everything. I reckon that the Lord gets blamed for a lot of things too for which he is not responsible. God is doing things. God is speaking. He is doing things in the depths of people's spirits and sometimes we can come in and confuse their ears, and we are filling their ears with words when God is already doing a great work. We need to allow for that time, and to ask God a fundamental question, 'Lord, what is it you need to do for your people this morning?' And it may not be the same as last week.

Worship that is not predictable

Prophetic worship is worship that is fresh and new. A particular song was sung last week and in it God really moved. So what happens? The first song you sing the following week is that same song — you are going to try to recapture the blessing of last week. God says, 'No. I was in it last time but I have something different this time.' Isaiah 43:18–19 says, 'Forget the former things; do not dwell on the past. See, I am doing a new thing! Now it springs up; do you not perceive it?' But we are creatures of habit who try to reproduce experiences, maybe even fabricate them! God is looking for those who will come before him with freshness and newness, with an open heart, an open mind and an open spirit.

I just want to refer back to planning. You could hit problems if you don't plan, but you overplan at your peril. Overplanning can become a problem. In Lincoln we ask the Lord how he wants us to set sail. And we think of it in very clear terms like that — of setting sail. I don't know a great deal about sailing — yachts, boats, dinghies or anything else. But I do know that before the wind can do its job you have to put the sail up. That's fundamental, isn't it? There is that 'setting sail' at the beginning of the meeting, of saying, 'Lord, begin to blow by your Spirit. Lord, we are going to set our hearts on this theme right now in you.' God says, 'Good. I have something I can work on here.' When the wind blows we don't struggle if he says, 'Now I want you to move in that direction.' We are free; we are flexible. I often fear that our large celebration gatherings feel as if they have to proceed at a hundred miles an hour. They don't. There is need for stillness, even in celebrations, allowing God to move us in different directions. We have this fixed idea that the celebration should operate at many decibels and at high speed. But that is not so. It is just another platform for God to move among us.

When I was in the Shetlands, there was half an hour of silence at about 11.00 pm during the meeting. It was a living silence. It was vital. And God was doing business and people were doing business with God. I must tell you what happened as a result of that because I shall remember it as long as I live. A woman, for the first time, began to sing a song to the Lord with a sweet voice. Somebody else picked up another refrain. Then somebody else — and the song of the Lord just went round the congregation until the whole congregation was involved. But there was no sense of predictability. There was no planning for that. That was the move of the Spirit of God. But we need to set sail. We need to plan but we must also provide opportunity for the Spirit of God to move.

We need to be fresh. We need to be new. We need to be fresh in our attitude, fresh in our desires before God. I am a great believer in having the right motives. It is fundamental to the outcome. I believe that one of the things that we need to stand against is lethargy, and that spirit of apathy that can so easily descend on the people of God. When this sort of tiredness comes upon them we need to minister something of the freshness of the Spirit of God.

Where does it come from? What causes apathy and where does freshness in the Spirit come from? It comes from the level of our expectation. What do you expect when you come together with your people on a Sunday morning? Well, I expect that the musicians will be playing by the time I sit down. I expect that the pastor and the elders will be there. I expect that the pastor will stand up and that he will begin to lead us. I expect that we will have a time of singing, and I expect that we will probably begin to sing in the Spirit. What you expect is probably what you'll get!

And by the way, have you noticed that when in doubt we sing in the Spirit? We have a problem there. It's almost like, 'What shall we do until it is evident what the next chorus should be? Let's sing in the Spirit. Musicians, make sure we stay in the right key. We'll keep it there until someone sings the relevant chorus to move on.' I'm not being cynical here. This is what really happens. We have entered into this, but we are actually now using something which is beautiful and we are abusing it.

I would rather there were times when we actually sang a new song to the Lord with our understanding because that is harder to do than singing in the Spirit. Sometimes to sing in the Spirit is a cop out. It is much harder to stand before the Lord and begin to sing, 'Lord, you are great. You are wonderful,' when other people around you can hear exactly what you are singing and saying. God is looking for us to sing a new song in words that can be understood: 'I will sing with my spirit, but I will also sing with my mind' (1 Cor 14:15). God is looking for new songs from us. How can new songs come? They can only come out of hearts that know what it is to be continually renewed in God.

If I was doing a workshop, I would say, 'Right. We will sing a song. Then we will sing a new song to the Lord. We won't sing in the Spirit. We will all sing with the understanding. We will all magnify the Lord using words that we understand so that we are clear what we are saying to God.' Yes. There eventually comes a time when we run out of words. Mere words eventually become inadequate to express our feelings to God. Some of my readers will be married men. When you sit down and tell your wife you love her, you don't then go off into some strange sort of language when you have told her once. You say, 'I do love you. I think you're terrific. I appreciated that meal you cooked for me tonight. I like the way you have your hair today.' There are so many ways we can express to our wives our gratitude and our love, using words they can understand. That makes sense.

Once a month I take the opportunity to sit in the congregation. I like to sit in the congregation, because you get a different perspective of what is going on around you. On one of these occasions I stood next to a woman, a single parent who was going through the mill. She had financial problems, there was sickness in the family and I just knew that she was having a hard time of things. During the time of worship I could hear this sweet little voice beside me singing, 'Lord, I do love you. Lord, I want to thank you for everything you are doing in my life. Lord, you are so kind to me.' I tell you this, it broke me. What it must have done to the heart of God I do not know. You see, something was coming out of her life that wasn't due to her circumstances, but arose from a heart-relationship with God. And because she sang with the understanding it did something for me. And I said, 'Lord, if she can sing like that, how much more can I. Lord, you are so kind to me as well.' And it released something in my spirit. You need to sing with the understanding. However, as Keri Jones puts it in his song, there is a time when 'from deep within the spirit sings unto God'. There comes a time when we just run out of knowing what to say, when the Spirit of God within us begins to give utterance before the throne.

But be fresh. Let's be new. Let's be creative in our expression of praise. Imagine that at 10.30 one Sunday morning I sit my wife down on the settee in our lounge and I say, 'I have something to say to you, Lesley. I love you. I appreciate you. I really think you are wonderful. Bless your heart.' Now the first time that happened she would smile back at me and perhaps say, 'Well, thank you very much. That's nice of you.' But then if the following Sunday morning at 10.30 I said, 'Love, it's time. I do love you. I think you're wonderful. Bless you,' there might still be a smile, and a frown. 'Thank you,' she would say. 'That's kind of you. Are you all right?' Then the following Sunday I say, 'It's time, Lesley. Sit down.' She would say, 'No, I won't.' 'What do you mean? It's the time when I say I love you, I appreciate you.' And she would say, 'Haven't you anything else to say?' Do you see what I am trying to say? Let's be creative before God. Let's be creative in our hearts before him and begin to express our love and gratitude. Let's be fresh. Let's be new in our worship. Let's be new in our application.

I wonder what it is in your life about which you have said to God, 'Never!' God has a habit of taking you at the points of your 'nevers' and making them challenging points in your life.

Muriel Shelbourne is a total contrast to John in physique and temperament. They are so different; it is unbelievable that the two are living in the same house. She is very small and quiet and John is the exact opposite. There was a time very recently when Muriel stood before the Lord and said, 'Lord, is there anything I have ever said "never" about to you?'

'Well,' God said, 'since you are asking, there is something.'

'What's that, Lord? I want to surrender that "never" to you.'

'Well, Muriel, you have said you can never dance before me.'

'Oh yes.'

Do you know what she did? She called Wesley, her sixteen-year-old son, and said, 'Wesley, don't laugh,' as she kicked off her shoes. 'I want you to sing a chorus and make it a quick one.' You can imagine a sixteen-year-old boy's reactions! 'Don't say anything, Wesley, and don't laugh. Sing something. Sing "The Lord has led forth his people with joy".'

'OK, Mum.' So he started.

She said, 'No, faster than that, Wesley.'

And he began to sing. To his dismay and horror his mother started to skip around the kitchen, and at the end of it Muriel just knew in her spirit that she had been obedient before God. By the end she felt a little smug. 'Did you see that, Lord?'

'Yes. I was watching. But what about on a Sunday morning?'

'Lord, that wasn't part of the agreement. The agreement was that I was going to surrender my "never".'

The Lord said, 'Yes, but that didn't cost you a great deal in the secrecy of your kitchen. Sunday morning, Muriel. In front of all the other people in the fellowship. I will be waiting.'

To Muriel's delight it was one of those quiet meetings. It was all gentle worship. 'Well, Lord. I was willing. You know I was willing. And I was ready, Lord.' The meeting came to its end and somebody stood up and said, 'I feel, before we go home, we ought to sing, "We shall go out with joy".'

Muriel thought, 'Oh no. I thought I had got away with it.' So the song started and there at the back of the church she began to skip. (Psalm 116:14: 'I will fulfil my vows to the Lord in the presence of all his people.')

The Lord challenged her, 'Who told you to sit at the back? No one can see you. Get into the aisle and start going down to the front.'

So she started skipping and dancing down the aisle, and I will tell you what happened. There were other people in the fellowship who were using Muriel Shelbourne as an excuse for not dancing. Suddenly the excuse had been removed, and it released several other people into something new in God. It makes you wonder, doesn't it, what effect we have on people by the way we are, into what dimension of release we enter or don't enter.

But we need to be fresh. We need to be new in our worship. Have you found yourself moving into a period of worship where you just want to kneel before God? This isn't something that is manufactured in our meeting. It is just happening. There isn't someone saying, 'Let's all kneel.' It's happening because God is beginning to move us into new expressions of worship before him. Be fresh. Be new.

A clear focus

I believe we need to be clearly focused in our worship. Let me tell you this. There are many costs involved in worship. David said he would not bring to the Lord that which cost him nothing (2 Sam 24:24). Many of us are actually doing that week after week. We are bringing to the Lord that which costs us nothing. But one of the costs is a cost of concentration. Those of you in leadership and those of you who actually look across congregations know that there are people who are having problems with their concentration. There is a cost of bringing our concentration into subjection to the praise and worship that is in hand. You can look across and see that people's brains are locked into neutral. Sure they will be singing. They will be clapping. But you know there is nothing going on between their ears! When you are singing a song the mind can so easily be on other things — that hat, that tie, the dinner. Our minds can be going anywhere and everywhere while singing and clapping our song to the Lord.

When my children were younger, there was nothing better than that time of the day when they were all in bed — most parents will appreciate that. I loved it on Saturday nights when they were in bed and I could sit on the settee drinking cocoa, or whatever, with my wife, waiting for *Match of the Day* to come on TV. The sheer excitement of the moment even caused me to put my arms round her. With that encouragement she snuggled up. Then maybe just before the first match I would give her a kiss on the cheek. She'd say, 'Either concentrate on me or on *Match of the Day*.' There is a level of concentration that is required in any loving relationship. There is nothing worse, so I am told by my wife, than my kissing her with one eye closed and the other looking at the television. In all seriousness, I believe there are times when God says, 'Will you give me your whole attention? Will you concentrate on me?'

How clearly focused is your worship and your praise? Do you bring that mind and that concentration into subjection and with all your heart concentrate on him? Listen to this: It is only to the extent that you have seen the Lord that you can truly worship him. Isaiah saw the Lord upon the throne. He was high and lifted up, and his train filled the temple. And the angels cried to one another, 'Holy, holy, holy is the Lord' (Is 6:1–3).

When Isaiah saw the Lord he gained a clearer perspective of himself and he also gained a clearer perspective of his generation. 'Lord, I am a man of unclean lips. I have seen you, Lord. Look at me. I have seen you, Lord. But look at the society I am living in. I have never really seen them in the light of your throne before.' Such a revelation could lead us into desperation and woes and yet more woes, and there would be some people who would enjoy that type of environment. But God didn't leave Isaiah there. God said, 'I know your problem. Here is the answer.' And he took some coals off the fire and touched his lips.

To every problem God has an application and an answer. There are many people who sit in our congregations week after week in the morass of self-condemnation. They enjoy their woes, and they go out still woeful. But God's purposes are not for us to remain in that condition. God's purposes are that we see his throne and know the provision of cleansing. What happened to Isaiah? He heard in a way that he had never heard before. God said, 'Look, you are in this generation. I need a messenger. Who can I send?' So a sense of destiny came into Isaiah's life because of what he had seen. Do you have a real sense of destiny in your life? Maybe it is that you haven't yet seen the Lord. Have you heard the voice of the Lord and have you responded, 'Lord, here am I. Send me'? Do you want to know what the ultimate of truly focused worship is? It is a life that is truly focused in living for God. Paul says, 'Therefore, in view of God's mercy, offer your bodies as living sacrifices' (Rom 12:1).

A clear direction

How many of you remember church services that were a little bit like spiritual bingo? 'What shall we sing? Number 44? We will sing Number 44, "He holds my hand, He holds my hand". Right, that was lovely. We haven't sung that for a few weeks, luv. That was great. Thanks for Number 44. What shall we sing now? Number 66. That's a good one. That was my mother's favourite "From the rising of the Sun".' Then we have 72, then we have 135 — so we have our spiritual bingo sessions.

We might say, 'We don't do that any more.' I know we don't. Do you know why? We've changed the game to 'Name that Tune'. How often are we halfway through a chorus before we know what it is? Before we know it we have drifted into a medley-sing-along style of worship, the only conceivable link from chorus to chorus being the key or the tempo of the song.

We need to be clearly focused in our worship and praise, and particularly focused in the theme. I believe in God speaking to a group of people in what I call 'the seasons of the soul' (cf. Eccles 3). I believe that a church will go through a period of time when God is speaking about the same thing week after week after week. Carlos Ortez, something of a radical, actually says that no church should have in its teaching programme more than three subjects in a year because he believes time should be spent on teaching a subject and giving opportunity for development and application. When the church is living in the truth and reality of the teaching, then, and only then, is it time to move on to the next theme. Sadly, we move on before the truth of what we have heard becomes a relevant part of our daily lives.

The Spirit of God, in a season in the life of the fellowship, will be speaking on certain themes and certain subjects. The choruses that God gave to us in

Lincoln started because of the desire to flow with what God was saying to us as a church at that time. We didn't just sing songs for the sake of singing songs. We wanted to sing songs that reinforced the things that the Spirit of God was bringing home to us. So if God was speaking about his lordship, for instance, then God began to give us songs confessing his lordship. There was a period of time when our Bible teacher, John Phillips, was giving a beautiful series of teaching on the workings of the Holy Spirit, and the typology of the Holy Spirit. At the end of this series of teaching the Lord gave me a song, 'Come Holy Spirit, Come just as You will'. There were several verses, each crystallising everything that John had been saying. God gave me this song and we taught it to the congregation. What was the result? They began to sing the truth that they had been learning.

Those things that we declare with the mouth, that we begin to sing, begin to speak, become a part of our lives. Such is the power of making confession. How many Scripture verses do you know simply because of the songs that are based on Scripture? God gave us songs that flowed in line with the teaching. We need to focus right into what the Spirit of God is saying at any particular time, not to go off at a tangent. That might mean that at your church God is going to raise up more and more song-writers who are going to bring the people the 'now song' of the Lord — songs that are clearly 'in tune'.

Something that we are learning right now in Lincoln is that the things we sing need to be brought into the perspective of the reality of experience. That is what prophecy is all about. It is a word from the Lord that needs to be applied. It's a challenging thought, isn't it?

Was there a challenging word from God last Sunday in your church? What did God say? Can you remember?

Most of us, by the time dinner is over, have actually forgotten what God said. That's incredible, isn't it? It is basically because we don't take these things to heart and see if there is need for application in our own lives. If there is a thing God is reinforcing to us right now in Lincoln it is that of lifting his name above every other name. Recently we knew a mighty breakthrough in God. Something of heaven broke out among us. How did it start? It started by the fact that we declared our intent to magnify the name of the Lord above every other name.

But we didn't leave it there. We named every other name that might come against it. So we spoke out the name 'apathy' and we exalted the name of the Lord above it. We spoke out the name 'lethargy' and we exalted the name of the Lord above it. We spoke out the name 'fear' and we exalted the name of the Lord above it. We spoke out about sickness and we named cancer and we exalted the name of the Lord above it. So often we allow circumstances to dictate to and dominate our spirits. There are fears that people have in their lives that so captivate their hearts and imaginations that the fears are actually exalted in their thinking. We need to reverse that and begin to lift up his name. 'Take captive every thought to make it obedient to Christ' (2 Cor 10:5). God has invested in that name all authority and all power.

That Sunday morning we saw things happen in the most tremendous way. We saw people healed; others were baptised in the Holy Spirit. There were people who moved into a new dimension of release in God, and there were people saved during the Sunday morning service. That was because we exalted his name. Radical worship is doing what we actually say we believe. So many of these things I have shared about predictability, about freshness, about being focused, we believe. But we allow ourselves to get sidetracked into something else.

One Sunday night in my congregation, we began to sing the song, 'Behold I am the Lord, the God of all flesh. Is there anything too hard for Me?' I stopped the meeting and asked what it was that people thought was hard, was a problem, and was difficult. 'Why not bring it into line with the One who is the God of all flesh, for whom there is nothing too hard?' I said. There were testimonies after that, where things were actually named and identified and brought into line with the God of all flesh, and God, as a result of this revelation, had his name returned to its correct perspective. Is there anything too hard for him? This is the dimension of prophetic worship that we need to move into more and more.

I trust that I have scratched a few parts that may be itching. I trust I have prodded a few parts that may be hurting, and that maybe one or two areas of our understanding have been opened up a little bit. But you see, my heart is set on being a worshipper because that is what the Father is seeking. I want to please my Father. I want to honour him. So the onus is on me and upon you to please the heart of the Father.

I want you to hear what God is saying and I hope that anything I mention which is mere debris will not be allowed to become cluttered in your hearts. It is possible for us all to be together, to listen to or to read the same things, but to understand and hear differing things. It is easy to jump ahead and think that things are being said that are not in reality. It's like a prayer meeting at which a Nigerian, for the first time, stood up and prayed a very halting prayer. He began, 'Lord, you are divine.' Then he just dried up. Some lovely sympathetic people began to fill that gap for him with, 'Hallelujah, glory to God. You're wonderful, you're the sovereign Lord, you're the divine Lord. Oh, you are a great God. You are mighty.' This encouraged him and he plucked up the courage to start again. He continued, 'And, Lord, we are de branches.' So don't jump to conclusions in the little gaps inbetween.

Honesty and sincerity

God is not wanting hypocritical praise. He does not require lip service. But he does require clean hearts, right spirits and those in whom joy is restored (Ps 51). The condition of our heart is central to the issue of praise. Pretence does not please God. Looking apparently enraptured by his presence when in reality heart and mind are wayward, distant or, at best, merely locked into neutral, does not please God.

Truth is a high priority in worship. The Father seeks truth. Far better to be honest and acknowledge that we are out of sorts than to seem outwardly to be consumed with love but be inwardly condemned for hypocrisy.

Someone once said that God is like a best friend: he doesn't mind if we're not speaking to him as long as he doesn't find it out from someone else. Begin to express the reality of your condition. Begin to state an intention to worship. My experience is that in giving praise and honour, a positive act of giving, something is renewed and rekindled in the depths of our spirits.

Responsiveness

Those of you who are leaders know what it is like when you are in front of people and the congregation are not with you. They're just not responding. It is hard work.

If you are not a leader who is up front, then encourage that leader who is. Be responsive to leadership. It doesn't cost anything. However, there is a dimension of leadership that most preachers know all about. There are times when the vibrancy and the anointing are missing in the meeting and you have to start from scratch. But you are a person under God, a person who is anointed, and you begin to minister in that anointing. Such is the gift of leadership.

Home-group leaders among you can encourage the people to be responsive. If there is lethargy in your church, don't blame anybody else but your leaders. If there is apathy in your church, look to the leaders. If there is criticism in the church, look to the leaders. The people will mirror that which the leadership sets before them. Leaders will feed through to the people various spirits and attitudes.

I am thrilled at the way my triplets — who are not saints — have responded to God, even when they were very young. If there was a worship tape playing they would be dancing round the room and lifting up their hands and they would be singing and clapping. They even managed to do it with *Songs of Praise* on the TV! You could say, 'They were only copying what they saw in you.' Yes. But there are other things that they could have copied. What are your kids picking up from you? What are your people in your home groups picking up from you? Because they will catch that sense of dissatisfaction and that spirit of criticism. Enthusiasm also breeds enthusiasm. What is sown in the hearts of people will be reaped. Leadership that is faithless also breeds faithlessness.

When you are in front of the people in a leadership capacity you have an awesome responsibility in how you respond and react. What do people do if something happens during the meeting and they are not quite sure what to make of it? They look to the pastor or to the leaders to see what their reaction is and then adopt the same attitude.

The reactions of a pastor I know are transparent. If something happens about which he feels heavy his head goes down — and so everybody else's head goes down. People will respond to that measure of leadership.

If you are on the platform as a pastor, elder, deacon, home-group leader or any position of leadership, people will look at you and will say, 'That is the way leadership responds.' Some people may have a desire in their hearts to be leaders and so might say, 'If that is the way a leader responds, I had better learn to respond that way too.' So it can work both ways. It can work for good and it can work for ill. You can bring a heaviness onto the meeting simply because you are standing there and not entering into praise or worship. Respond to the leadership. Encourage them.

I learned on a visit to Australia the three Es. One was the pursuit of *excellence*, another was the *energy* they exuded in God and the other was a sense of *encouragement* that came through.

Don't some people read the notices well? We appreciate them. Then let's say so. That is not just back-slapping if the spirit in which we show our appreciation is that of encouragement.

People will always rise to that level of encouragement. They will also fall to that level of discouragement. If you are for ever exercising the ministry of a Fire Brigade, people will eventually say, 'I will not get up because every time I do I get a soaking!'

We need to give people the privilege of failing. God isn't so put out by things as we are. We often imagine that when certain things happen God is rushing around heaven in an absolute frenzied panic: 'I don't know what to do. There were four tongues messages this morning.

What do I do?' God is not put out. God is bigger than our puny imaginations. He works outside the sight-lines of our blinkered vision. He is seated in the heavenlies. He is laughing in derision at his enemies. That's my God. Who is yours?

An environment of encouragement is a great thing. Nurture it. Don't lose it. But be responsive also, not just to the leadership but to the movings of the Holy Spirit. God is wanting worship that comes out of a desire to respond to his presence.

If there is a difference between praise and worship, it is, I believe, that praise can actually create an environment for the presence of God. Yes, God is there. God is present because 'God Is'. But there is that special manifestation of his presence where his glory fills the place. That is a level of praise that God inhabits. It is the praise of warfare. We need to respond to his presence.

I love the story of Mary before Jesus. Maybe Martha had just got used to Jesus being in Bethany. But not Mary. Mary could remember the time that Jesus came to Bethany when the smell of death was on the place. Mary could remember that where there was death Jesus brought life. Mary did not allow herself to forget. Sometimes we have grown accustomed to his presence. We no longer respond to him; we have taken him for granted.

Maybe you need to get out that alabaster box; that which will really cost something. It won't just be a matter of pouring out the contents and replacing the box on the shelf because it is a nice box and because it would be a nice memento of the occasion. Mary was prepared to do it as though it were for the last time. She wasn't hanging on to it for a keepsake afterwards. She wanted it to be a total expression of love.

Men, do you perhaps find it hard to pay that cost of emotion because, after all, you are a man? We need to learn to break the alabaster box and pour some of that emotion on the feet of Jesus.

The Spirit of God wants to reach those parts which nothing else can reach. You love God with all your heart, but have you put a barrier up? Have you got some 'nevers'? You might have been taught, ever since childhood, to bottle-up your emotions; taught that boys don't cry, boys don't show emotion; taught to 'be a man'. I want to encourage you to be a worshipper. Begin to learn to pay that cost and say:

> Lord, touch my heart just once again,
> Fill me anew with wonder;
> The wonder of Your love so free,
> The wonder that it included me;
> That I am now Yours eternally,
> Fill me anew with wonder.
>
> (*C. A. Bowater, 1985*)

There might be some other area in which you find difficulty in responding to the Lord. God isn't wanting technicians in worship. He's wanting responders, those who will respond to his presence. I don't know how you will respond to him. I don't know how you need to respond to him. But be responsive to his Spirit.

The world is waiting for prophetic worship. It awaits a people whose worship and daily lives demonstrate the reality of God's presence. My prayer is that God will teach us, help us and lead us; that he will bring into our lives the reality of his presence; that our lives will be real manifestations of the truths about him; that wherever we go there will be a fragrance about us because we are saturated in his presence; that we will live lives of reality and be relevant to the society we live in — in our homes, in our place of work; that we might be a prophetic people bringing the 'now word' of the Lord to this generation.

My prayer is that God will not only hear our words but scan our hearts that he might see that desire to bless him, to surround his throne with blessing; that he might see our love for Jesus and thankful hearts full of adoration and gratitude and worship.

Jesus, I worship You,
Worship, honour and adore Your lovely name.
Jesus I worship You
Lord of lords and King of kings
I worship You
From a thankful heart, I sing
I worship You.

(*C. A. Bowater, 1982*)

PART 3

Discovering the Potential of Your Priesthood

Discovering the full potential

Hands up all those of you who are old enough to remember the days when the only musical instruments used in worship were the organ or the massive old piano, played by the dear lady who had been 'in the way' for forty years. If that's still the scene, please ignore this comment and continue.

The radicals then combined in duo the piano and organ (frequently the Hammond variety) but for some reason put them at least a platform's length apart, often creating a torturous stereophonic effect. Needless to say that musically and sometimes literally 'never the twain did meet'.

The advent of guitars in worship caused many hands to be raised . . . not in praise but in horror! They 'twanged' and were said to be worldly. Guitarists swayed in time to the music and were viewed as being sensuous. I can remember being part of a gospel group nearly two decades ago who were firmly instructed by an austere church leader to play 'but not wiggle'.

The introduction of drums and electronic instruments was surely therefore the last straw, seen by many as the decadence of Babylon, the sign of the times, demonic. We were told, 'There'll be dancing in the church next,' and there was . . . and is (and is to come, world without end, etc).

Very important message

Anyone having problems in accepting the development and proliferation of musical instruments in the context of praise and worship should perhaps take a pair of scissors and remove, for starters, whole passages from the Book of Psalms.

It is so important to know and accept that God actually enjoys music. Can we imagine what a chorus of ram's horns would sound like? God even makes room for *noise* as long as it is joyful: 'Shout for joy to the Lord, all the earth. Serve the Lord with gladness; come before him with joyful songs' (Ps 100:1–2).

God is not offended by joyful, loving exuberance, though lukewarm religious hypocrisy makes him sick.

The restoration of many varied sounding instruments is right in line with what God really enjoys. He loves to see all our creative resources released as an expression of praise and honour.
Note:

1. Drums are not worldly — but you can get drummers who are.
2. Electric guitars are not unsanctified — but sometimes the people who play them are.
3. 'Holy things' (buildings, icons, organs, etc) do not exist — just holy people.

Let everything be done (let all the instruments be played) *decently and in order*, but for God's sake.

Let everything be done

Let's respond and not be reactionary when it comes to coping with change. I am convinced that one of God's many dealings with his people in the wilderness wanderings was to teach them the challenge of change. They were called to be a people who 'followed the cloud'. If they were to know God's continued presence and guidance, along with other criteria, when the cloud moved they had to move on, regardless of how inconvenient or unsettling it was. Strange how the Comforter can sometimes make us feel so uncomfortable!

Lessons from history

From as long ago as the sixth century the contemporary and traditional became a point of conflict. The chants sung in the monasteries during the ecclesiastical reign of Pope Gregory I were monophonic — hovering around a few notes without any sense of harmonic colour. Without doubt the style was initially improvisation and not without similarity to the free worship the early church must have enjoyed (cf. singing in tongues). Free expression became canonised by the Roman Catholic Church and the style became a mandatory part of the liturgical service.

Contemporary spontaneous expression of spiritual life became forced into the death mould of tradition as soon as religious authorities declared, 'This is the way it has to be done.'

In the sixteenth century a new move of God brought with it many new songs. Martin Luther said: 'Next to theology, I give music the highest place and honour. Music is the art of the prophets, the only art that can calm the agitation of the soul; it is one of the most magnificent and delightful presents God has given us.'

Luther adapted and translated Latin hymns, making them available to the ordinary, non-scholastic person, and wrote many new hymns in the German language — some to secular tunes. He was much criticised for doing this!

Calvin, however, rejected these new trends and *banned* all songs of human composition, harmonies and musical instruments. His followers continued in the traditional ways, singing in unison to the 'Geneva Psalter'.

Fear always reacts by banning, being legalistic and becoming segregated from contemporary reality.

The Methodist revival of the early eighteenth century caused many things to change, as God used men like Isaac Watts and Charles Wesley in a whole new wave of music.

In 1861, however, controversy was once more in the air as *Hymns Ancient and Modern* was published for the Anglican Church. Breaking away from unison singing, chordal progressions and harmonies were added. These harmonies were considered to be sensual! The established church found it hard to receive the new music.

D. L. Moody teamed up with Ira Sankey to produce the *Sankey and Moody Hymn-book* in 1875, using contemporary dance styles such as the waltz. The established church reacted negatively towards this 'worldly music' — even though thousands of sinners received the gospel through these songs!

William Booth of 'Why should the devil have all the best tunes?' and Salvation Army fame was criticised by the religious establishment for using secular and militant tunes. However, masses of the world's poor and needy met Jesus through this music.

The Pentecostal revival in Britain at the beginning of the twentieth century renewed zeal and enthusiasm, as well as a new generation of hymns, many focusing on the second coming of Christ. A new phenomenon was the abundance and increasing popularity of choruses. Short and memorable, these embryonic statements of faith reflected renewed joy and fervour. They were criticised as being mere ditties, musically and poetically trite, and, not without some truth, as being theologically and doctrinally weak.

The charismatic renewal, along with Scripture in Song, brought spiritual refreshment to even some of the most tradition-bound denominations in the early 1970s. And because the life and expressions of the Holy Spirit are not bound by cultural, political or religious boundaries or traditions, the true church of Jesus Christ is in a constant state of renewal and restoration.

The earth will be filled with the glory of the Lord, and his kingdom will come on earth as it is in heaven. Individually and together we are in the process of change. All that God requires is hearts that are willing.

The purpose of instruments

Church musicians are vital contributors to the atmosphere experienced at services. If they get it right, technically and spiritually, they will almost surely help to bring the congregation into blessing. If they get it wrong, at best they will be an embarrassment; worse still, an obstruction to the spiritual flow of the gathering.

We are seeing an extraordinary proliferation of musicians actively participating even in the most liturgy-based services. In what was once the domain of the organ alone, guitars, drums, woodwind, string and brass instruments, percussion and all kinds of electronic gadgetry are now commonplace in many worship and praise celebrations.

Musicians, as you serve the body of Christ and minister to the Lord on your instruments, may I encourage you to extend the boundaries of known abilities and enter into the fullness of your potential — the potential of your priesthood.

1. 'Sing for joy to God our strength; shout aloud to the God of Jacob! Begin the music, strike the tambourine, play the melodious harp and lyre' (Ps 81:1–2).

The most obvious purpose for instruments is to accompany singing, to provide melodic, harmonic and rhythmic support to hymns and praise and worship songs. It's vital for the instruments to make the songs feel right in respect of pitch, volume and tempo. The art of accompaniment is an advanced skill. Accompaniments must never dominate, but can direct. To provide appropriate and differing timbre according to the style and message of the song is a vital consideration.

2. 'He appointed some of the Levites to minister before the ark of the Lord, to make petition, to give thanks, and to praise the Lord, the God of Israel . . . and Benaiah and Jahaziel the priests were to blow the trumpets regularly before the ark of the covenant of God' (1 Chron 16:4, 6).

Amid other duties the Levites, priestly musicians, were appointed by David to surround the ark of the Lord continually with thanksgiving and praise, in song and on the instruments. On their instruments they ministered to God in his presence. God must love music. The psalmist exhorts us to 'come before him with joyful songs' (Ps 100:2), and frequently implores, 'Sing to the Lord a new song' (Ps 96:1).

How limiting it would be if our involvement as musicians was merely to accompany singing. We minister to the Lord directly, we serve him as we play. Therefore, make every note intonated, every harmony completed, every rhythm created and every melody weaved a meaningful, worshipful act of service to the Lord. That, as we will see later, implies greater care and preparation in what we do.

3. 'Praise the Lord with the harp; make music to him on the ten-stringed lyre' (Ps 33:2).

The playing of instruments must be an extension of a praising instrumentalist. A player with a worshipful heart can create worshipful music. We must first of all be praising people — worshippers first, instrumentalists second. That's why God entrusted to the priestly tribe, the Levites, the awesome responsibility of surrounding his presence with music. They could handle it. Their priorities were right.

4. 'Elisha said, ". . . now bring me a harpist." While the harpist was playing, the hand of the Lord came upon Elisha, and he said, "This is what the Lord says . . ."' (2 Kings 3:15–16).

So many times I have experienced that Holy Spirit anointing upon instrumentalists where, from that platform of inspiration, the word of the Lord, the prophetic utterance, has been brought to the people of God. The instruments prepared the people for prophecy. Music has inherent power — it can stir or soothe the spirit, it can inspire or incite, bring deliverance or destruction. Under the anointing of God the Holy Spirit it can lay bare and prepare the heart to receive the word of the Lord.

5. They '. . . prophesied, using the harp in thanking and praising the Lord' (1 Chron 25:3).

'I will turn my ear to a proverb; with the harp I will expound my riddle' (Ps 49:4).

How about the thought that as well as the playing of instruments preparing the people for prophecy, the instruments can in fact be played in a prophetic manner themselves? Given that the instruments are extensions of the players, the music an expression of their hearts, should it therefore be impossible to believe that the prophetic spirit can be stirred within the heart of the instrumentalists who declare it in the way they know best, through the music? I would imagine that most of us have at some time listened to music — symphony, sonata or whatever — and confessed that it had spoken volumes to us. We actually attribute speech, words, thoughts to something that is without lyrics. The music spoke to us. Sometimes, music can touch on those areas of emotions, dreams and aspiration that no amount of words could express. I believe in prophetic playing. None the less there may be times when it is necessary to clothe the melody with understanding.

6. 'Make two trumpets . . . use them for calling the community together . . .' (Num 10:2).

The instruments should call the people together and lead them in worship. Remember, it was the Levites, those who lived and moved in the dimension of their priestly calling, who were the instrumentalists. They did not play before they were prepared in heart and spirit. Truly they could lead — they had got themselves ready! In truth that cannot always be said about most of our congregations. They arrive and stumble into church in varying stages of readiness and willingness to worship and praise the Lord. The musicians should be ready, if their calling is true, to lead the people in the journey of praise into the intimacy of throne-room worship.

How profitable to the local church to have anointed and separated musicians who, as they begin to minister to the Lord, begin to draw in the people so that together they can make that ascent from things temporal to timeless worship!

7. 'When you go into battle . . . against the enemy who is oppressing you, sound a blast on the trumpets. Then you will be remembered by the Lord your God and rescued from your enemies' (Num 10:9).

'Spiritual warfare' is an in-vogue subject, and quite rightly so. Ephesians 6:12 says, 'Our struggle is not against flesh and blood, but against the rulers, against the authorities, against the powers of this dark world and against the spiritual forces of evil in the heavenly realms.' The enemy of the church is not people, systems or military powers, but spiritual powers and forces. We must therefore not dissipate our energies by fighting and standing against things that are not really our enemies. If our enemy is spiritual then the resources given to us by God to do combat and win victories will also be spiritual. 'The weapons we fight with are not the weapons of the world. On the contrary, they have divine power to demolish strongholds' (2 Cor 10:4).

I recommend a book by Terry Law entitled *The Power of Praise and Worship* (Victory House Publishing). He identifies our weapons not as guns, swords, knives or the like, but as rockets:

Rocket Weapon 1. The word of God: giving to us health, new birth, light, food, cleansing and victory — in all resisting Satan.

Rocket Weapon 2. The name of Jesus: recognising that God has invested power and authority in the name of Jesus to resist the activities of Satan.

Rocket Weapon 3. The blood of the Lamb: the blood that resists the accusations of Satan, the enemy, and declares our righteousness so that we, who are made clean by his precious blood, can face the 'accuser of the brethren' and with Paul say that by the blood of Jesus, we are justified and made righteous just as if we had never sinned (Rom 5:9), and having been redeemed, forgiven, cleansed, made righteous and sanctified (1 Cor 6:19–20), Satan has no place in us and no power over us.

Spiritual rockets require spiritual launching-pads. These include prayer, preaching, the word of testimony, praise and worship.

Terry Law says:

> When praise and worship are loosed by a group, there is a tremendous amount of power generated. Psalm 22:3 says that God inhabits the praises of His people. When we praise

God together, God inhabits our praise. Because corporate praise involves the power of agreement, the power of coming into harmony, there is a tremendous spiritual energy generated (op. cit. p. 117).

Musicians, be equipped by the Spirit of God to lead the people into a dimension of praise that will make inroads into the enemy's territory. As the spirit of praise explodes among you, you will begin to see the fall-out of blessing and deliverance from the enemy.

Paul and Silas prayed and sang praises to the Lord in the midst of their prison darkness, when hurt and in pain. In offering their sacrifice of praise, their prison, the stronghold, was shaken and they were set at liberty.

Has it ever occurred to you how it was that young David had the confidence to take on the warlike Goliath? What was his training school? Did he read books on 'How to Kill Giants'? His preparation was in the hillsides as he looked after his sheep. There he got to know God, the God of all creation. He would look around at the hills, the fields, the flowers and the birds and declare, 'The earth is the Lord's, and everything in it' (Ps 24:1). He would look up at the night sky and see the moon and the stars and state, 'The heavens declare the glory of God; the skies proclaim the work of his hands' (Ps 19:1). Before you take on giants you need to know that the God in whom you trust is all-powerful.

Not only did David develop an awesome awareness of the greatness of God, but in those many hours of solitude he developed a relationship with God: 'The Lord is my shepherd . . .' (Ps 23:1); 'The Lord is my light and my salvation — whom shall I fear?' (Ps 27:1). Before you face giants it's necessary to have a personal walk and relationship with God.

We know too that in the course of his work, David

killed a bear and a lion — God delivered them into his hands. Before you fight giants, know what it is to defeat the bears and the lions of daily experiences: habits, attitudes and desires. Unless they can be overcome, the 'Goliaths' in our lives can never be defeated, but God will deliver them into our hands for us to do something about them. God will only reward us with public victories when we know victories privately.

May our worship 'in spirit and truth', and divine inhabited praise, bring many captivated hearts into liberty and release, and healing to hurting and broken hearts.

8. 'God has ascended amid shouts of joy, the Lord amid the sounding of trumpets' (Ps 47:5).

There is a dimension of praise that God feels sufficiently pleased with to 'inhabit'. Another paraphrase suggests that he sits enthroned in the midst of the praises. A throne is intended for a king. The praises of God's people can herald in the presence of the King. How often we sing, for instance, 'Jesus, we enthrone you, we proclaim you our King.'

The song goes on to develop the concept that he is standing among us, but as we worship we build a throne. God does not desire to stand among his people as if unwelcome or a spectator. He wishes to reside, and to sit down on something that is appropriate to who he is. He is the King of kings and Lord of lords. He deserves a throne. Instrumentalists, know this: the music that is required is that fit for a king. Herald in his presence. Swing wide the gates and let the King of glory come in. Let us declare his majesty, with joy, dignity, clarity and that very special unction of the Holy Spirit which transforms the ordinary into something that is mighty in God.

In 2 Chronicles 5 we read of how the people of God

practised and prepared to receive the return of the ark of the Lord into Solomon's Temple. After years of floundering and mistakes, the total symbolism of the presence of God was returning to where it belonged. As the people sang and the trumpets sounded, the Bible reveals that God was so overjoyed at being welcome, that even he must have felt that he had 'come home'; that he could not be confined even to the proportions of human imagination, and his glory, his manifested presence, filled the temple.

We may know very little of such an experience, but let our spirits long and thirst for a revelation and manifestion of the presence of our God.

Fill the place Lord with Your glory
At this gathering of Your own.
Reign in sovereign grace and power
From Your praise surrounded throne.
Fill the place Lord with Your glory
At this gathering of Your own.
We exalt You, we adore You,
Thankful hearts now join as one.
You're the Christ, the King of Glory,
Father's well beloved Son.
Fill the place Lord with Your glory,
At this gathering of Your own.

(C. A. Bowater, 1984)

The organisation of the music team

The chief musician

The chief musician has very strong scriptural foundations. He was someone who was directly accountable to the king and had the responsibility to choose, develop and direct the musicians and singers in the temple services and feast days.

In David's tabernacle there were three main chief musicians: Asaph, Heman and Jeduthan or Ethan. We also read in 1 Chronicles 15:22 of Chenaniah who because of his skill and his position as the head Levite 'was in charge of the singing'.

Something about the names of these chief musicians reveals the qualities necessary for those aspiring to, or already in, such a position in the local church.

Asaph: There is not an abundance of information to show us the kind of man Asaph was, other than that along with other chief musicians he was specially anointed, gifted and chosen to minister in music. There is something, however, more revealing about the man's name.

114

Today, little thought is given to the naming of our offspring other than, perhaps, fondly naming them after a favourite Bible character, relative or friend. There was a time when names were given because their meanings were perfectly representative of the person's appearance, occupation or personality, or merely summed up the aspiration of the parents for their child.

Asaph meant 'one who gathers together and removes reproach'. Isn't that a beautiful name?

The chief musician needs to be an Asaph. Music goes beyond being just an art form. It is not neutral. It has the power to influence, damage, corrupt, destroy, bless, soothe, build up, heal and deliver. Satan is using music as a supernatural tool in these days to bind and destroy many young lives. How much more then can God, the Creator of all good things, use music as a powerful means of blessing, inspiration and fulfilment of his purposes in these last days.

There can be a great unifying work of God done through music. Every week, as your congregation comes together from so many differing circumstances and conditions, varying in willingness and readiness to worship and praise, be an Asaph, gather the people together into one central purpose, to exalt the Lord our God. People tend to carry into church many heartaches, senses of failure, disillusionment and sorrows. They need to have their hearts and minds gently centred on the Lord and away from the place, people or programme.

As the people are gathered together and the musicians minister the anointing of God, in his presence, those with feelings of loneliness, bitterness and self-reproach can know, as it were, healing ointment being poured out into their lives. So often self-condemnation lies like a thick cloud over people. They come into the service and leave at the end in exactly the same state of heart and mind. They have neither been gathered together with the other worshippers nor made any personal sacrifice of praise, and consequently they have not allowed themselves to be changed in his presence. The spirit of self-condemnation must be replaced with a sense of being God's child, of belonging, and the eyes that are downcast and inward-looking must be uplifted to behold the Christ. For when we behold him, we are changed.

Gather together, remove reproach and focus hearts and minds on Jesus.

> When I look into Your holiness,
> When I gaze upon Your loveliness,
> When all things that surround
> Become shadows in the light of You.
> When I've found the joy of reaching Your heart,
> When my will becomes enthroned in Your love,
> When all things that surround
> Become shadows in the light of You,
> I worship You,
> I worship You.
> The reason I live is to worship You.
> (*Wayne & Cathy Perrin, © 1980 Integrity's Hosanna! Music/ Thankyou Music, PO Box 75, Eastbourne BN23 6NW, UK*)

Heman: He too was gifted and chosen, but his name meant 'one who is faithful'. Much emphasis in society today is given to spectacular, fantastic and generally over-the-top styles of behaviour, but the essential quality required in the kingdom of God is that of faithfulness. The ultimate benediction is, 'Well done, good and faithful servant' (Mt 25:21). The final commendation is not for how skilful or ingenious we have been in the work of the Lord, but how faithful.

Faithfulness requires endurance and determination to continue, particularly when it would be the easiest thing to quit. There are times, particularly when dealing with people — specifically musicians — that frustration and exasperation can seemingly overshadow every good desire and vision. Then, qualities of faithfulness are put to the test.

Psalm 88, interestingly, is associated with Heman. It's not a psalm of glorious victory, a sense of overcoming or general well-being. It speaks of being near to death (v. 3), of being without strength (v. 4), of being forgotten (v. 5), of being separated from friends (v. 8), of being rejected (v. 8) and more! Not exactly a 'walking in faith and victory' style song! But Heman the Ezrahite was a faithful man, faithful to his calling and faithful to his God.

Jeduthan/Ethan: The name means 'one in whom is consistent or permanent praise'. Praise had become a part of his lifestyle. It wasn't switched on when the occasion demanded. It was as much a part of him as was breathing.

Have you met people like that? How beautifully infectious and influential is their spirit. They are just as exposed to the rigours and hassles of life as the rest of us, but in everything, every experience, they can still return praise to God. No longer are they dictated to by circumstance or feeling. They have learned to reign in life and not lose that sense of desire continually to return to give God his due. No problem in life changes the fact that God is worthy to receive all honour and praise. Jeduthan did not live a yo-yo spiritual existence — in giving praise to God, he was consistent.

Fundamentally, I believe that praise is caught and not taught. Principles can be imparted but that sense of heart adoration can only be ignited by the Holy Spirit of praise within us.

Often, as I have travelled with my musicians and singers, I have seen congregations change from icy indifference or abject apathy, to real enthused expressions of praise. That they were merely being stirred up could be a valid criticism. God, however, is in the business of stirring up spirits. Haggai 1:14 says, 'The Lord stirred up the spirit of Zerubbabel' (see also 1 Chronicles 5:26; 2 Chronicles 36:22). Surely God in us would desire us to encourage, exhort and motivate his people into an expression of praise: 'It is fitting for the upright to praise him' (Ps 33:1); 'How pleasant and fitting to praise him' (Ps 147:1).

Chenaniah: This name means 'one who is established by Jehovah'. Do not desire, seek, or even remain in the position of chief musician if you do not have unshakeable confidence in the certainty of your calling. At best you will be a square peg in a round hole, but more important you must discover that place and function in the body of Christ that is meant specifically for you. Furthermore, by being the wrong person fulfilling the chief musician's role, you are hindering the right man or woman from entering into their God-ordained ministry. Perhaps, even more seriously, by being the wrong person in this key position you could in fact be an obstruction to the clear flow of the Holy Ghost among the people in your fellowship.

Give careful consideration to these issues. They may save you many years of frustrated ministry. The church of Jesus Christ has been littered over the years with the debris of well-intentioned people — pastors, teachers, evangelists and the like — ill-equipped misfits, frustrating the workings of God. Chenaniah had an inner security that was not based on what other people thought about him, or even on a recognition of his obvious skills, but on the fact that he was established, called and equipped by God.

Practical implications

Realistically, the chief musician must have:

Good grounding in the word of God. It is not sufficient to be super-abundant in natural skills, knowing all there is to know about harmony and counterpoint, compositional techniques, arranging skills and performance credibility. But the chief musician does need to be fully established in scriptural principles. Not necessarily a theologian, but well conversant with the Scriptures.

Leadership qualities. If you are to lead, people will have to want to follow. There must be a strength of character manifesting itself in communication skills, faithfulness, ability to exercise authority and to behave at all times with compassion. Musicians can often be temperamental, frequently over-sensitive and, generally speaking, hard to handle.

Organisational ability. In many growing churches the quality of musical activities can be mind-blowing: choice for different ages, worship groups, gospel rock groups, soloists, teams of musicians, productions involving drama and dance, recording sessions, video recordings, theory classes, instrumental tuition, travelling ministry and maybe more. All these are a normal part of the musical life in my church. There are also the services to minister at, of course! The organisation and co-ordination in itself can be a full-time job without the added desire actually to be creative in the writing of original material.

By the way, the philosophy held by many, that it is only necessary to 'rely on the Lord' or wait for the 'moving of the Spirit', holds little credibility. Planning and organisation do not have to be divorced from the need to wait on God and know the Holy Spirit's guidance. They are compatible. Most people operate with more security if they know in advance when and where they are needed. Do not take your musicians or singers for granted. Plan ahead and communicate your plans precisely. However, do not become bound up with a legalistic spirit but make allowances for the unexpected!

A prayerful love for the ministry and musicians. If you try to function without prayer, it is like a car being run without oil. Inevitably the crunch comes. Friction arises, something blows up, and the whole thing becomes non-functional. Every step and decision must be exposed to the oil of prayer.

Every person in your care needs your prayers. The musicians too are having to struggle with their own emotions, perhaps senses of inadequacy, and of course they have to cope with you!

A love for the congregation. You are a servant. To minister is to serve. Our service for God stems best from a love relationship with God and with God's people.

I was recently meditating on the scripture in Ephesians 4:15 in which Paul implores the people to speak the truth in love. Have you ever been on the end of an 'I love you, but . . .' statement? Usually the 'but' covers a multitude, dare I suggest, of sins! As I considered the verse, I began to recognise that the only environment in which truth is secure is that of 'being in love'. A couple in love can share truths, maybe about each other, without a sense of being under attack and without the need to become defensive. In that environment of love for each other it is understood that the well-being of the other person is the main priority.

Chief musician, you must fall in love with your congregation. You may not always feel that love reciprocated, or feel appreciated, but your love for them has got to be without measure or favour.

Does that remind you of someone? Of course. As we become more like Jesus we will love as he loved. His compassion will become ours. His priorities will find a central place in our hearts.

Choosing and appointing musicians

Pray for the musicians you need. I had the privilege in 1984 of visiting Australia and, in particular, the New Life Centre in Sydney. This church had seen phenomenal numerical growth in the six or seven year period of existence under its pastor, Frank Houston. He recalled that in the early days of his church he had received very clear direction from the Lord that music, or more specifically worship and praise, was to be a key for future development. He began to pray that God would send in the right person to head up the music in the church. The more he prayed, the harder the heavens seemed to become. He could not understand how it was that, having been given this secret by God, the answer to his prayer was so delayed. By spiritual revelation, he realised that he wasn't getting an answer because he wasn't asking the right question. It was something like the time when God said to Moses, 'What is that in your hand?' (Ex 4:2). God was wanting to show Moses that he already had the resources at hand to be a man of authority under the power of God, as long as he was prepared to surrender even those things that humanly speaking appear to be insignificant.

As God revealed to Frank Houston these principles, to his alarm God also identified the answer to the prayer: a young man already in the fellowship. Trevor King at that time was a recently converted ex-drug addict hippie. The long hair, casual clothing and laid back attitudes were still a part of his lifestyle. After much argument with God, Pastor Houston eventually, almost reluctantly, agreed to approach Trevor. In asking him to play at the next Sunday service, Frank inwardly prayed that the long hair might be cut, the shorts replaced by normal trousers and the open sandals by shoes. At that Sunday service, to his pastor's horror, Trevor appeared in his usual non-conformist clothes but, as he started to play, the anointing of God the Holy Spirit became evident.

Trevor King eventually became full-time Director of Music, founding with Frank Houston a creative ministry centre *par excellence*, and is now a pastor in his own right.

'What is that in your hand?' Only a pianist, maybe a guitarist, nothing terribly significant. Pray for them, pray with them and release them to the Holy Spirit. Encourage other latent gifts and talents within the church. I have often known people who gave up their involvement in music as soon as they became Christians, thinking that perhaps it might cause unnecessary problems in their new way of life. Stir up these hidden abilities, expose them to the potential of the anointing of the Holy Spirit.

Taking lessons. Encourage younger musicians in the church to be involved in junior groups. I have initiated a system among my own musicians whereby senior instrumentalists coach and develop the younger people. There is an excellent principle here of giving encouragement which I believe God can bless.

Do not expose your very young musicians to playing in the main services — even out of a desire for involvement or boosting the size of the band. It is a mistake for two reasons. Inexperience can promote discouragement, and frequent discouragement can lead to youngsters with potential giving up unnecessarily. Also, playing for worship is not merely an activity, an extension of a hobby. It is a spiritual ministry. As with all ministries, together with the pleasures there are the responsibilities. It is not fair to let young musicians, who are often spiritually immature, face such responsibilities.

Maintaining standards. I was delighted when a number of my frontline musicians asked for advice regarding taking private lessons. They all wanted to be 'stretched' technically so that they could be more effective in their playing. This was obviously going to be an investment of time and money and, for some, real sacrifices had to be made. It is very easy to become musically stale, and even a brief series of lessons can help to freshen up attitudes and understanding.

However high the standard of performance is, it is without real merit if it is not matched spiritually. In choosing musicians, who are exposed to the possible dangers of pride and jealousy and so much more, consideration of their spiritual maturity and consistency is altogether valid.

Establishing ministries. Pray for and with each musician, individually. Seek always the blessing of the Holy Spirit upon each of your instrumentalists. Make sure of their calling. It is essential that they are not misplaced in their ministry. Constantly cover them with prayer, that they might become established and rooted in God in such a way that there can blossom something that will have fruit for the glory of God.

The hurt of not being asked to be part of the music team is not as great as the hurt of being asked to step down from that position. Be careful when appointing musicians.

Practise together regularly

Pray together as a team. Not the hurried 'God bless us!' prayer, but lingering times of waiting on God and praying for and with each other. Many of us hide behind our instruments. Our involvement covers up a multitude of hurts and anxieties. In fact, in church life in general a role or a position held can be used as a convenient mask. Musicians must learn to pray as well as play. There is a great unifying quality in prayer. That environment of being open before God, honest and forthright with him in front of colleagues, is spiritually healthy. One learns more about people from hearing them pray than from hearing them play their instruments.

Honesty and commitment. Musicians are very defensive creatures, especially if ability or musical interpretation is brought into question. However, if a level of gracious honesty does not exist between members of the team, real progress will not be made, either spiritually or musically. The know-it-all, got-it-all and done-it-all syndrome is deadly for the team relationship. It's a cul-de-sac from which there is no going on.

Note that I use the words 'gracious honesty'. My experience has been that truth has not always been clothed in love. Truth, taken out of that setting of being 'in love', is not always edifying. We must certainly be open to the truth — about our playing, attitude, reliability, and so on.

Commitment is one of the current 'in' words. But really there is no air of mystery surrounding it. Commitment is faithfulness — faithfulness to God and to his people; to the vision of the church and its outworkings. Where there is love there should be commitment. What are the implications?

We need to be committed to each other's spiritual growth, development and success. A competitive spirit is not conducive to making progress in committed relationships. Commitment is all to do with relationships. When marriage vows are taken, the promise is made to stand by each other 'in sickness or in health . . . for better or worse . . .' and so forth. There is no opting out of real commitment just because times may become hard. I have a poster on the wall of my office, showing a baboon neck-high in mud. With large penetrating eyes he implicates everyone that looks at him and says, 'We're all in this together!' There are no exclusion clauses in commitment.

I will stand by my musicians publicly and privately. There may be things that I don't like. Certain attitudes may need to be corrected, but I will always show them complete loyalty. I expect that loyalty to be returned and shown among the whole team.

Have a goal. If you aim at nothing, you'll probably hit it! For a practice to disintegrate into a free-for-all 'jam session' is perhaps the most common of all side-tracks. Know where you are going. Have a goal for your rehearsals. It may be to learn a new song. To teach a song with confidence takes time — time to be sure of the lyrics, tempo and arrangement. When it comes to teaching the song to your church, your confidence (or lack of it) will be conveyed and mirrored. The aim of the rehearsal may be to conquer difficult keys or new chords or to prepare a 'special' for the Sunday night service. Whatever, always have a goal. Be disciplined and you'll be more productive.

Insist on punctuality. If the practice is scheduled to start at 8.00 pm, be there on time. And that doesn't mean 7.59 pm. Allow enough time to set up and prepare so that the real rehearsal can begin at 8.00 pm. There are some people who can always be relied on to be late. Without being legalistic, if anything is worth doing, then let it be done properly. Time is easily lost and wasted through indiscipline. It has been my experience that the one who is always late to the practice is usually a principal player, and consequently the main thrust of the rehearsal cannot begin until that person has arrived. Patience is stretched, and frustrations rise among those who scheduled their day to be there on time.

Establishing priorities. It has been my observation that the committed musicians can be among the busiest members of the fellowship. This may induce certain stresses and pressures that must be recognised and relieved. The establishing of priorities is paramount. This may be taken for granted but needs restating: the first priority is a personal relationship with God — for from this alone can any blessing flow. A first-hand, relevant and refreshing relationship with God must be established in the lives of all who seek to minister. Anything less will produce mechanical, lifeless service. Musicians, be sure of your calling and discover more of the heart and mind of the One who called you!

Vitally important too is the keeping of good relationships within the family. Do not neglect family responsibilities. It has been said often that God made families before he made the church. How often, though, we see even Christian families suffering neglect because a father or mother is taken up with 'the Lord's work'. My desire is that my children are not switched-off because my involvement in ministry robs them of a dad around the place. I want to be a good father. I want them to see just how exciting life is, how great is is to live in the revealed will of God. I want them to love life, to love God and serve him with a full heart. In it all, I am the priest in my home. I have a responsibility to love and serve my wife even as Jesus loved and served the church. There is no credit if in the midst of all my serving the Lord I actually fail to give my wife love, time and attention. We now try, with some success, to write into the weekly schedule a family time and a time for being together. If communication on a domestic level falls apart, everything else will become meaningless.

Young musicians too, honour your parents. Treat them with love and respect. I believe in having good strong family relationships as the foundation for ministry.

If you are involved in secular employment, make sure your testimony is clear and strong. Don't be one thing at work and something else in the church. Let your ministry flow out of a lifestyle that honours God.

Take care of your health. Be sensible. Over-tiredness can so easily lead to sickness. If you're ill it's hard to fulfil your musical responsibilities. You could be letting down a pastor who relies heavily on you. Our bodies are the temples of the Holy Spirit and need to be treated with care and respect.

Do not commit yourself to a ministry that consistently won't be fulfilled. Be aware of the cost of time factors involved. Keep yourself and your ministry in correct perspective to life. We need to be complete people, separated to the purposes of God but living life to the full. We must be visual aids of what it means to have abundant life. With regard to other interests: clean, healthy pursuits are vital if we are truly to relate and communicate with society today. Let us not be known for what we don't do but for what we are!

Strive always for excellence. Most of us settle for something below what we are capable of. Do not avoid playing in the key of E^b major simply because you find it difficult. Certain songs are written in that key because it is the one best suited to its mood and melody. You can rob a song of its intrinsic qualities by transposing it simply for convenience into E major. If the theory of music baffles you, ask God to give you understanding. If playing by ear is a mystery, ask God to give abilities. Whatever the situation, work hard at improving technique. Give yourself whole-heartedly to the task.

At the service

Arrive early — not just in time for the pre-service prayer meeting but before it — to tune up your instrument and make sure the musicians' area is tidy. I hate having to step over trumpet cases, bags and coats, music stands and the like. When you're ready, don't mess about. Remember, folk are arriving at church and don't need the atmosphere of several impromptu recitals. Join the prayer meeting. You've tuned your instruments, now get tuned in yourself. Pray and worship together with the other musicians (who have also arrived early!).

Position instruments so that there is a good sense of ensemble. There must be visual contact with the chief musician and maybe also with the pastor. Watchfulness and alertness are essential. Many of our charismatic-type times of praise and worship have so much variety, making eye contact vital. I have known musicians who have not only kept their eyes closed but have seemingly blocked their ears too. I once knew a lead guitarist who would frequently get lost in wonder, love and oblivion. He would plough right on through prayers and the like. I eventually pulled the plug on him. Even then there was a fraction of a moment before he realised anything was different!

Don't play all the time. It's not a race where we all start together and try to finish as close to each other as possible. Sometimes a song will be best served by leaving out certain instruments. Listen to each other. Sense the tapestry of sound as instruments weave in and out of the texture. Sense the movement of the Spirit of God.

Enhance the song with the qualities your instrument can bring. Don't destroy the atmosphere.

Take time out from playing. Put your instrument down and get involved in the praise and worship. Your playing must be an extension of your praising. Technical proficiency is not sufficient. You need to be a worshipper first, a musician next. If your own personal walk with God is faltering, have the courage to stand down from musical involvement. Take time when you can be ministered to instead of always giving out. You cannot minister out of spiritual dryness. Become refreshed in God, then with renewed joy serve the Lord with your playing.

Provide continuity — musically and spiritually. There are times when the musicians can underscore, for instance, the reading of the word of God, out of which can flow a relevant song. An instrument played gently during spoken links can preserve the flow and spirits of a service, but this must be done sensitively and must never dominate.

Pitch and tempo are two contributing factors to the success of a chorus or hymn. The pitch of the song must be comfortable for the large majority of the congregation: too high and most people will give up; too low and the song will lack impetus, drive and penetration. Carefully selected modulation from verse to verse can in fact enhance a song and help to bring a sense of climax.

Tempo also is frequently not considered. Sometimes we settle for a mid-tempo feel for most of the songs which tends to produce a mid-tempo level of praise. Excitement often needs to be injected for the song to become genuinely up-tempo. There are some worship songs that become more intense, more personal, if the tempo is really slowed down. Certain choruses and hymns with real growth potential lend themselves to multi-tempo treatment.

Simplicity. While it's great to learn all the beautiful augmented, diminished, major seventh and ninth chords, there are times when simplicity is of the essence. Genius is doing the simple things well. Congregations that like to sing in harmony can be easily confused and discouraged by musicians heavily into chord experimentation. Our motivation is not to be obscure or 'clever' but supportive of meaningful, fulfilling worship.

Begin and conclude the songs tidily. A clear, well-thought-out introduction can assist confident singing. There is no need to stop and give the starting note each time as if to say, 'On your marks, get set, go!' Learn to create introductions that provide the correct impetus for songs, and when the song is finished, let the music clearly suggest the drawing of it to a close. Introductions and endings require plenty of rehearsal.

Bless the people with your servant's heart. Allow God to minister through you to them. Don't isolate yourself or only meet with those who can talk about music. Be an encourager of the people. You have an immeasurable privilege in serving them. Serve them joyfully. Don't grouse or moan, murmur or back-bite. Reject the 'no one understands us' syndrome that obsesses many young musicians. Seek always to play under the anointing of the Holy Spirit. It's difficult to define. It's not always easy to know what it is but it is very easy to recognise what is isn't!

Selah. Musicians, pause for a moment. Consider all that God is saying to you. Think on his claims for your life and ministry. Remember, first and foremost, it's not your ability that God is after — but your availability. Just as the musicians were considered a treasure in the courts of the kings of Israel and the rich, so the Lord will consider you a treasure in his house as you minister him.

The singer and the song

Singers, by the very nature of their inherent skill, are frequently over-rated in their own eyes and, in the eyes of others, under-rehearsed. The human voice needs to be gently coerced, shaped and developed. Lose your voice and you've lost your ministry. However, this finely balanced area of good voice and good spirit is vital.

Singers, dare to take a good look at yourself and allow God to make you into a 'vessel of honour' (2 Tim 2:21).

Singing to the Lord involves our whole being: our spirits, our emotions and will, and our intellect. But the most important ingredient is our spirit. 'God is spirit, and his worshippers must worship in spirit and in truth' (Jn 4:24). Secular music is performed to impress or to move others emotionally. God's music goes beyond that, because it ministers life and truth by presenting and glorifying Jesus. This can only be done when the singers, the instrumentalists, the instruments themselves and the songs, are anointed — that is, saturated in God's Holy Spirit. Without the presence of the Holy Spirit in our lives and ministries we have nothing to offer except mere words and pretty music. But when we are anointed, and the presence of the Holy Spirit is upon our instruments and voices, we minister according to what is God's desire and will for a particular service. It is not talent that breaks the yoke over people's lives and sets the captives free but, as Jesus said, 'The Spirit of the Lord is on me, because he has anointed me to . . .' (Lk 4:18–19). The same Spirit that was upon Jesus is capable of radically revolutionising our ministry, causing us to serve with power and authority.

> The Spirit of the Lord,
> The Sovereign Lord, is on me
> Because He has anointed me
> To preach Good News to the poor.
>
> And He has called on me
> To bind up all the broken hearts,
> To minister release
> To every captivated soul . . .
>
> Proclaiming Jesus, only Jesus,
> Jesus, Saviour, Healer and Baptiser,
> The Mighty King,
> The Victor and Deliverer,
> He is Lord . . .
>
> (*C. A. Bowater, 1985*)

The singer and the Spirit

'Out of the overflow of the heart the mouth speaks' . . . and sings (Mt 12:34).

Prepare your heart through prayer. There is no short cut to knowing blessing on your ministry.

> Oh, ye who sigh and languish
> And mourn your lack of power,
> Hear ye this gentle whisper:
> 'Could ye not watch one hour?'

For fruitfulness and blessing
There is no royal road;
The power for holy service
Is intercourse with God.

> (*Author unknown.*
> *From Dick Eastman,* No Easy Road
> [*Baker Book House*])

God is looking for those with dedicated hearts, willing to work at prayer. The word of God declares: 'The effectual fervent prayer of a righteous man availeth much' (Jas 5:16, AV) or, to put it another way, 'The one who is in good relationship with God and gives himself to prayer will see much accomplished.' Perhaps we don't see a lot happening spiritually through our ministries because we don't truly apply ourselves to prayer.

Teach me,
Teach me how to touch Your throne,
Teach me how to bring Heaven down,
To release Your power.
Teach me,
The wonders of the secret place,
Teach me,
Teach me how to pray.

Teach me,
Teach me how to touch Your heart,
Teach me what it means to have faith
That can mountains move.
Teach me,
How even I can seek Your face,
Teach me,
Teach me how to pray.

Prayers of the righteous man availeth much,
And righteousness exalts a nation,
Come holy fire of God and sanctify,
To intercede for restoration.

Where shall we turn?
Turn to the Lord!
How shall we cry?
Cry with all our hearts.

My soul shall wait on Thee
O Lord, my God,
From Thee alone
Comes our salvation.
O God, be merciful,
Turn not away,
Let saving health
Flow through the nation.

(C. A. Bowater, 1984)

The preparation must begin with praying for the forgiveness of sin: 'If we confess our sins, he is faithful and just and will forgive us our sins and purify us from all unrighteousness' (1 Jn 1:9).

Sin allowed to linger in the life wrecks all real usefulness for God. It will rob us of joy and potential power. For us to be effective in serving God, sin must be removed. The psalmist said, 'If I regard iniquity in my heart, the Lord will not hear me' (Ps 66:18, AV). Unconfessed sin automatically blocks the ears of God. Humble prayer and confession — 'Have mercy on me, a sinner' — in an instant releases a flood of forgiveness (Lk 18:13).

Prayer defeats Satan. His accusations and innuendoes are stifled as he is presented with the blood of our Lord Jesus Christ that makes us clean from every sin (1 Jn 1:7). See also Revelation 12:11: 'They overcame him by the blood of the Lamb.' Forgiveness removes Satan's finger-hold on our lives.

'Prayer, real prayer, intelligent prayer, it is that which routs Satan's demons for it routs their chief. David killed

· the lion and bear in the secret forests before he faced the giant in the open' (S. D. Gordon, *Quiet Talks on Prayer* [Grosset and Dunlop, New York]). Each time you sing, pray for God's anointing. Without the anointing we can do nothing, we are nothing (Jn 15:5). It is only the Spirit of God flowing through us that will genuinely affect lives. Many can be impressed, stirred, even emotionally moved by fine singing, but it is the Holy Spirit's working in us that actually changes people: 'You will receive power when the Holy Spirit comes upon you' (Acts 1:8). God is ready to extend this power to those who will pray (Acts 2:17–18).

We can so easily plough on 'working for the Lord', relying on fleshly energy, ideas and ideals. It is not service or work that is required, but fruit. What is the fruit of your ministry? 'If a man remains in me and I in him, he will bear much fruit; apart from me you can do nothing' (Jn 15:5). See also Zechariah 4:6: 'Not by might nor by power, but by my Spirit.'

If the ministry in song is clearly recognised and is not seen as simply a programme filler, it will then come into line with the criteria for all ministry. Christian work, whatever the manner of extending Christ's kingdom, inevitably means a collision with opposing forces. We keep forgetting that 'our struggle is not against flesh and blood, but against the rulers, against the authorities, against the powers of this dark world . . . spiritual forces of evil in the heavenly realms' (Eph 6:12). We get nowhere until these are overthrown. Religious pomp often provides a hiding place for dark spirits. Mere preaching or fine singing will not remove them. Only an openness to the Holy Spirit, an aligning with the throne of God, and a realisation as to our true position in Christ, will bring effectiveness against our enemy. Furthermore, we need not and cannot expect to see

Holy Spirit manifestation if our lives are not continually saturated by his power. We cannot live how we like and still expect God to reveal his power (Jas 4:7).

> Come Holy Spirit, come just as You will,
> Softly and gently as breezes so still.
> Come as a rushing wind, mighty in power,
> Come Holy Spirit, come now.
>
> Come Holy Spirit, as flames from the fire,
> Cleanse me, empower me, my being inspire.
> Come as the healing oil liberally poured,
> Come Holy Spirit, come now.
>
> Come as a torrent, as waves on the sea,
> Sweeping away all that would hinder me.
> Come as refreshment, as streams from the hills,
> Come Holy Spirit, come now.
>
> Come Holy Spirit, come just as You will,
> Work in and through me, Your purpose fulfil.
> Make me much more like my Saviour, I pray,
> Come Holy Spirit, come now.
>
> Cause me to live as a child of the King,
> One from whom worship and praise freely spring,
> Bring Holy Spirit revival to me,
> Come Holy Spirit, come now.
>
> (*C. A. Bowater, 1982*)

Evaluate your motives. Keith Green has said:

> What we idolise, we ourselves desire to become with our whole heart. A lot of people want to be just like their favourite gospel singer and performer, and they seek after it with the same fervour that the Lord demands we seek after Him. We insult the Spirit of Grace to make a place for ourselves rather than a place for Jesus.

The Bible says, 'As a man thinketh in his heart . . . so he is' (Prov 22:7, AV).

As a youngster, I never fully understood why it was that my dad would put such emphasis on the importance of motives. Just about every week he would warn his congregation about guarding motives. Enlightenment must come with age, and now more than ever I see this area of our lives as a key. The carnal life seeks to make a reputation, preserve it and project it. The Christ-like attitude is to make ourselves of no reputation.

It is essential to die to self-made ambitions and goals. Singer, know what it is to be dead! This is not an excuse for false humility. 'I'm really nothing very special,' can sound very humble and spiritual. The true test is to see the reaction when someone else tells the same person, 'You're really nothing very special'! One learns most about people by their reactions and not by their actions. Paul said, 'I have been crucified with Christ . . .' (Gal 2:20). In every respect the 'I' in our lives must be crucified. What 'I' am, what 'I' think, what 'I' want to do and so forth. The 'I' is central to sin and therefore to separation from the purposes of God. The 'I' must be crucified and must only know resurrection in the life of Christ. Without his life, I am nothing.

What I am speaking about is not a sporadic experience; it must become a part of our lifestyles. We need daily to learn to deny ourselves (Lk 9:23). Following Jesus demands a day-by-day, moment-by-moment willingness to be identified with his cross if we are to know Easter fruits in our ministries.

When people die they forgo any rights on life, rights of reply or bargaining rights, and they are buried. The chapter on this life is closed. In spiritual terms, the problem is often that we claim to be dead but refuse to be buried. There needs to be a death and burial of all that is represented by the old life if we are to bring forth the fruits of Christ's new, indwelling life (Jn 12:24–25).

We may as well delete the verse in Scripture which declares that 'the old has gone, the new has come' (2 Cor 5:17) if we are not prepared for it to be worked out in our own lives. If it is to be powerful in our lives, the truth of the word of God must not only be acquired but applied. Let's be radical and actually do what he says.

Hands up all those of you who have never been asked, 'What's your ministry?' Not many, I imagine. Have you noticed that when they say 'ministry', it's said as if there were some mystical quality attached to it. I must confess to becoming a little weary of the 'My Ministry' syndrome. It is time to take the capital 'M' out of ministry.

Don't get me wrong. I do not for one moment disregard the importance of finding a place in the body of Christ. I reckon though that I know a few who have found theirs — they're pains in the neck! Praise God for his giftings to the church, but the superstar image is inappropriate to those whose true desire is to minister. 'Let this mind be in you, which was also in Christ Jesus who . . . made himself of no reputation, and took upon him the form of a servant . . . humbled himself, and became obedient unto death' (Phil 2:5–8, AV).

So, you have a ministry? Then be like Jesus, become a servant. To minister is to serve.

First, surrender that inflated ego. Singers, be honest now. How much time, either consciously or subconsciously, do you spend feeding off people's reaction to what you do? We all like and need encouragement. There should be more of it around. However, ultimately it could become a very self-centred exercise and lead to a self-gratifying existence. What we are is more important than what we do. A reputation is what other people think about us. Character is what we really are. That's why Jesus made himself of no reputation. It didn't really matter what people thought about him. He knew who he was. If you have the potential to minister, it need not be supported by boastful claims. What you are will be recognised by those with the ability to 'see'.

Secondly, be a servant. Jesus took upon himself the form of a servant. This concept is so contrary to the in-vogue claim that we, the Christian population, are going to take over the world. Sure, I believe we are 'in training for reigning', as John Phillips would put it. Certainly those who are 'in Christ' are seated with him at the place of real authority (Eph 2:6). The conquest, however, will not be by authoritarian, dictatorial methods but through servanthood. The spirit of the kingdom of God is that of a servant. Then God will cause those who serve to be exalted, but exaltation must not be confined by our narrow thinking.

To minister is to serve. No promise of glamour or frills. Simply serve. Those who seek to minister will, by necessity, develop a lifestyle of service and let that spirit of servanthood be proved (1 Tim 3:10). Servants will have a deep awareness of their responsibilities and a particular regard for authority. A servant will always come under authority. To serve is to have a submissive spirit. 'Lone Ranger' ministries are not a part of the kingdom of God (see Matthew 20:26–28).

Thirdly, there is a need for separation. The call to holiness is as pertinent today as it ever was. 'Be holy because I, the Lord your God, am holy' (Lev 19:2). There is a need for separation from the trends and standards of this age. We are to be an alternative people — a holy nation set aside for God's glory.

> You shall be unto Me
> A kingdom of priests
> A holy nation
> Set aside for My glory.

Hear My words and obey,
Keep My covenants every day,
You're My chosen special treasure,
Mine alone . . .

> (*C. A. Bowater, 1985, from Ex 19:5–6*)

Maybe you have sung, 'Fill this place, Lord, with your glory.' You and I are the temples of the Holy Spirit, and his glory can only fill that which is anointed and separated to his purposes (1 Cor 6:19).

Finally, let those of us who seek to minister, to serve, be steadfast. 'Stand firm. Let nothing move you. Always give yourselves fully to the work of the Lord, because you know that your labour in the Lord is not in vain' (1 Cor 15:58). Faithfulness is a prerequisite. It's no good having a servant who cannot be relied upon. It appears that the musicians referred to so often in Chronicles had a set time to minister. They fulfilled their calling faithfully, stood at the posts, played when, how and for as long as they were required. Faithfulness is one of the most overlooked virtues in the lives of Christians today.

The world should know what God is saying, because the church is living and saying it. We should see that in all areas of our lives, wherever we are, we are steadfast in all we do.

So we have a ministry? We're servants of Jesus Christ and his body? Then let us 'wait on our ministering' (Rom 12:7, AV). Let us humble ourselves before God, in awe that he should ever choose to work through us. Let's be more like Jesus.

Study and meditate on the word of God. Colossians 3:16 beautifully shows how the abundance of song will emerge from the richness of God's word in our lives: 'Let the word of Christ dwell in you richly as you teach and admonish one another with all wisdom, and as you sing psalms, hymns and spiritual songs with gratitude in your hearts to God.'

The word of God provides perspective. It keeps us in our rightful place and puts God firmly in his, as the One who is 'seated in the heavenlies', laughing in derision at his enemies (Ps 2). The word of God is penetrating, causing motives and intentions to be truly evaluated. It is powerful, sharper than a 'double-edged sword' (Heb 4:12).

Your Word, O Lord,
Is truth unchanged, unchanging,
A constant firm foundation,
So steadfast and secure.
All that there is written
Remains, and ever shall be.
Life itself shall fade away.
Your Word alone endures.

Your Word, O Lord,
Directs in paths of righteousness.
Lamp and radiant Light,
The way is clear to see.
Word of God, instruct Your people
And in our hearts be hidden,
Planted there, Lord, let it bring forth
Fruit, abundantly.

Your Word, O Lord,
Is healing to the nations.
Your Word reproves, corrects
And ministers peace.
Lord, cause us to turn once more
To the precepts You have given,
To the life-imparting words
Of pardon and release.

Your Word, O Lord
Is full of penetrating power,
Piercing even the parts
That sin would cause not to yield.
Living, energising Word, now
Activate Your people.
Revolutionise our living
And in our hearts be sealed.

(C. A. Bowater, 1984)

Dealing with two enemies: jealousy and pride

Jealousy robs you of your God-given goals and gives you bitterness of soul. Without wishing to offend, my experience has been that singers are prone to jealousy more than most. I think it's because the human voice is considered to be inseparable from the person — unlike with instrumentalists. Implied criticism becomes much more of a personal issue. Therefore the interrelationships between singers are prone to more personal problems.

Realise that jealousy comes from the devil. Such an attitude of heart 'is earthly, unspiritual, of the devil' (Jas 3:15), and where it exists '. . . you find disorder and every evil practice' (Jas 3:16). That's pretty clear, isn't it? The devil, Lucifer, is the author of confusion. He's an expert on jealousy.

The name Lucifer means 'light-bearer' or 'daystar'. It also means 'the anointed cherub that covereth' (Ezek 28:14, AV). Lucifer had been given a special, distinctive commission from God, different from that of the other archangels, Michael and Gabriel. Lucifer was the anointed cherub who covered the glory of God. He had a special anointing from God for ministering to God and covering the glory of God with music. Before his fall, Lucifer led the angelic host in praise and worship to the Father.

However, sin entered the picture. Isaiah 14:13–14 describes how it happened: Lucifer took his eyes off God and onto his own beauty and brilliance. He became filled with jealousy and pride. He began to desire worship for himself instead of being willing to give worship to God. As a result, Lucifer gained one-third of the angels and they were cast out of heaven because of their rebellion.

Jealousy is rooted in Satan. Guard against it. Reject it. Desire success for your brother and sister, encourage them, prefer them to yourself. 'Be devoted to one another in brotherly love. Honour one another above yourselves' (Rom 12:10).

Keep your eyes on your own attitude and standards; don't keep comparing yourself with others in a negative way (Gal 6:3–4); strive for excellence in ability and spirit. By all means learn from those with greater gifting and desire equal measure, but let your desires be without spite or bitterness — let them be holy desires. Always acknowledge the giftings of others and be prepared to consider them as better than yourself (Phil 2:3). Refuse to be drawn into the competitive spirit of the age. Don't let striving become sin.

Whole church fellowships can be devastated if jealousies are allowed to run rampant. Learn, and let the truth go deep into your spirit, that what you are right now, is only because of the grace of God; and so it is with your brother and sister in Christ. And that grace is sufficient (2 Cor 12:8).

Pride will blind you to the truth. You are deceived if you think of yourself more highly than you should (Gal 6:3).

Pride does not survive the scrutiny of the throne of God. We cannot enter deeper into God until all 'flesh-life' has disappeared. The knife of the cross must be applied as never before. Our availability to God is not based on the principle that he would be at desperation point if it wasn't for us. He probably experiences more desperation because of us. Our service, our availability, is not on our terms, but on his. Singers, we must be wholly available, to be used, or not to be used. If you can't cope with that, don't sing a lie, 'Here I am, wholly available. . . .' Availability in the spirit of servanthood means that when God beckons, we move; when he doesn't, we stay put. It's a hard lesson to learn. Often we think we have learned it then someone else is selected in our place and we find all the old feelings of rejection, hurt, bitterness, jealousy and pride resurfacing. Folks, it's time for another funeral service. The remedy can only be repentance, humility and developing a teachable heart.

'If we confess our sins he . . . will forgive us' (1 Jn 1:9).

'Humble yourselves before the Lord, and he will lift you up' (Jas 4:10).

'Clothe yourselves with humility towards one another' (1 Pet 5:5).

'Act justly and love mercy and walk humbly with your God' (Mic 6:8).

How to handle applause

It's a funny thing. That outrageous ego that makes a person dare to stand on a platform and say, 'Listen to me,' has to be crucified, it has to be dead and buried, but then still be able to stand up in front of people with a selfless motivation.

Applause can be hard to handle. How many of you have been totally at a loss to know what to do when a congregation has broken into spontaneous applause? What do you do? Smile out of embarrassment? Bow?

Look bewildered? Don't be afraid of applause. Rather, receive it as though gathering praise offerings to the Lord. Deflect applause that is offered to you, as a thank offering to God. Maybe you can join in and with the congregation offer your own thanks to the Lord.

At the end of the day, be sure to offer an evening sacrifice to the Lord, blessing him for all that he has enabled you to do. Give him the glory, recognising that it is only what he has done in you that has enabled him to work through you.

Maybe you have been lost for words when someone has come and thanked you for a song that you have sung. It has perhaps ministered in a real way into their lives and they want to convey gratitude. Always receive these compliments graciously. It's good that people can feel free to say 'thank you'. Encouragement never hurts anyone. It's when we allow all the well-intended encouragement and compliments to change our perspective of ourselves that things can begin to go wrong. Anything that gets out of its true perspective can become sin. It has been said of secular entertainers that problems begin when they start to believe their own press releases.

Keep in mind at all times that we are what we are only by the grace of God (1 Cor 1:26–31). As soon as we start taking too much credit for giftings and abilities, that's when any anointing leaves us. We may impress and influence many with the natural ability we possess; people may pass remarks on the quality of our voice, diction, breath control, sincerity; but none of even these desirable attributes will actually cause a life to be transformed. Ultimately it's 'not by might nor by power, but by my Spirit' (Zech 4:6). Take the ministry in song seriously — but don't take yourself too seriously. It's good to strive for perfection, but there will be times when you will make mistakes; times when you'll want the floor to open up so that you can just disappear; times when you'll not want to face anyone; times when you'll feel a fool.

How to overcome stage fright

I can remember the very first time I sang a solo in front of a congregation. My voice had only recently broken and I had delusions of grandeur. George Beverley Shea could now stand aside — the voice that was to melt a million hearts was to be launched.

The rehearsals were fine. They always are! But when the time came to stand up, my legs turned to jelly. There suddenly seemed to be a million miles of communication between my brains and my legs. I tripped up the steps on to the platform. I looked up at the congregation and whatever was causing my legs to malfunction now began to affect my eyes — the people literally seemed to be enveloped in a blurring mist. The organist began the introduction and gave me the starting note. By now my ears had caught the dreaded disease: was this the song that we had rehearsed? I must have conveyed my dilemma by the blankness of my expression. We had a second, a third and a fourth go at the introduction. In sheer panic during the fourth introduction, I stepped out into the unknown. By the third line of the song, after a series of squeaked notes, wrong words and variable pitch, I managed to home in on a close resemblance to the tune.

I still get nervous, but nerves and stage fright are vastly different. Nerves can be a useful way of getting the adrenalin pumping. Stage fright destroys.

The best remedy for stage fright is to place your confidence firmly in the Lord. Without fail I always say to the Lord, 'Lord, without your help I can do nothing,

I am nothing.' Confession of a need is a great starting point. God never lets down those who are prepared really to rely on him.

'The Lord is my light and my salvation — whom shall I fear? The Lord is the stronghold of my life — of whom shall I be afraid?' (Ps 27:1).

'When I am afraid, I will trust in you . . . in God I trust; I will not be afraid. What can man do to me?' (Ps 56:3, 11).

'Dear friends, if our hearts do not condemn us, we have confidence before God and receive from him anything we ask, because we obey his commands and do what pleases him' (1 Jn 3:21–22).

Be God-conscious and not people-conscious. What is the true source of our motivation? Whom are we singing for? For people, yes, but more realistically for God. We must want to please him first by our attitudes and desires. 'So we make it our goal to please him' (2 Cor 5:9). We are going to be answerable ultimately to God for what we do in his name. The day will come when every motive will be clearly seen for what it is.

Be prepared

Along with every spiritual preparation there must be a practical application. Time, energy, effort and prayer must go into our ministries; any calling must be substantiated by work. It says in James 2:17 that faith without works is dead; work without faith is useless. Any real ministry will find its proof in our full commitment to it.

'Do your best to present yourself to God as one approved, a workman who does not need to be ashamed . . .' (2 Tim 2:15). There is more to singing a song than might be immediately apparent.

1. The choice of material is determined by the occasion, by the listener and not the least by your own abilities. Great care should be taken over the choice of songs. If more than one or two songs are to be sung in sequence then the question of balance has to be considered. Experience alone will teach how this is done.

2. The accompaniment will either enhance or ruin your song. The relationship with your accompanist is vital (whether it's a single pianist or an instrumental group). They need to be involved in all stages of preparation, including prayer, and fully appreciated for the way they serve the more 'up front' ministries.

3. Don't necessarily sing the song in the original key. That key may not suit your voice. Discover the right key for each song.

4. 'Practice makes . . .' Well, let us at least strive for perfection! Take time to learn each song thoroughly. Find out the places in the song where there are problems of pitch or phrasing, diction or delivery. Memorise the songs. Using a book can become an unnecessary prop. It may even become a distraction for the audience if not handled correctly.

5. Always be natural. There is no greater turn off than a poseur. Be yourself. Look and feel comfortable. Don't be for ever apologising to the people; if a song is worth singing it doesn't need apologies. Be careful that you don't talk too much between songs. Your gifting is singing — don't detract from it with links that are too lengthy. If a song has to have a great build-up or explanation then perhaps it's not that good a song.

6. Always be flexible enough to change a song or the order of songs if prompted by the Holy Spirit, either before the meeting or on the platform.

I am so blessed with the singers God has placed in Lincoln. Flexibility is not an easy lesson to learn, but it sometimes means we have to be adaptable enough *not* to sing — in spite of all the planning. Sometimes the Spirit of God will move during a meeting making the ministry in song totally surplus to requirements. My singers have learned what it is to lay aside their ministry as God requires. It sometimes involves a change of plan. Here, the singers now know that all plans are 'God willing'! Some people cannot cope with this. They have to have written details and plans in triplicate. Flexibility is the only way in a Holy Spirit-led environment. You can only truly be flexible when you are truly fully prepared.

The song-writer

'Dear Chris, the Lord has given me this song. I wonder if you could tell me what you think of it . . .'

Apart from the problem of passing an opinion on what 'the Lord has given', more and more these days there seems to be a blossoming of song-writers who are looking for some guidance and direction. My files at the moment are bursting with new material sent to me, from old and young, each reflecting a freshness but also revealing a measure of frustration — what to do with this new flow of creativity.

As I looked through the pages of manuscript recently, I began to reflect on my own development as a song-writer, and particularly with God's dealings in my life.

My first efforts as a writer were inflicted on children! When I was fifteen I would spend weeks of the school holidays helping on beach missions on the Lincolnshire coast (this was years before the Lord led me to live in the county). To think of some of the things I did to piano accordions in those days! But how the children sang! In fine weather and more often not-so-fine, the gospel was sown into many young hearts. It was here that God first challenged me. He showed me the potential of spiritual truth, clothed in an easy-to-remember tune, in the hearts and lives of young people. The children would take these songs into their homes and many letters confirmed the impact they made.

Opus 1 No. 1 was a gentle, waltz-like tune:

Gentle Jesus, Saviour and Friend,
I will love You right to life's end
For You died on Calvary's tree
To save a sinner like me
Like me,
To save a sinner like me.

And a little later:

With my God, nothing is impossible
With my God, all things can be done.
Yes, my God can revolutionise the one
Who looks to Him
To cleanse from every sin,
Yes, my God can do it
Yes, my God will do it
For He's a good God.

During my years at the Royal College of Music in London I drifted into a 'strange land' where the 'songs of Zion' were neither sung, played nor written. But the Lord, in his abundant mercy, rescued me and when I was at my lowest ebb, spoke into my life and graciously restored me to himself. A very short while after my reconsecration the Lord began to give me new songs. The one at that time that was particularly special and relevant was 'Kneeling at the Cross'. The second verse says:

How could I reject such pardon?
This heart though hardened
Dear Lord would yield.
Now I see my real condition
Sinful position
In Christ revealed . . .
See how agonised He suffers
His only words . . .
Lord forgive . . .
Kneeling at the Cross of Calvary
In deep contrition
I humbly bow.

Then and now that song has a special place in my heart.
It was like an altar built, a reference point with God.

At the same time I wrote a chorus that I still believe
to be important:

Calvary love, grow in my heart,
Calvary love, glow in my heart,
Calvary love, fill every part
Revealing Christ in me,
Revealing Christ in me.

(1976)

And so began a flow of songs that were direct products
of a relationship with the Lord. Songs that expressed
what God was saying and conveyed what God was
doing. Songs to encourage to love and to holiness. Songs
to exhort and challenge people to 'reclaim the territory'.
But with the flow I also knew the frustration. Would
these songs — that I believed were God-given — ever
be released beyond the local fellowship? It seemed they
never would.

Then eighteen years ago came the move to Lincoln.
Where's Lincoln? If you look on the map it seems that
nowhere leads to Lincoln . . . and that's where God
took us: Rachel, a very poorly two-year-old; Lesley, a

very pregnant wife; and me, a very ambitious school teacher. During the first twelve months we would gladly have gone back to Solihull! God, however, was beginning to reprogramme my life, to rechannel my ambitions.

The Lord began to move in the Lincoln Assembly. It manifested itself in renewed vision, a flow of love, a depth of commitment and a release in praise. Songs, too, began beautifully edifying the fellowship: 'I'm enjoying being loved by Jesus'; 'I delight greatly in the Lord'; 'I confess that Jesus Christ is Lord'; 'Jesus, your love has melted my heart'. There had been a major turnabout in our attitude to songs in praise. They changed from being programme fillers, pre-meeting warm-ups, to becoming an outward expression of what God was doing in us.

It was here, almost by accident, that the songs began to be released to the body of Christ. But in all this time of waiting, God had taught me a vital lesson. There was little merit in the songs being released in isolation, as an entity in themselves; they flowed out from a reservoir of blessing, from an atmosphere where the Spirit of God was at work. The songs were just a part of the great thing God was doing among us. Thus the tapes 'Abba Father', 'In the Presence of the Lord', 'Jesus Thou Art Precious' and others have reached every continent. When God releases, he does it well!

PART 4
The Power of God's Presence

Comparison of worship

Much has been written developing the theology and principles of the restoration of the tabernacle of David, and I am not attempting to add to this. Sufficient to say that God is no longer interested in animal sacrifices, because of Christ's perfect atoning sacrifice. God's desire today is to hear the sacrifice of praise coming from the lips of his people, the church. The voice of praise will be heard in a new way in these last days as the praise and worship of the tabernacle of David is restored to the church, the bride of Christ.

The tabernacle of David gives us the New Covenant way of praise and worship for the New Testament church and church age. David, by faith, tasted of what really belongs to us. We are the 'new creation' people of Psalm 102:18 and therefore we will experience the fullness of Zion, which is praise and worship and the power of God's presence achieving great things for us. See Acts 16:25–34, for what God's power did for Paul and Silas in prison.

David had brought back the ark of the covenant (or the ark of God's presence) and placed it in his tabernacle

153

on Mount Zion (1 Chron 15:1). But as it is with so many today, many in David's time preferred to remain with the old way of worship. While David and many of the people worshipped God in great freedom before the ark in the tabernacle of David on Mount Zion, ten kilometres away at Mount Gibeon people continued to worship under the old ritualistic order in the tabernacle of Moses. But the tragedy was that God had forsaken the old tabernacle (Ps 78:60) and chosen Mount Zion (Ps 78:68; 132:13). The power of God's presence was at Mount Zion, not at Gibeon!

The purpose of comparison is not to be divisive but to be decisive. Ultimately, we must come into line with that to which God has given his seal of approval. His presence is the ultimate seal of approval.

The tabernacle of David

In the tabernacle of David, worship was characterised by vibrant sound; new songs in abundance; music (1 Chron 23:5); praise (1 Chron 16:4); clapping (Ps 47:1); shouting (Ps 47:1); dancing (1 Chron 16:29; Ps 149–150); lifting up of hands (Ps 134:1; 1 Tim 2:8). None of these was known in the tabernacle of Moses. In the old tabernacle only the High Priest ministered before the ark, whereas in the tabernacle of David all the Levites ministered before the ark (1 Chron 16:37). In the tabernacle of Moses there were animal sacrifices, but the tabernacle of David knew only spiritual sacrifices (Ps 27:6; 116:17; 1 Pet 2:3–5; Heb 13–15). As the writer of Hebrews said, we have not come to Mount Sinai, 'but you have come to Mount Zion' (Heb 12:22).

The Psalms give us a picture of how they praised and worshipped at the tabernacle of David (Ps 146:1–7; 148:1–6; 149–150). The overriding principle is this: God is enthroned on, or dwells in the praises of, his people (Ps 22:3).

> The Lord inhabits the praises of His people
> The Lord inhabits the praises of His people,
> The presence of the Lord addeth joy
> The blessings of the Lord maketh rich,
> The flow of Holy Ghost anointed worship and praise
> Brings release, brings release.
> Hallelujah, the Lord's joy is my strength!
> Hallelujah, my inheritance is sure!
> Hallelujah for this liberty
> In Christ I am kept free —
> Hallelujah, Hallelujah — Praise the Lord!
>
> *(C. A. Bowater, 1981)*

The people of Zion

'From Zion, perfect in beauty, God shines forth' (Ps 50:2).

In the power of God's presence, there will be salvation, baptism in the Holy Spirit, healings, deliverance and victory (Ps 87:5–6; Obad 17; Is 12:6; 33:5, 14). God is going to give his Zion people a double portion of his anointing to come against the powers of spiritual darkness. 'Be glad, O people of Zion, rejoice in the Lord your God, for he has given you a teacher for righteousness. He sends you abundant showers, both autumn and spring rains, as before' (Joel 2:23).

Isaiah 61:6–7 tells us more of the blessings in store for the people of Zion:

And you will be called priests of the Lord, you will be named ministers of our God. You will feed on the wealth of nations, and their riches you will boast. Instead of their shame my people will receive a double portion, and instead of disgrace they will rejoice in their inheritance; and so they will inherit a double portion in their land, and everlasting joy will be theirs.

Satan is letting loose all he can against the church to cause it to topple over. He is trying to finish the church, but we, as the feet, bear up the whole body!

Our forefathers had a measure of revelation but we are going to enter into the fullness of 'all truth' (Jn 16:13). 'The path of the righteous is like the first gleam of dawn, shining ever brighter till the full light of day' (Prov 4:18).

God has a glorious path for the people of Zion to tread, but we need to realise that there will be great pressures on us and that we will need to stay alert. Jesus said, 'Watch out that no-one deceives you' (Mt 24:4), and, 'Watch and pray so that you will not fall into temptation' (Mt 26:41).

Amos brings a timely word of caution: 'Woe to you who are complacent in Zion' (Amos 6:1). The time of great blessing can also be the time of great temptation. Don't become comfortable, careless, complacent, proud or unfaithful. The study of Abiathar and Zadok, the priests during the tabernacle of David period, teach us about this.

Abiathar was faithful to David during his wilderness testings and during the rebellion of Absalom. But was he reliable to the end? Sadly, no. He failed to support David at the rebellion of Adonijah and consequently lost his position and forfeited his ministry (1 Kings 2:26–27, 35). Just one moment of complacency and careless unfaithfulness. That was all that was needed. Abiathar was at the place of blessing but still fell to the temptation of a momentary lapse of zeal.

Zadok, who was the priest at the tabernacle of Moses at Mount Gibeon, was elevated to priest at the tabernacle of David and the temple of Solomon. Why? Because he remained faithful to God and to God's anointed men. And so, in Ezekiel 44, there are two groups of priests mentioned. The higher group is named after faithful Zadok. They will come nearer to the Lord and stand in his presence (Ezek 44:15).

Even David fell to temptation. He became careless amid all the blessings of Zion (2 Sam 11:14). He trusted in his own strength, in making a count of his fighting men (2 Sam 24).

But, like David in his earlier days, let us remain humble, faithful to God and dependent upon God and it will be for us as it was for him, who '. . . became more and more powerful because the Lord God Almighty was with him' (2 Sam 5:10).

And so: 'To him who loves us and has freed us from our sins by his blood, and has made us to be a kingdom and priests to serve his God and Father — to him be glory and power for ever and ever! Amen' (Rev 1:5–6).

Bibliography

Roxanne Brantk, *Ministering to the Lord* (Mustard Seed Press: Florida, USA).

Jamie Buckingham, *Risky Living* (Kingsway Publications: Eastbourne).

Jamie Buckingham, *Where Eagles Soar* (Kingsway Publications: Eastbourne).

Judson Cornwall, *Let us Worship* (Bridge Publishing, Inc: New Jersey, USA).

Dick Eastman, *No Easy Road* (Baker Book House: USA).

Graham Kendrick, *Worship* (Kingsway Publications: Eastbourne).

Terry Law, *The Power of Praise and Worship* (Victory House Publishing: Tulsa, Oklahoma, USA).

Daniel Strazor, *Restoration — What is it?* (Maranatha Christian Centre: 1077 Angus Street, Regina, Saski, Canada, 54T1Y1).